"Nijay Gupta has produced an accessible ~~who~~ for students who are seeking to grasp the contours of scholarly debates on several key issues in New Testament studies. Gupta presents a fair and balanced treatment of diverging opinions and whets the reader's appetite vis-à-vis the issues discussed."

—**Abson Joseph**, Wesley Seminary, Indiana Wesleyan University

"In *A Beginner's Guide to New Testament Studies*, Nijay Gupta demonstrates the skill of a master guide as he takes readers on a fast-paced tour of the world of New Testament studies. This volume doesn't shy away from the complexity of critical New Testament debates and yet manages to offer concise, accessible overviews that invite further study and reflection. Nijay's pastoral sense is also evident as he anticipates the challenges presented by popular (mis)perceptions of the New Testament (in church and culture). A new generation of students will find that Nijay has demystified some of the most contested areas of scholarly debate and provided them with the opportunity to navigate their own course in studying the New Testament."

—**Ronald Herms**, Fresno Pacific University

"A concise and accessible guide with salient details for beginners. The short chapters aptly expose students to the main issues and differing views among scholars, and each concludes with questions for critical reflection—questions that may be reappropriated for online, in-class, or small-group discussions. An excellent book for undergraduate students."

—**Daniel K. Darko**, Gordon College

"What do New Testament scholars think about the historical reliability of John's Gospel? What is the relationship between the historical Jesus and the apostle Paul? What is the New Testament's view of women in leadership roles? What is the center of Paul's theology? Do Paul's statements about the Jewish law have any coherence? Who really wrote Jude, 2 Peter, or the Pastoral Epistles? Is the New Testament silent on the Roman Empire or does it engage in a veiled but powerful critique? It would take beginning students a lifetime to answer these questions! Or they could just read this book. Gupta has a detailed grasp of the New Testament, its sociocultural world, and the history of New Testament interpretation, and he communicates in remarkably accessible prose, providing an ideal entry point for students seeking a way in to the field of New Testament studies."

—**Joshua Jipp**, Trinity Evangelical Divinity School

A BEGINNER'S GUIDE TO
NEW TESTAMENT STUDIES

A BEGINNER'S GUIDE TO

NEW TESTAMENT STUDIES

UNDERSTANDING KEY DEBATES

NIJAY K. GUPTA

Baker Academic

a division of Baker Publishing Group

Grand Rapids, Michigan

Published by Baker Academic
a division of Baker Publishing Group
PO Box 6287, Grand Rapids, MI 49516-6287
www.bakeracademic.com

Printed in the United States of America

Library of Congress Cataloging-in-Publication Data
Names: Gupta, Nijay K., author.
Title: A beginner's guide to New Testament studies : understanding key debates / Nijay K. Gupta.
Description: Grand Rapids, MI : Baker Academic, a division of Baker Publishing Group, [2020] |
    Includes bibliographical references.
Identifiers: LCCN 2019027440 | ISBN 9780801097577 (paperback)
Subjects: LCSH: Bible. New Testament—Study and teaching. | Bible—Hermeneutics.
Classification: LCC BS2530 .G87 2020 | DDC 225.6/1—dc23
LC record available at https://lccn.loc.gov/2019027440

ISBN 978-1-5409-6271-3 (casebound)

20   21   22   23   24   25   26   7   6   5   4   3   2   1

Contents

Acknowledgments

This book wouldn't have been possible without the help of James Ernest, who accepted the original proposal, and the ongoing support of Bryan Dyer, who took over the project after James. Many of the essays in this book were field tested with my own students over the last several years, and I received substantial feedback that has helped me refine, clarify, and strengthen this work. My deepest thanks to those students, especially Alex Finkelson and Benjamin Black, who both provided focused advice and feedback that I needed at the last minute. Some chapters I sent out to subject experts for comments and a bit of extra help, so thank you to Mike Bird, Adam Winn, Anthony LeDonne, and Dean Flemming.

This book is dedicated to two of my own teachers. First, I want to honor Dr. David Aune (Ashland University) who introduced me to the academic study of the Bible when I was a teenager. I was a high school student who was able to take a college course for credit. I signed up for Dr. Aune's introduction to the Bible. I remember asking him all of these newbie questions after class, and he would graciously take me over to his office and look things up in the Greek text to help me find specific answers. Needless to say, his love of learning inspired me. Second, I want to honor Dr. Sean McDonough, the seminary professor who taught me how to interpret the New Testament ("Look at the fish!"—let the reader understand).[1] Dr. McDonough challenged me to learn from all the best resources across the spectrum of views and *then* to weigh and discern the strongest position.

1. For the uninitiated, see an explanation here: Justin Taylor, "Agassiz and the Fish," *The Gospel Coalition*, November 16, 2009, https://www.thegospelcoalition.org/blogs/justin-taylor/agassiz-and-the-fish/.

Last, but not least, I wish to acknowledge my family. My wife, Amy, always presses me to get to the "so what?" of academic debates. And the nightly exercise of reading the Bible with my young children constantly challenges me to reflect on how a better understanding of the Bible ought to lead toward love of God and love of neighbor.

Introduction

When I first entered theological education as a seminary student, I found my-self completely lost in the world of biblical scholarship. Not only were there so many technical terms I couldn't define and histories of interpretation with which I was not acquainted, but it seemed like there were two, or three, or ten views on various debated issues, and I had trouble keeping them straight. Oh, how I wished I had a map that could help me find my way through the maze of scholarship, or a guide to clue me into this view and that view!

More than fifteen years later, I can now say that I have a reasonable grasp of New Testament studies. Don't get me wrong—there are lots of subdisci-plines and specialized topics that I know little or nothing about. But I have taught introduction to the New Testament and New Testament exegesis and hermeneutics many times, certainly enough to feel comfortable tracing the main views and positions—hence, this book, *A Beginner's Guide to New Testament Studies*. This textbook aims to aid the uninitiated in understanding, in a simple way, some of the most important and hotly debated issues in academic study of the New Testament.

Before diving in, I want to clarify the audience, approach, and aims of this book. It is written for relative newcomers to the world of New Testament studies, not experts. Chapters are short, and for the most part, I avoid aca-demic jargon. In each chapter, you will find a short introduction to the issue at hand, explication of two or more views, and a final set of reflections. These reflections are very important in terms of the book's overall intentions. I do not expect that after consulting the short treatment of views I have offered, a reader will either (a) take a side or (b) change views. As will become clear, in nearly all of these debates, highly competent, well-intentioned scholars have good reasons for holding differing views. The reflections at the end of each chapter consider the key problems, paradoxes, methodological issues, and questions that undergird and generate the disagreement. In many cases I also point to tools and new perspectives that are shedding fresh light on these debates today. I sincerely hope readers will see the rich complexity and textures of the debates with a view toward holistic understanding of the issue, gain sympathy for the "other side," and be inspired to learn more beyond what could be presented in this single book.

On the matter of further reading, each chapter ends with suggested academic works of three kinds: (a) beginner works (basic but longer readings that will orient readers to the subject); (b) readings tied to the presented views (to get firsthand knowledge of a view's perspective and argumentation); and (c) advanced (more technical) works.

A bit of warning and encouragement for those wanting to turn the page and go down the rabbit hole: it can lead to a bit of despair when readers are confronted with so many views and so much disagreement. Why is it so complicated? Can we know anything in the end? Is there any agreement? Such inquiries are inevitable when one is faced with this ostensible cacophony in scholarship. But we must believe knowledge is always good. Knowledge always has the capacity to lead us to better understanding. We do our best to collect all the information we can, and then we live and act and believe based on faith, reason, and conscience. The alternative is to live in ignorant bliss—ignorance is still out there, but I'm not sure it is all that blissful. I have appreciated these famous words of Oliver Wendell Holmes when I struggle with the messiness of biblical interpretation: "I do not give a fig for the simplicity this side of complexity, but I would give my right arm for the simplicity on the far side of complexity."[1] I have tried my best to provide in this book a bit of complexity *and* simplicity for readers, and I wish you well on the journey ahead toward more complete understanding of the interpretation of the New Testament.

---

1. Quoted in Donald A. Hagner, *The New Testament: A Historical and Theological Introduction* (Grand Rapids: Baker Academic, 2012), xi.

ONE

The Synoptic Problem

One of my favorite stories in the Gospels is about the woman who anoints Jesus. Recollecting this story from memory, I remember that she brings a very expensive jar of ointment made of spikenard—a costly herb native to India. She anoints Jesus and washes his feet with her tears. She is a sinful woman, and Jesus recognizes her repentance and forgives her. The Pharisees are upset because this suspicious woman is behaving improperly, but Jesus commends her because she has been forgiven for so much and all the more is her love; her story will be told for generations wherever the gospel is preached.

Which Gospel is this story from? Well, if you look it up in the New Testament Gospels, you will find that I have inadvertently combined and mixed up details from Matthew, Mark, and Luke. The gist of my summary above resembles the story of the sinful woman who is forgiven in Luke 7:36–50. But a few pieces of information that I accidentally added appear only in Matthew or Mark. Mark mentions that this ointment is made from spikenard (Mark 14:3; neither Luke nor Matthew has this detail). Matthew is the one who mentions that this woman's fame will go out to all the world (Matt. 26:13). Though in Matthew's telling her repute involves her *anointing* Jesus with this ointment, not necessarily her extraordinary love. When we compare Luke against the other Gospels, Luke says that she weeps on Jesus's feet; Matthew and Mark do not offer this information. Luke mentions that she is a sinful woman, but Matthew refers to her only as a woman. Matthew and Mark seem to be telling the exact same story with only slight variation in some of the details. Luke appears to be sharing a story with a few overlapping aspects, but it potentially *could* be a different story—and yet how likely is it that on separate occasions two different women unexpectedly come to Jesus in a home with an alabaster jar of expensive ointment, cover him with it in some fashion, are criticized by dinner guests, and are defended by Jesus?

When we compare Matthew, Mark, and Luke in this way—lining up their versions of a particular story or saying and trying to puzzle out how they are similar and different—we are engaging in what scholars call the "Synoptic Problem." The word "synoptic" means "seen together," and it is used to refer to these three Gospels, since they can be placed side by side and compared and contrasted because of their similarities—what we might call "family resemblances." How can it be that these Gospels seem so similar in ordering (for the most part), inclusion of material (for the most part), and verbal overlap (sometimes), and yet there are some major differences (e.g., very different beginnings and endings) and numerous small differences?

And what about John? John is often studied separately from the Synoptic Gospels, because it is so different. John has no exorcisms and a very limited number of Jesus's miracles, for example, compared to the Synoptics. John is more likely to recount Jesus talking about "eternal life" than about the "kingdom of God." So, when we bring John into the mix, it is all the more clear that the Synoptics (Matthew, Mark, and Luke) belong together; they seem to have *some* sort of shared background, or they share some kind of original set of traditions. Or perhaps one or two of them is dependent on the third.

Have you ever wondered why the early Christians came to include *four* Gospels in their canon? Why not just one (such as Matthew) or two (Luke and John)? Why not just the earliest one because it is closest to the time of Jesus, or the latest one because it would include the most time-tested traditions? Does it not set Christians up for confusion to have *four different* Gospels? Sometimes I have heard this explained by the analogy of multiple witnesses to a crime. Imagine three different people who view a car accident. When they are independently interviewed by the police, surely they will end up agreeing on a few key elements of what happened: maybe that the incident happened around 10 a.m. on Thursday; there were two vehicles, a car and a truck. And maybe also that one car was wrecked and the other was fine. But we might also expect that, based on human error and various viewpoints, some details would be different between the witnesses: one witness might say the truck had one person, but another saw two people. Or they might disagree about who was at fault for the accident.

This analogy relates to the Synoptic Gospels in some ways, but the matter is more complex than chalking up differences to human error or point of view. What if two of the witnesses of the car accident are brothers and they talk at length about the incident before being interviewed? What if all three could recall both license plates perfectly, but then they disagreed about the states of the license plates? The scholarship on the Synoptic Problem attempts to address how these three Gospels—Matthew, Mark, and Luke—are noticeably

similar and yet have many differences in how they word things, how they ar-
range material, and what they include or leave out.

A Long History of Investigation

Many of us discover the Synoptic Problem in college or seminary, but in truth
this conversation and investigation has been going on for almost two thousand
years. A third-century theologian named Origen attempted to trace the development of the writing of the Gospels and gave this account: "I have learned
by tradition that the Gospel according to Matthew . . . was written first; and
that he composed it in the Hebrew tongue and published it for the converts
from Judaism. The second written was that according to Mark, who wrote
it according to the instruction of Peter. . . . And third, was that according to
Luke, the Gospel commended by Paul, which he composed for the converts
from the Gentiles. Last of all, that according to John."[1] As you can see, Origen
was especially interested (as others were in his time) in priority (who wrote
first), ordering, influences, and audience/purpose. The Gospels were clearly
not written as free-floating literary works for intellectual consumption. They
had some unique interests and objectives. But the Synoptic Problem has to do
with their interrelationship: How is it that they are part of the same family?
And how are these family members related?

We will engage with these questions with two different perspectives in
view. The most common approach to answering these questions focuses on
textual or literary relationships (who copied from whom). We will call this
the "literary-dependence perspective." In recent years, though, some scholars
have tried to incorporate what they have learned from oral cultures into their
answers to the Synoptic Problem. Many of these scholars are still interested in
the question of copying, but they acknowledge that this process would have
looked different in a primarily oral culture.

Literary-Dependence Perspective

As a professor, sometimes I have to deal with plagiarism, that unfortunate
occasion when you get two papers or exams that have a lot of word-for-word

1. Origen, *Commentary on Matthew* 1.1, trans. John Patrick, *Ante-Nicene Fathers*, vol. 10,
ed. A. Menzies (Buffalo, NY: Christian Literature Publishing, 1896), 412, quoted in Stanley E.
Porter and Bryan R. Dyer, "The Synoptic Problem: An Introduction to Its Key Terms, Concepts,
Figures, and Hypotheses," in *The Synoptic Problem: Four Views*, ed. Stanley E. Porter and
Bryan R. Dyer (Grand Rapids: Baker Academic, 2016), 1–26, at 14.

overlap. Clearly somebody copied off of someone else. Usually, even without talking to the people involved, you can highlight the similar or identical portions and detect the copied bits, but unless someone confesses to copying, it is actually pretty difficult to figure out who wrote first and who copied. We have a somewhat similar challenge with the Synoptic Gospels, insofar as scholars have debated and disagreed about who's first. Let's say that one of the Gospels was composed first, and others depended on that first one for a large amount of information but also incorporated information from other sources. How would you decide which one was written first?[2]

St. Augustine came up with a theory about the interrelationship of the Synoptics. He argued that Matthew was written first; Mark came second, abbreviating Matthew's Gospel. And Luke came next, utilizing both Matthew and Mark.[3] Until the nineteenth century, the view was rather popular that Matthew was first. But eventually scholars by and large came to believe that Mark was written earlier than Matthew and Luke. There are many reasons for this conclusion of Markan priority—for example, Mark supplies some Aramaic words where Matthew and Luke offer only the word in Greek; and it makes more sense that Matthew and Luke (both longer Gospels than Mark) would *add* information about Jesus's teachings (like the Sermon on the Mount), rather than that Mark would choose to *cut out* material (if the shorter Mark borrowed, let's say, from the longer Matthew).

At present, the most popular theory (presuming literary dependence) is that Matthew and Luke depended on Mark; that is, they had access to Mark's Gospel and wrote their Gospels based on his (with some editorial freedoms), but clearly they had other sources as well. If you take out of Matthew and Luke passages or stories that are also in Mark, you are left with two kinds of material: (1) material unique to their respective Gospels (e.g., Luke's song of Mary, 1:46–55; Matthew's Great Commission teaching, 28:16–20) and (2) material that Matthew and Luke have in common (that is not in Mark). Scholars refer to this shared material (2) as coming from a hypothetical source that we call "Q."

In the study of Jesus and the Gospels, Q is short for the German word *Quelle*, which means "source." It is important to know that this is a *hypothetical* document. There is no such real text in existence—we don't have a physical copy of Q, or a fragment, and no ancient writer referred to

2. Though I have mentioned plagiarism here as an illustration, it is important to know that no one in the ancient world would have accused the Gospel writers of any sort of theft or bad intentions. See further chap. 8 for more on literary dependence in the ancient world.

3. Augustine, *De consensu evangelistarum* 1.2–3.

anything called Q—but some scholars believe some kind of document like this must have existed. Take, for example, the teaching of Jesus about the man who builds his house on the rock. This teaching is not in Mark, but it is in Matthew (7:21–27) and Luke (6:46–49). How is it that Matthew and Luke both have this teaching if it is not in Mark? The Q theory explains this. According to scholars invested in relying on Q as a source, this theoretical document would not have been a narrative-based Gospel but more like a collection of teachings of Jesus. Some Q proponents hold loosely to this hypothesis and refuse to go too far down the road of outlining Q in detail. Others have worked hard on mapping out the contents of Q in minute detail. And still others believe there are important reasons to question the existence of Q altogether. For example, Mark Goodacre has argued that the shared material between Matthew and Luke is better explained by Luke using and editing Matthew rather than the two of them separately depending on another source (Q).[4]

Whatever the case, from a literary-dependence perspective, it appears that Luke and Matthew also had special sources for the information that is found only in their respective Gospels. The reality is that scholars are put in a position here where they have to do a lot of guessing and piecing together of sources. It is somewhat like seeing a crime scene and developing theories about what happened, by whom, and how, based on the final scene.

The goal of this enterprise is to map sources and the origin of materials in order to trace them back to the beginning and understand the influences, flow, and editing processes involved. If Matthew depended on Mark, and copied material from Mark, what did he employ untouched, and what did he leave out or change—and why? What about Luke? Did he use Mark or just Matthew? Or something else? Did he use the same Q document as Matthew? Did he have a different version of Q? Is there a Q at all?

Here it might help to lay out four important scholarly theories that try to resolve the Synoptic Problem.

Augustine's Solution

As I have already mentioned above, Augustine saw Matthew as coming first, then Mark, with Luke written later and depending on both Matthew and Mark. Some scholars think that he was influenced by the canonical order of the Gospels (Matthew → Mark → Luke), despite the fact that biblical book sequence does not necessarily assume order of composition.

4. Mark Goodacre, *The Case against Q* (Harrisburg, PA: Trinity Press International, 2002).

Figure 1.1
Augustine's View of the Synoptic Problem

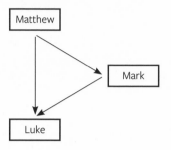

Griesbach's Solution

J. J. Griesbach (1789) suggested that Matthew came first (in agreement with Augustine), but he put Luke second. Mark came along third, attempting to bring Matthew and Luke together in a short form.

Figure 1.2
The Griesbach Hypothesis

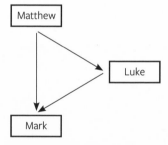

Two- or Four-Source Hypothesis

In the nineteenth century, there developed an interest in placing Mark first (Markan priority), for reasons suggested above (among other reasons). This theory claims that alongside Mark, Matthew and Luke also used Q—hence two sources, but if we include special L and special M material (material unique to their respective Gospels), we have four sources that existed (hypothetically) before Matthew and Luke were written.

Figure 1.3
The Four-Source Theory

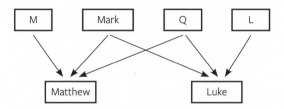

Farrer's Solution

A fourth theory worth noting is traced especially to Austin Farrer (1950s). Farrer argued in favor of Markan priority but denied the necessity of Q. If Luke relied on both Mark *and Matthew*, Q as a hypothesis is not really necessary, he posited.

Figure 1.4
The Farrer Hypothesis

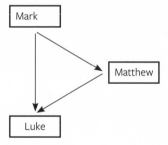

For many years the scholarly debate of the Synoptic Problem largely dwelled on these matters of textual sources and redaction (editing). But in recent years there has developed concern with theories that focus exclusively on textual composition, literary dependence, and intentional (literary and theological) redaction. There is a surge of interest in what can be gained from better understanding the nature and impact of the development of traditions that are passed on orally in community.

Dynamics-of-Oral-Tradition Perspective

Virtually all New Testament scholars agree that in the earliest years of Christianity (approximately 35–45 CE) stories about Jesus and his teachings would have been passed on orally. Perhaps some things would have been written and recorded for posterity, but inevitably much would have circulated as communities proclaimed these things out loud in mission and worship. But written Gospels did emerge—such as Mark—and an industry of Gospel writing began (not only Matthew, Luke, and John, but many others in the second and third centuries). Thus academic discussions have tended to focus on textual sources and dependence and on the intentional authorial habits of collating, removing, supplementing, and nuancing.

In the last few decades especially, though, there has been a swell of interest in the dynamics of oral tradition and how communities shared their cherished and important teachings. What if, some have wondered, the differences between the Synoptic Gospels are not primarily about one individual (e.g., Luke) sitting down with different sources and fashioning a new version of a Gospel? What if the majority of differences and similarities can be better explained in relation to the stability and flexibility of oral tradition?

One of the scholars who has stimulated this conversation is Kenneth Bailey, who argues that oral cultures can transmit teachings in an informal manner, and yet that community can maintain some control over the proper preservation of these teachings (hence his theory of "informal controlled oral tradition").[5] Bailey spent many decades in the Middle East and gave anecdotal evidence of this sort of phenomenon where a community gathered regularly to share stories, poems, and other important teachings. In such settings, there may not have been a designated teacher, but naturally the elders of the community carried the burden of passing on the wisdom of the past accurately. Some communities were rather strict with how material was recited, but Bailey found that many communities demonstrated flexibility in retellings—while small details might have been left out or paraphrased, the key pieces of the tradition were regularly transmitted in a faithful way. Bailey applies this to the Synoptic Problem—what if the small differences between these Gospels are not authorial changes, mistakes, modifications, or contradictions? Perhaps these are the natural and acceptable differences that emerged as early Christian leaders passed on the Jesus tradition over many years and as this group of Jesus followers expanded and moved into different regions.

James D. G. Dunn has further worked to strengthen this kind of approach to the Synoptic Gospels. He urges that we modern Westerners must

5. Kenneth E. Bailey, "Informal Controlled Oral Tradition and the Synoptic Gospels," *Themelios* 20, no. 2 (1995): 4–11. In scholarship, it is recognized that Werner Kelber's work has had the greatest impact; see Kelber, *The Oral and the Written Gospel* (Bloomington: Indiana University Press, 1983).

learn to break out of a literary paradigm when it comes to studying the Bible. We must reckon with an oral culture. Dunn explains that there was relatively low literacy in the ancient world. Much was learned and presented in person and by voice.[6] And the earliest Jesus tradition developed in rural communities, again where teachings were regularly passed on by mouth, not written text. Dunn argues that taking into account this mentality about instruction in early Christianity can help to address some of the concerns about small differences among the Synoptic Gospels. While it is true that Matthew or Luke must have played some role in selecting, reshaping, and interpreting Jesus material, we must also take into account the natural way that oral tradition bends and flexes while still adhering to some sense of stability with respect to the core features of a teaching or story. The coherence and overlap between the Synoptics stem from the way traditions maintain the heart or core of the tradition. But probably some of the variance results from the passing on of traditions orally from one community to another.

At the same time this study of orality was taking place, biblical scholars were reflecting on the nature of personal and social memory. Scholars like Dale Allison have argued that cognitive science shows how humans can remember events well as a whole, even if the details get fuzzy.[7] If the Gospels are testimonies based on memories of Jesus, then Jesus scholarship has long been wrongheaded in its use of authenticity tools that weigh the validity of individual sayings or event details.

Until now, we have been referring to the nature and dynamics of oral tradition theoretically, but it may be helpful to look at a case study: the Lord's Prayer. Most Christians who know and recite the Lord's Prayer concentrate on Matthew 6:9–13, but there is another version of the Lord's Prayer in Luke (11:2–4) (see table 1).

When we compare these two versions of the Lord's Prayer, there is obviously much overlap and verbal repetition. Key words or phrases are shared: "Father," "Hallowed be your name," "Your kingdom come," "daily bread," "forgive," "temptation." Luke's version is much shorter, and almost terse. Scholars have long wondered how these two texts relate. A common assumption is that

---

6. Just as a simple example, you might recall that in 3 John the author explains that he wishes to write much to the reader but prefers to talk face-to-face rather than communicate via ink and pen because the former is superior to the latter (3 John 13–14).

7. See Dale C. Allison Jr., *Constructing Jesus* (Grand Rapids: Baker Academic, 2010); for a basic overview of his approach, see Allison, "The Study of the Historical Jesus and Human Memory," *Catalyst*, March 1, 2012, https://www.catalystresources.org/the-study-of-the-historical-jesus-and-human-memory/.

Table 1. The Lord's Prayer in Matthew and Luke

Matthew 6:9–13	Luke 11:2–4
Pray then in this way:	He said to them, "When you pray, say:
Our Father in heaven, hallowed be your name.	Father, hallowed be your name.
Your kingdom come. Your will be done, on earth as it is in heaven.	Your kingdom come.
Give us this day our daily bread.	Give us each day our daily bread.

And forgive us our debts,
    as we also have forgiven our debtors.
	And forgive us our sins,
	    for we ourselves forgive everyone in-
	        debted to us.

And do not bring us into temptation, but rescue us from the evil one.	And do not bring us into temptation."

Note: In Matt. 6:13 and Luke 11:4 "into temptation" is in the NRSV footnote.

Matthew expanded and filled out a short form of the Lord's Prayer that we see in Luke, though that does not mean Luke was written before Matthew. But if the Lord's Prayer was so important to early Christian tradition, why would Matthew lengthen it or Luke shorten it?

If we take into account what has been said about the workings of oral tradition in this time and culture, some scholars believe we are not best served by relying on theories of literary dependence and editing, even though that has been the default attitude of scholars for many decades. Rather, the two different versions of the Lord's Prayer we find in the Gospels could be explained via the flexibility of many tellings and liturgical performances of the Lord's Prayer in many places in the first century. Leaders and elders would have exercised *some* control over the transmission of this prayer to ensure it stayed true to the teaching of Jesus Christ, but individual communities would naturally adapt the wording in small ways to their context and cultural vocabulary. Could this explain the two different versions of the Lord's Prayer in the Gospels better than a primarily literary or authorial (intentional) editing choice? Many scholars today are drawn to this perspective, or at least more open to it. But at the end of the day, scholars who press for oral-tradition perspective do not discount or reject source-comparison questions or the impact of literary dependence. Instead, they urge that the dynamics of oral tradition should be taken into consideration from the start and should factor into solutions to the so-called Synoptic Problem.

Reflections

As long as there is a biblical studies guild, work will continue steadily on the Synoptic Problem. But why? What has continued to fan this flame and keep the fire of interest and explanation burning? What are the deep questions that prick the minds of Gospels scholars and spur them on to revisit this matter time and time again? Almost certainly one driving impulse is to look for the historical Jesus (see chap. 2). As the theory sometimes goes, the better we can outline how the Synoptics are related, and what methods and techniques the evangelists used to modify, eliminate, add, or combine material, the better we can sort out what belongs to "true history" and what might be embellishment, extra commentary and interpretation, or later liturgy and teachings. Another driving impulse is the desire to peer into the busy, chaotic, and exhilarating world of the early Christians of the middle and late first century as they retold the story of Jesus that they believed had brought transformative good news to the world. What inspired the first evangelist to write? And why was another Gospel written? And another? And another? There are also natural curiosities about genre and purpose that are intricately related to the Synoptic Problem: Did the evangelists think they were reporting history? What kinds of artistic license were allowed? How did they know if their editorial changes went too far beyond transmitting their received traditions faithfully? Was any material considered sacrosanct?

But lately there has been disillusionment (and even despair) in the whole enterprise of sorting out sources and layers of history and tradition, and there has been concern that we may never be able to retrieve (objectively) what the historical Jesus actually said or did. What we have is the testimonies found in these Gospels (and other written sources). That is not to say these sources are fictitious, deceptive, or misinformed. But as of late there is a growing interest in both oral tradition (as we have noted above) and the nature and operations of personal and social *memory*. Virtually all scholars who study the Gospels agree that what we find in the Synoptics is not myth or legend, but neither is it modern journalistic reporting. Instead, we have testimony and proclamation about a real person (Jesus), and that witness is based on how Jesus was *remembered* by his followers. This reality has led to industrious work on the psychology and sociology of memory and collective commemoration. And it has complicated and enriched how we talk about what the Gospels are and how they relate to one another. With these new questions about memory, testimony, and oral and written traditions, the Synoptic Problem will continue to have a new life. What we are seeing is a broadening of approaches to this problem such that many more factors are taken into consideration beyond the more simplistic charts and figures of a few generations ago. Perhaps what is most fascinating is how the Synoptics now, more than ever, are being appreciated not for what they might contain that points to other important texts (like Q) but for what they themselves offer as pieces of literature and testimony.

Suggested Reading

Beginner

Goodacre, Mark. *The Synoptic Problem: A Way through the Maze*. Harrisburg, PA: Trinity Press International, 2001.

Pennington, Jonathan T. *Reading the Gospels Wisely: A Narrative and Theological Introduction*. Grand Rapids: Baker Academic, 2012.

Perkins, Pheme. *Introduction to the Synoptic Gospels*. Grand Rapids: Eerdmans, 2007.

Porter, Stanley E., and Bryan R. Dyer, eds. *The Synoptic Problem: Four Views*. Grand Rapids: Baker Academic, 2016.

Powell, Mark Allan. *Fortress Introduction to the Gospels*. Minneapolis: Fortress, 1988.

Rodriguez, Rafael. *Oral Tradition and the New Testament: A Guide for the Perplexed*. London: Bloomsbury T&T Clark, 2013.

Watson, Francis. *The Fourfold Gospel: A Theological Reading of the New Testament Portraits of Jesus*. Grand Rapids: Baker Academic, 2016.

Literary-Dependence Perspective

Goodacre, Mark. *The Case against Q*. Harrisburg, PA: Trinity Press International, 2002.

Robinson, James M., Paul Hoffmann, and John S. Kloppenborg. *The Critical Edition of Q*. Minneapolis: Fortress, 2000.

Oral-Tradition Perspective

Dunn, James D. G. *Jesus Remembered*. Christianity in the Making 1. Grand Rapids: Eerdmans, 2003.

———. *The Oral Gospel Tradition*. Grand Rapids: Eerdmans, 2013.

Advanced

Allison, Dale C. *Constructing Jesus: Memory, Imagination, and History*. Grand Rapids: Baker Academic, 2013.

Bauckham, Richard. *Jesus and the Eyewitnesses: The Gospels as Eyewitness Testimony*. 2nd ed. Grand Rapids: Eerdmans, 2017.

Kirk, Alan. *Q in Matthew: Ancient Media, Memory, and Early Scribal Transmission of the Jesus Tradition*. London: Bloomsbury T&T Clark, 2016.

Watson, Francis. *Gospel Writing: A Canonical Perspective*. Grand Rapids: Eerdmans, 2013.

TWO

The Historical Jesus

If you look carefully at Tim Whyatt's comic "Have You Found Jesus?" (included here), you'll see that Jesus is in a woman's house hiding behind a curtain even as she is asked if she has found him. (Hint: his feet are sticking out.) This comic pokes fun at the way Christians sometimes talk about Jesus, but it is a worthwhile question to ask—How do you "find" Jesus? Or, put another way, how do you come to know about Jesus? Most people would immediately say that we know about Jesus through the Bible, especially the Gospels. But information about Jesus can seemingly be found elsewhere as well. For example, the ancient Jewish historian Josephus had a few things to say about Jesus. And Jesus is talked about in the Islamic Qur'an as well. And in the Jewish rabbinic literature (e.g., the Babylonian Talmud). Ancient Roman writers, like Tacitus, refer to Jesus. So, how do we know which sources are the most accurate or trustworthy in terms of relaying historical facts? Christians tend to take the information in the New Testament Gospels at face value, but other people are also interested in Jesus as a figure in history, and there has been a long-standing discussion among scholars—Christian and otherwise—regarding the best ways to examine and interpret the New Testament Gospels and other relevant texts so as to shed the most light on the historical Jesus. Even that phrase, "historical Jesus," has its own complex history and jargon-like nuances. Mark Allan Powell helpfully defines the "historical Jesus" as "the person who emerges from an analysis of sources in accord with generally accepted principles of historical science."[1]

A common first reaction to this historical-Jesus enterprise is to label it an anti-Christian or antifaith endeavor. Truth be told, many who have engaged

1. Mark Allan Powell, *Introducing the New Testament* (Grand Rapids: Baker Academic, 2009), 87.

with this matter in the past and present do not profess religious faith in Jesus or subscribe to any form of traditional Christianity, but there are also many who consider this approach to "finding Jesus" beneficial even for those who trust the Bible. This approach to studying Jesus is about analyzing the sources (including the canonical Gospels) carefully and developing as well as possible a holistic theory about his life, influences, aim, and actions.

One might think of this another way. Even if someone concludes that the canonical Gospels are historically accurate, these four portraits of Jesus still give us a lot of seemingly disparate information about Jesus's identity, vocation, and activities. Not one of them boils his life down to a main thread of intention or accomplishment. The search for the historical Jesus attempts to analyze all the information available to develop a sensible, even compelling, arc of Jesus's life and ministry that sheds light on his significance. Eventually I will lay out how Jesus scholars today approach this subject, but before I do that, it is helpful to offer a quick summary of the history of the so-called quest for the historical Jesus.

A History of Questing for Jesus

For seventeen centuries of Christian history, interested readers of the Bible by and large took the testimony of the Gospels at face value—whether Jesus's miraculous birth, his amazing miracles, his controversial teachings, or, of course, his resurrection. But during the Enlightenment, academics started to use tools of historical science and historiography to analyze the Bible, and specifically the Gospels. Hermann Reimarus (1694–1768) is often credited with launching the first "quest" for the historical Jesus. Reimarus produced a theory about the life and intentions of Jesus that looked more human and mundane, once his miracles were set aside as fanciful. Reimarus argued that Jesus wanted to claim the earthly kingship of Israel but ultimately failed. No scholars today find Reimarus's exact hypothesis compelling, but his work seemed to have opened the doorway to further theories about the real life of Jesus, where the canonical Gospels can be stripped of fictional elements and the true ministry of the Galilean can come to light.

Another key figure of this first period is David F. Strauss (1808–74). Like Reimarus, Strauss thought it important to approach the canonical Gospels with a critical historical lens. But instead of discarding fictional elements like a shell to focus on the nut of historical truth, Strauss concentrated on the Gospels as primarily *myths*—formative stories that shape the identity of a community, such as the early Christians. Strauss moved scholarship, then, in the direction of thinking about the theological and community-shaping aims of the Gospels, and not just how they might be useful as a potential repository of historical information.

William Wrede (1859–1906) continued this quest with his important work on the so-called messianic secret in the Gospels. This refers to those several occasions where Jesus gives a teaching or performs a miracle and then commands the observer or recipient to be silent about it. For example, in Mark 1:40–45 Jesus heals a leper but then says, "See that you say nothing to anyone" (1:44a). Why would Jesus do this when he says that he came to proclaim the gospel publicly? Wrede theorized that Jesus himself did not issue these silence commands, but the church imported into the Gospels these pronouncements to cover up the embarrassing reality that Jesus's fellow Jews by and large did not believe in him. Again, Wrede moved forward the realization that the evangelists were storytellers (and not merely transmitters of historical sayings and events), but with respect to the first quest he played a role in further putting into doubt the historical reliability of portions of the canonical Gospels.

At the beginning of the twentieth century, Albert Schweitzer (1875–1965) challenged this quest for the historical Jesus by observing that the Synoptic Gospels all point to a Jesus who is focused on the end of the world, a matter not taken very seriously in Jesus scholarship at his time. Many questers ended up portraying a life of Jesus that made him out to be a good teacher offering timeless truths and an overall message of love and goodwill. But Schweitzer presented Jesus as an eschatological prophet heralding the coming of a Son of Man (not Jesus himself). When this Son of Man failed to show up, Jesus adopted this role, and he believed his own death would prompt God's kingdom to come—but it didn't. Jesus was wrong and his mission a failure. Still, his self-sacrifice was inspiring, and that leaves Jesus with an important legacy, so Schweitzer argued. His focus on Jesus and eschatology pushed scholars to face a Jesus of antiquity very different from "modern man." Some scholars have described Schweitzer's work as a bombshell, disrupting the Jesus quest.

As a result of this Schweitzerian interruption, scholars refer to a break from research on the historical Jesus, sometimes called the "no quest" period. During this era, Jesus was still in fact a topic of research, but much interest in New Testament studies shifted toward the theological work of Rudolf Bultmann (1884–1976). Bultmann believed that uncovering or discovering the historical Jesus was insignificant. Rather, what really mattered was existentially responding to the Christ of faith. Ironically, a "new quest" for the historical Jesus was launched by one of Bultmann's students, Ernst Käsemann (1906–98). Käsemann agreed with his teacher that faith in the risen Christ is important, but he disagreed with Bultmann about the irrelevance of studying the figure of the earthly Jesus. In the wake of the Second World War and the Holocaust, Käsemann considered it crucial to keep the knowledge of Jesus rooted in history, so people would not be tempted to remake Jesus in their own image, as some Nazis and Nazi sympathizers had done. This phase of Jesus study was marked by a focus on methods, especially how to recover the *exact words* of Jesus. Scholars like Norman Perrin (1920–76) helped to establish certain factors or criteria to judge a statement as authentic or rule it out as inauthentic. Let's say that some material in the canonical Gospels is truly historical, a direct and more-or-less verbatim saying of Jesus or an event that has credible grounding in history. And let's say other material (according to these questers) is either fabricated by the evangelist or has made its way into a Gospel as a (fictional) part of early Christian legend about Jesus. These criteria were meant to offer tools to sort out such layers and to move toward identifying the most-historical portions. I will mention three notable criteria that developed in this period.

Criterion of Dissimilarity

This factor judges as dubious any event or saying of Jesus that is too similar to what early Christians came to recognize as orthodox. This material, in the judgment of some Jesus scholars, demonstrates layers or traditions that must have been produced by Christians and reinvested into the mouth or life of Jesus. And the same goes for material that resonates with early Judaism. What this criterion does is look for the unique person and personality of Jesus by honing in on things he said and did that were *striking* and *distinctive*. There has been much criticism of this criterion; as Helen Bond writes, this factor is "almost engineered to produce a Jesus strangely dislocated from both his Jewish environment and the church which followed him."[2]

2. Helen Bond, *The Historical Jesus: A Guide for the Perplexed* (London: T&T Clark, 2012).

Criterion of Multiple Attestation

Another tool that Jesus scholars have used involves the value of multiple sources confirming a particular event, story, or teaching. For example, the fact that all four Gospels point to Jesus's interest in the kingdom of God supports the historicity of this theme for the historical Jesus. Or we could note the wide attestation that Jesus taught in parables. That is not to say that a saying found in only one Gospel was automatically proven inauthentic; rather, this criterion allows for material to be considered more reasonably factual where more than one unique source offers confirmation.

Criterion of Embarrassment

Sayings or actions that would have been embarrassing or inexplicable for the early church would be counted as more likely to be authentic because the church would have had no benefit from fabricating the information. A classic case here is the baptism of Jesus by John the Baptist (Matt. 3:14)—John portrays baptism as a rite of repentance for forgiveness, and it would have been awkward for Christians to explain why Jesus was so insistent that he should be baptized when he was considered sinless by the church. A clear challenge with this criterion, though, is that what is embarrassing to modern people in the West may be different from what was embarrassing in the ancient Mediterranean; this factor requires numerous assumptions.

These criteria and others have continued to be used in Jesus scholarship over the last half century. Some scholars use the authenticity criteria strictly, and others use them as a loose guide. Others still have completely rejected them.

Looking back, Jesus scholars now sense that a new kind of quest started in the 1980s, even while the second ("new quest") continued in some circles. This third quest put a stronger emphasis on reading and interpreting the canonical Gospels and Jesus in the light of early Judaism in the Roman world. For a number of reasons, New Testament scholars became more invested overall in gleaning historical, cultural, ideological, and literary insight from Jewish texts, such as the writings of Josephus and Philo, the Dead Sea Scrolls, and the Old Testament Apocrypha and Pseudepigrapha. It was not uncommon in the nineteenth century for Jesus scholars to conclude that the historical Jesus rejected Jews and Judaism in favor of a new religion, which became Christianity. But in this third quest several scholars, especially in view of the depth and breadth of the Judaism of Jesus's time, saw Jesus as resonant with restorationist, political, and prophetic strands of Israel's heritage and contemporary culture. Here it was easier to imagine that Jesus's critical words against his fellow Jews were not signs of outright rejection but rather insider critique, a devout Jew calling his kinspeople to repentance and faith in Israel's God. In a former era, many Jesus scholars assumed Jesus rejected torah, considering it impossible, primitive and superstitious, or void. But in the third quest a new perspective on Jesus opened up the possibility that he was a law-observant and pro-torah Jew despite some of his radical teachings.

At the same time as the "Jewish Jesus" third quest, scholars more aligned with the second quest have continued to examine the historical Jesus. In the 1980s the Jesus Seminar was founded, which brought together dozens of critical scholars to judge individual sayings and events of Jesus as authentic or inauthentic.[3] At the end of it all, this group deemed less than 20 percent of the material from the canonical Gospels to be authentic.[4] When they analyzed this material that met their satisfaction of historical authenticity, they came up with the following descriptions of Jesus.

1. "Jesus' characteristic talk was distinctive—it can usually be distinguished from common lore."

2. "Jesus' sayings and parables cut against the social and religious grain [of his society]."

3. "Jesus' sayings and parables surprise and shock: they characteristically call for a reversal of roles or frustrate ordinary, everyday expectations."

4. "Jesus' sayings are often characterized by exaggeration, humor, and paradox."

5. "Jesus' images are concrete and vivid, his sayings and parables customarily metaphorical and without explicit application."

6. "Jesus does not as a rule initiate dialogue or debate, nor does he offer to cure people."

3. One of the critiques of the Jesus Seminar at that time was that it included several men who were not bona fide Gospels scholars, and even someone who was not a part of the academy (he was a movie producer).

4. The Jesus Seminar had a notoriously quirky voting system, using beads of different colors for individual votes. One could vote a saying or story was authentic, somewhat likely authentic, somewhat unlikely authentic, and unlikely authentic. Their final verdict on authentic material included only sayings and actions deemed definitely authentic. For more information on the Jesus Seminar, see "The Jesus Seminar," Westar Institute, accessed April 25, 2019, https://www.westarinstitute.org/projects/the-jesus-seminar/. See also Robert W. Funk and Roy W. Hoover, eds., *The Five Gospels: The Search for the Authentic Words of Jesus* (Sonoma: Polebridge, 1993); R. W. Funk, ed., *The Acts of Jesus: What Did Jesus Really Do? The Search for the Authentic Deeds of Jesus* (San Francisco: HarperCollins, 1998).

7. "Jesus rarely makes pronouncements or speaks about himself in the first person."

8. "Jesus makes no claim to be the Anointed, the messiah."[5]

According to many critics of the Jesus Seminar, their approach to studying the historical Jesus in relation to the Gospels and their final analysis of Jesus are deeply flawed methodologically. First of all, their "scientific" system is highly restrictive and leads to a collection of somewhat random information. Second, it is noticeable that the historical Jesus that emerges is not very Jewish—their strict application of the criterion of dissimilarity tends to produce a contextless, heritage-less Jesus. Third, given the meager information they surmise that one can know about the historical Jesus, is it even possible to construct a life of Jesus with any confidence or to any profitable end? For these reasons and others, the influence and prominence of the Jesus Seminar has largely waned, but historical work of this nature continues in many different circles.

Four Approaches to the Historical Jesus

With the above background and academic context in mind, I will now outline four different approaches to the historical Jesus. One of the key factors that weighs heavily into how one looks at Jesus is the sources of information—what kind of material is included and excluded, and how much of that material is taken at face value. How is Q used and with what importance? Or the Gospel of Thomas? Is John's Gospel included in the discussion? Is Mark prioritized?

Jesus the Prophet

Perhaps more than any other view that has emerged in the last forty years, the idea that Jesus was some kind of *prophet* has gained the most widespread agreement. According to Matthew, Jesus's disciples recount that some people believe Jesus to be a prophet (Matt. 16:14). And during the so-called triumphal entry the crowds confess, "This is the prophet Jesus from Nazareth in Galilee" (Matt. 21:11; cf. 21:46). According to Mark, Jesus makes a kind of roundabout self-reference when he states, "Prophets are not without honor, except in their hometown" (Mark 6:4). And Luke mentions certain followers of Jesus who describe him as "a prophet mighty in deed and word before God and all the

---

5. Funk and Hoover, *Five Gospels*, 30–32.

people" (Luke 24:19). Obviously many were attracted to Jesus as a miracle worker, and most of the wonder-workers in ancient Judaism (including the Old Testament) were prophets of one kind or another.

Geza Vermes has described Jesus as a kind of charismatic holy man within the Jewish sphere. Vermes is insistent that Jesus should not be located primarily among the ancient Pharisees, Essenes, or political zealots but rather was a spiritual miracle worker like Honi the Circle Drawer and Hanina ben Dosa. Jesus disrupted the religious status quo and dared to heal and support the poor and marginalized.[6] Another Jesus scholar, Marcus Borg, has portrayed the historical Jesus as a mystic, a "spirit person" who sought to renew Israel through the transforming work of God. Borg sees Jesus as using himself as a channel for the Spirit's presence and power to allow Israel to encounter their God in a new and fresh way.[7]

E. P. Sanders has taken a different approach to Jesus as prophet: with Schweitzer's work as a major influence, Sanders presents Jesus as an eschatological prophet who proclaimed a future day of reckoning for Israel and the dawning of a new world order.[8] In 1998, Dale Allison also supported this kind of view (see below how he has changed his mind since), referring to the historical Jesus as a "millenarian prophet." At that point Allison focused on Jesus's teachings about final judgment, resurrection, the restoration of Israel, and a great tribulation to come.[9] Those who have emphasized Jesus as a prophet tend to point to distinctive features of his ministry, such as his miracles and his teaching about judgment.

Jesus the Wise

We can contrast the Jesus-the-prophet perspective with one that fixates instead on Jesus as a sage or philosopher. Several scholars have tried to relate Jesus to the Cynic philosophers of antiquity.[10] The Cynics were known for valuing freedom of speech, self-sufficiency, and indifference (apathy). They

6. Geza Vermes, *Jesus the Jew* (London: Collins, 1973).

7. Marcus Borg, *Meeting Jesus Again for the First Time: The Historical Jesus and the Heart of Contemporary Faith* (San Francisco: HarperSanFrancisco, 1994), 32.

8. E. P. Sanders, *Jesus and Judaism* (Philadelphia: Fortress, 1985); for a helpful and short summary of his view, see Sanders, "In Quest of the Historical Jesus," *The New York Review of Books*, November 15, 2001, https://www.nybooks.com/articles/2001/11/15/in-quest-of-the -historical-jesus/.

9. Dale Allison, *Jesus of Nazareth: Millenarian Prophet* (Minneapolis: Fortress, 1998).

10. See F. Gerald Downing, *Christ and the Cynics: Jesus and Other Radical Preachers in First-Century Tradition* (Sheffield: JSOT, 1988); Downing, *Cynics and Christian Origins* (Edinburgh: T&T Clark, 1992); Burton Mack, *A Myth of Innocence: Mark and Christian Origins* (Minneapolis: Fortress, 1988).

often rejected social conventions of society; in fact, their name Cynic refers to being "doglike," pointing to their intentionally shabby appearance and rugged way of life. Some scholars have compared the Cynic attitude with the instructions that Jesus gives to his disciples in Luke 10 (also believed to be in Q). Jesus tells them to carry no worldly goods (Luke 10:4) and to travel from place to place lightly. In order to make this connection between Jesus and the Cynics, these scholars put into doubt material in the canonical Gospels that is especially eschatological; instead, they focus on Jesus's aphorisms, specifically his teachings about renouncing worldly norms and systems. This Cynic Jesus is understood to be deeply influenced by Greek culture in the region of Galilee. For some scholars this is an interpretation of the historical Jesus as a not-so-Jewish philosopher, but others, such as John Dominic Crossan, have argued that Jesus was a Jewish-style Cynic.[11] According to Crossan, Jesus originally was attracted to the teachings of John the Baptist but later decided to go out on his own, wandering about teaching his people a profound message of unbrokered egalitarianism and radical commensality.[12] This Jesus's concern was not especially spiritual or religious but more directly focused on classism and economic oppression in his sociopolitical environment. Scholars who read Jesus as a Cynic philosopher are generally considered to be part of an ongoing "new quest," not the so-called third quest.

Ben Witherington also interprets Jesus especially as a wise man, although he is deeply invested in locating Jesus within the traditions and culture of early Judaism with no recourse to Greco-Roman models as dominant. Witherington argues that Jesus would have seen himself as a prophetic sage (teacher of wisdom), and even God's Wisdom incarnate. Despite some indicators that Jesus saw himself as a prophet-like figure, Witherington urges that key features of prophetic speech and self-identification are not found in the canonical Gospels. For example, Jesus in the Synoptic Gospels tends to speak on his own authority rather than positioning himself as a unique mouthpiece of the God of Israel ("Thus saith the Lord . . ."). When it comes to Jesus embodying Wisdom, Witherington notes texts like Matthew 11:19, where Matthew's Jesus says, "Wisdom is vindicated by her deeds," which appears to be a self-reference *as the wisdom of God*. This kind of evidence has convinced Witherington that Jesus often and regularly thought and taught in "sapiential ways."[13]

11. John Dominic Crossan, *The Historical Jesus: The Life of a Mediterranean Jewish Peasant* (New York: HarperCollins, 1991).

12. See Crossan, *The Historical Jesus*, 225–264.

13. Ben Witherington III, *The Jesus Quest: The Third Search for the Jew of Nazareth* (Downers Grove, IL: InterVarsity, 1995), 161–96.

Obviously those scholars who focus on Jesus as wise teacher or philosopher concentrate the personality and vocation of the historical Jesus on his teachings first and foremost, and they tend to put *less* emphasis on his actions. This is largely in keeping with special attention on Jesus-tradition sources such as Q and the Gospel of Thomas, which are both composed largely of Jesus's aphorisms. Witherington, again, is much more inclusive of historical material that is found in the canonical Gospels, and he treats the four Gospels of the New Testament as having more accuracy and authority than the so-called apocryphal Gospels. Even still, he locates Jesus's identity and activity especially within the role of the wise teacher.

Jesus the Social Revolutionary

Scholars like Richard Horsley have focused more on Jesus as a social change agent in a political environment.[14] According to Horsley, what was most important to Jesus's agenda was not conveying a set of important ideas—that is, Jesus was not primarily a wise teacher—but challenging Roman colonial oppression. The historical Jesus identified with the rural peasant population and launched a program to condemn the ruling elites. Jesus did this not from the top down as a governor or magistrate in hopes of leading a regime change but from the bottom up as a grassroots activist. Horsley argues that when the historical Jesus gave apocalyptic utterances, this was not about an otherworldly spirituality but rather was an appropriation of Israel's eschatological hopes that imagined a restored social reality where imperial domination would be exposed and overthrown once and for all. From this perspective, Jesus's emphasis on the kingdom of God did not pertain to spiritual insight into a heavenly institution; it is the vision of a real community that is just and peaceable for all. Horsley, and other like-minded Jesus scholars, have paid close attention to the sociopolitical landscape of Judea in the first-century Roman Empire. They interpret Jesus not as a wandering spiritualist but as an individual in a particular time and place deeply aware of the real-life conditions of Jews within a highly stratified and economically depressing world. Obviously, if the historical Jesus did engage with the politics of his time, one can see how he made many enemies and eventually caught the attention of high-level Jewish leaders, and Roman ones as well. While the sayings of Jesus could point to Jesus's revolutionary attitudes, interpreters in this camp also take very seriously the actions of Jesus—in

---

14. See Richard A. Horsley, *Jesus and the Spiral of Violence: Popular Jewish Resistance in Roman Palestine* (Minneapolis: Fortress, 1993); Horsley, *Jesus and Empire: The Kingdom of God and the New World Disorder* (Minneapolis: Fortress, 2003).

particular, threats in word or deed against political entities like the temple institution and the Sanhedrin.

Jesus the Messiah

It might seem strange for someone who has read the New Testament Gospels to hear that many Jesus scholars discard the notion that Jesus thought of himself as the Messiah. After all, this is a cornerstone claim of Christians ancient and modern, and it appears to be a key feature of the canonical Gospels (e.g., Matt. 1:1; 16:16; Mark 14:61–62; Luke 23:2). But we must remember that the historical-Jesus enterprise for the past two hundred years has put into question the historical reliability of the canonical Gospels—usually not as a whole, but in part, as the parts must be weighed and analyzed scientifically or academically to (re)discover the real Jesus. Those who rely heavily on Q as an early and trustworthy source argue that this document does not portray Jesus as a messianic claimant or prospective king. But even for those who give some historical credibility to the Synoptic Gospels, they point to the so-called messianic secret and the way Jesus deflects announcements of his messiahship (e.g., Luke 22:67). However, before examining specific texts of the Gospels, some scholars believe that it is anachronistic to presume that Jesus imagined and represented himself as Israel's Messiah. Such a concept was not widely established in Jesus's time, some argue; and the little discussion there was in early Judaism was not uniform. Nevertheless, others have found that "Messiah" is the best designation for the interests and aims of the historical Jesus.

N. T. Wright has written extensively on Jesus and asserts that the messiahship claims by and for Jesus make historical sense.[15] Like Horsley and Crossan, Wright takes very seriously the religious, social, political, and economic environment of Judea in the first-century Roman Empire. For Jesus to have considered himself Israel's Messiah does not mean that he claimed divine status or revealed himself as the Second Person of the Trinity. Jesus as Messiah acted as a representative leader of his people, a king, who brought redemption to his people by taking sin and death upon himself. That is not to say that he was not a prophet or wise teacher—Wright argues he functioned in these ways as well. But Wright posits that if Jesus was crucified—as almost all Jesus scholars agree that he was—he must have operated in such a public and political manner that he was deserving of public execution in the eyes of Jews and Romans; such a damnation would make sense for a pretender king

---

15. See N. T. Wright, *Jesus and the Victory of God*, Christian Origins and the Question of God 2 (Minneapolis: Fortress, 1996).

or a messiah.[16] Part of the stimulus for this approach to examining Jesus is the more-recent study of Jewish figures from the Second Temple period who aspired to take over leadership in Israel to fulfill the divine promises of restoration for Israel, purifying God's wayward people and freeing them from their oppressors.[17]

Is the Quest for the Historical Jesus a Dead End?

As I have explained already, there have been many paths taken on the quests for the historical Jesus, with some focused on a Greek-like teacher, and others on a Jewish prophet. And some believe the quest leads nowhere. Recent years have seen much skepticism toward questing for Jesus. One impression is that Jesus cannot be discovered by cutting and pasting sources together, no matter what sources you deem reliable. Allison, in his important book *Constructing Jesus*, argues that we need to reckon with the nature of memory and the Gospels as remembered testimony.[18] Memory is neither perfect nor objective. That does not mean memory is useless. But Allison argues that when it comes to "remembering" the historical Jesus, memory fails regarding specific details. Nevertheless, memory *can* pass on the main elements of a story or teaching. That means traditional tools of the quests (sifting words and sayings in documents) are rather pointless. What we gain from the canonical Gospels (and other sources) are general impressions, such as that Jesus was an apocalyptic prophet ushering in a new era. A similar attack on traditional quest methods has come from a group of scholars heralding the demise of the "authenticity criteria."[19] They point to a prescient essay by Morna Hooker from 1970 that basically claimed that if all you have is a hammer, then everything you see is nails; that is, the tools used by questers are flawed and limited at best and should be abandoned.[20]

More serious attacks on the quest for the historical Jesus have come from others, including Scot McKnight, who—once a card-carrying historical Jesus

---

16. Wright's approach to Jesus is more multifaceted than can be explained here; suffice it to say that Wright also sees Jesus as fulfilling in himself Yahweh's covenantal promises of returning to Zion to reign as king; see N. T. Wright, *How God Became King* (New York: HarperOne, 2012).

17. See Richard A. Horsley and John S. Hanson, *Bandits, Prophets, and Messiahs: Popular Movements at the Time of Jesus* (San Francisco: Harper & Row, 1985).

18. Dale C. Allison, *Constructing Jesus: Memory, Imagination, and History* (Grand Rapids: Baker Academic, 2010).

19. Chris Keith and Anthony Le Donne, eds., *Jesus, Criteria, and the Demise of Authenticity* (London: T&T Clark, 2012).

20. Morna D. Hooker, "Christology and Methodology," *New Testament Studies* 17 (1970): 480–87.

scholar—has now professed its futility. In a *Christianity Today* article titled "The Jesus We'll Never Know," McKnight argues that the questing enterprise is too flawed in conception, history, methodology, and orientation to be beneficial to the guild.[21] Once upon a time, McKnight participated in these pursuits as a Jesus scholar, but he has since given up. He comments how he would regularly meet with scholars and work together to construct and analyze the historical Jesus, only to end up with divergent views and little consensus. Ultimately McKnight came to consider the "quest" a dead end not for outlining data about Jesus (e.g., born, lived, was crucified) but for making *meaning* of Jesus. Ultimately, no amount of historical Jesus research can inspire faith in the divine identity of Jesus, his resurrection, his atoning death, or his lordship over the church. So McKnight has washed his hands of that endeavor.

While McKnight has not been shy about his pessimism toward the quests, others continue with a more sober hope. Wright believes that historical Jesus scholarship keeps biblical studies scholars focused on history—which is a good thing.[22] And, as noted above, Jesus scholarship seems to die and rise again with new methods, interests, energy, and participants, and it is currently in a fresh phase of interest in personal and social memory. Furthermore, archaeology is also yielding new insights into the life and times of Jesus of Nazareth.[23]

Reflections

In this chapter, I can offer only a short and cursory introduction to the quests for the historical Jesus. It is an academic enterprise with a very long history and involves several different disciplines (historical criticism, tradition criticism, archaeology, social-scientific studies, etc.) and numerous perspectives— sometimes the joke is made that there are as many theories of Jesus's life as there are Jesus scholars! But *why*? If there is only one real Jesus of history, why can't scholars agree on what he did and said and his aims and accomplishments?

Presuppositions and Agendas

Ever since I read Allison's *The Historical Christ and the Theological Jesus*, I have been haunted by his sobering words about the Jesus questers. He writes,

---

21. Scot McKnight, "The Jesus We'll Never Know," *Christianity Today* 54, no. 4 (April 2010): 22, https://www.christianitytoday.com/ct/2010/april/15.22.html.

22. See N. T. Wright, "No, We Need History," *Christianity Today* 54, no. 4 (April 2010): 27.

23. See, e.g., Kristin Romey, "What Archaeology Is Telling Us about the Real Jesus," *National Geographic Magazine*, December 2017, https://www.nationalgeographic.com/magazine/2017/12/jesus-tomb-archaeology/.

Who doubts that authors who themselves have a high christology tend to write books in which the historical Jesus himself has a high christology? Or that those who are uncomfortable with Nicea and Chalcedon more often than not unearth a Jesus who humbled rather than exalted himself? The correlations between personal belief and historical discovery must be endless. Jesus seems friendly to evangelical Protestantism in books written by evangelical Protestants, and he is a faithful Jew in books written by non-Christian Jews who want to reclaim Jesus. It is easy to be suspicious here. You can do anything with statistics, and you can do anything with Jesus, or at least a lot of different things.[24]

Allison is not the first scholar to come to this realization. George Tyrrell, at the beginning of the twentieth century, famously commented that Jesus scholars are prone to peer down the well of history looking for Jesus, only to see their own reflection.[25] All humans have flaws and biases; and we can try our best to approach difficult issues fairly and objectively. But in a retrospective analysis of the history of the quests it has become clear that different scholars arriving at the same singular identity and impact of Jesus is all but impossible. Why is this so? Can we compensate for this in any way?

Sources

We can easily identify that the many interpretations of Jesus are directly related to the kinds and numbers of sources we use as foundational evidence. The tendency has been to trust earlier sources—or, perhaps more accurately, to mistrust documents composed later. For many years the sole focus was on the Synoptics. And then interest developed around the Gospel of Thomas and other noncanonical Gospels. And now there are lively conversations about what the Gospel of John might contribute. In all investigations, evidence is prime, but in the study of the historical Jesus there exists much disagreement about the best sources that count for evidence and how they ought to be weighed.

Methods

Almost all Jesus scholars agree that method is crucial to skillful study of the historical Jesus. But there is endless debate about which methods and tools are the most useful for this task. Some continue to follow a practice of weighing the authenticity of words, phrases, and passages from canonical

---

24. Dale Allison, *The Historical Christ and the Theological Jesus* (Grand Rapids: Eerdmans, 2009), 16.

25. See George Tyrrell, *Christianity at the Crossroads* (London: Longmans, 1909), 49–50.

and noncanonical sources. Others focus more on generalities gleaned from the sources. This is one reason why there are several different quests going on at the same time, but ones that can still exist in separate conversations.

Backgrounds and Contexts

Part of the challenge that Allison raises above—you can do anything with Jesus—has to do with the scholar's interests, education, and experiences. Some see Jesus fitting into a Hellenistic context, perhaps in part because those scholars have a vivid understanding of Greek culture and see connections others do not (for one reason or another). And the same goes for Jewish context. Or economic and sociopolitical context. The truth is that the Roman world of the first century was lively politically and very diverse in terms of the intersection of many cultures.

Conclusion

All Jesus scholars engaged in this subject agree—Jesus is fascinating. But that is pretty much all they agree on. From method to sources to the personality of Jesus and his vocational agenda, the areas of debate are numerous. Even though some have argued that this discipline is on its way out, history has proven it to be remarkably resilient. There will probably always be interest in the intersection between the "historical Jesus" of Nazareth, the Jesus found in record and legend, and the Jesus of the Christian faith.

What does the future of historical Jesus research hold? Some current quests will continue. I imagine study of noncanonical Gospels will grow in interest. Archaeological work on cities in and around Galilee will produce new insights and questions. And certainly the more recent work on personal and social memory will proceed. Other scholars will exit the quest. This period of academic history will undoubtedly be marked by many streams of thought and continued proliferation of many miniquests.

Suggested Reading

Beginner

Beilby, James, and Paul R. Eddy, eds. *The Historical Jesus: Five Views*. Downers Grove, IL: InterVarsity, 2009.

Bond, Helen. *The Historical Jesus: A Guide for the Perplexed*. London: T&T Clark, 2012.

Borg, Marcus, and N. T. Wright. *The Meaning of Jesus: Two Visions.* San Francisco: HarperSanFrancisco, 1998.

Powell, Mark Allan. *Jesus as a Figure in History: How Modern Historians View the Man from Galilee.* 2nd ed. Louisville: Westminster John Knox, 2013.

Taylor, Joan E. *What Did Jesus Look Like?* London: Bloomsbury T&T Clark, 2018.

Jesus the Prophet

Allison, Dale. *Jesus of Nazareth: Millenarian Prophet.* Minneapolis: Fortress, 1991.

Sanders, E. P. *Jesus and Judaism.* Philadelphia: Fortress, 1985.

Jesus the Wise

Crossan, John Dominic. *The Historical Jesus: The Life of a Mediterranean Jewish Peasant.* San Francisco: HarperCollins, 1991.

Witherington, Ben, III. *The Jesus Quest: The Third Search for the Jew of Nazareth.* Downers Grove, IL: InterVarsity, 1997.

Jesus the Social Revolutionary

Horsley, Richard. *Jesus and the Spiral of Violence: Popular Jewish Resistance in Roman Palestine.* Minneapolis: Fortress, 1993.

Oakman, Douglas E. *The Political Aims of Jesus.* Minneapolis: Fortress, 2012.

Jesus the Messiah

Bird, Michael F. *Are You the One Who Is to Come? The Historical Jesus and the Messianic Question.* Grand Rapids: Baker Academic, 2009.

Wright, N. T. *Jesus and the Victory of God.* Christian Origins and the Question of God 2. Minneapolis: Fortress, 1996.

Advanced

Allison, Dale C. *Constructing Jesus: Memory, Imagination, and History.* Grand Rapids: Baker Academic, 2010.

Dunn, James D. G. *Jesus Remembered.* Christianity in the Making 1. Grand Rapids: Eerdmans, 2003.

Holmén, Tom, and Stanley E. Porter, eds. *Handbook for the Study of the Historical Jesus.* 4 vols. Leiden: Brill, 2011.

Keener, Craig S. *The Historical Jesus of the Gospels.* Grand Rapids: Eerdmans, 2009.

Keith, Chris, and Anthony LeDonne, eds. *Jesus, Criteria, and the Demise of Authenticity.* London: T&T Clark, 2012.

THREE

The Fourth Gospel and History

When I was a kid, I remember reading the children's magazine *Highlights* whenever I sat in a waiting room. One of the activities that regularly featured in *Highlights* was to spot the differences between a pair of nearly identical pictures. Well, if the four Gospels were like a series of four pictures, the differences of the Gospel of John would stick out like a sore thumb! One scholar goes as far as calling it the *maverick* Gospel—John just does things differently.[1] Of course, it bears some very basic similarities to the Synoptics: narrative arrangement; similar details about the kinds of things Jesus said and did (miracles, preaching, disputes); emphasis on the suffering, death, and resurrection. And there are a small number of stories that are in both the Synoptics and John (e.g., the feeding of the multitudes and the triumphal entry). But, again, when you study the four Gospels in close detail, side by side, John is recognizably *different*. Note the following.

Beginnings. Perhaps one of the most prominent things about John is the way it begins. Luke, for example, commences with a historical report, and Matthew with a genealogy; but John has his famous theological prologue that is reminiscent of Genesis: "In the beginning was the Word, and the Word was with God, and the Word was God" (John 1:1; cf. Gen. 1:1). From the start, John engages with the eternal existence of Jesus, the Word of God, and his unique relationship to Israel's God.

Miracles. Obviously John and the Synoptics both recount the wonder-working activity of Jesus. But whereas the Synoptics record numerous miracles, John takes a unique approach. First, John restricts this material to only seven miracles. This apparently demonstrates the special and climactic ministry of Jesus that ushers in new creation. Second, John prefers to call these

1. Robert Kysar, *John, the Maverick Gospel* (Atlanta: John Knox, 1971).

miracles "signs"—events that point or testify to the messianic and heavenly identity of Jesus the Son of God.

Belief. In relation to John's signs, we have the matter of human belief. The Synoptic writers tend to underscore how faith *preceded* Jesus's miracle, and thus he would afterward pronounce, "Your faith has made you well" (e.g., Mark 5:34). But in John the signs are meant to *inspire* belief (e.g., John 11:15).

Teachings. Another prominent feature of John is the extensive teaching blocks throughout the Gospel. The impression one gets from the Synoptics is that Jesus most often taught in clever one-liners and short and pithy parables. While John includes a little parabolic or riddle-like material, we tend to find extensive teaching blocks where Jesus offers lengthy advice and wisdom—such as in the Farewell Discourse (John 14–16).

Concepts. It is not just *how* Jesus teaches that looks different in John; it is also *what* he teaches. In the Synoptics we commonly find Jesus preaching about the kingdom of God and human preparation for the eschaton and final judgment. Again, these issues are not absent entirely from John, but John's Jesus spends much more time talking about belief, truth, testimony, love, and eternal life. And we also find in John the important "I am" sayings (I am the bread of life, light of the world, good shepherd, true vine, etc.).

Spheres of Ministry. We see much difference between the Synoptics and John when it comes to *where* Jesus does his ministry. The common flow of the Synoptics places Jesus in Galilee for the majority of his ministry, only to turn toward Jerusalem later and meet his fate there at the hands of his enemies. But in John, Jesus appears to travel regularly to Jerusalem for special festivals and events.

Enemies. The Synoptics identify multiple groups that take issue with Jesus: Pharisees, Sadducees, scribes, chief priests, Herodians, and so on. John, of course, does mention the Pharisees, but he tends to lump Jesus's disputants together under the title "the Jews." It is not exactly clear what John means by this—after all, Jesus and his disciples were Jews as well. But it could simply be John's way of referring to Jewish leaders. Nevertheless, it is distinctive of John's Gospel.

Christology. At the risk of putting it too simply, in the Synoptics, Jesus serves as a special agent who points to the kingdom of God. Jesus never claims divinity outright, and he even deflects others' attempts to exalt him—"Why do you call me good? No one is good but God alone" (Mark 10:18). In John, Jesus says such mind-boggling things as "The Father and I are one" (John 10:30) and "Whoever has seen me has seen the Father" (John 14:9).

The list could go on regarding how John uniquely presents the life of Jesus, but this is enough of a teaser to raise these questions: Why is John so different? How does John relate to the Synoptics? What are his sources of information? What are the major influences on his Gospel? What are his ultimate aims? We will discuss a general dividing line between scholars with two views: "The Fourth Gospel is not historical" and "The Fourth Gospel is historical."

The Fourth Gospel Is Not Historical

The early church recognized the Fourth Gospel as special among the four Gospels. Many early theologians appealed to the four creatures of Ezekiel and Revelation to point out the complementary nature of the four Gospels. These creatures had four different faces: human, lion, ox, and eagle (Ezek. 1:10; Rev. 4:7). Irenaeus associated the Fourth Gospel with the eagle, insofar as it dwells on the work of the Spirit, which superintends over the church from far above. Clement of Alexandria famously commented, "But, last of all, aware that the physical facts had been recorded in the Gospels, encouraged by his pupils and irresistibly moved by the Spirit, John wrote a spiritual Gospel."[2] Cyril of Alexandria explains that the Fourth Gospel was written as doctrinal interpretation, to supplement the Synoptic Gospels by offering a spiritual understanding of Christ.[3] As Frances Young explains, "Cyril concentrates . . . on ways in which John helps to bring out the significance of events, and largely ignores the problems of chronology and the differences in detail."[4] Now, that is not to say these early theologians treated the Fourth Gospel as suspicious or unhistorical, but clearly they recognized a difference of approach and intention in the Fourth Gospel, and that John wears his theology on his sleeve. J. Louis Martyn captures well the impression one gets when reading the Fourth Gospel versus the Synoptics:

> The very mention of this Gospel causes most of us to think of those marvelous discourses of Jesus, in the reading of which one feels immediately warmed by such "spiritual" and timeless affirmations as, "I am the way, and the truth, and the life." Some of the Johannine Jesus' words seem to be so free of any first-century Palestinian provincialism that we chisel them into the walls of our university libraries, from Chicago to Freiburg, implying that they are philosophical

2. Eusebius, *Ecclesiastical History* 6.14, in *The History of the Church: From Christ to Constantine*, trans. G. A. Williamson (London: Penguin, 1965), 254–55.

3. See Frances Young, "John and the Synoptics: An Historical Problem or a Theological Opportunity?," *Louvain Studies* 33 (2008): 208–20, at 216.

4. Young, "John and the Synoptics," 217.

aphorisms, immediately understood in every enlightened age: "You shall know the truth, and the truth shall make you free."[5]

So, again, many students of the Fourth Gospel have concluded that this is something other than a historical account of the life of Jesus. How scholars account for this varies rather widely. And part of this conversation involves how the Fourth Gospel relates to the Synoptics. For many centuries it was assumed that the Fourth Gospel was dependent on the Synoptics. In the 1930s a new view emerged that argued for the Fourth Gospel's *independence* from the Synoptics.[6] This catalyzed further research into the formative sources and influences of the Fourth Gospel—if not the Synoptics, then what?

There have always been some scholars who assume John simply fabricated material, and though there may be sources of inspiration, what we find in the Fourth Gospel is primarily John's theological imagination. But most scholars have attempted to track down identifiable influences. Rudolf Bultmann, for example, argues that John borrowed imagery from a Greek (pagan) Gnostic redeemer myth in order to transmit the Christian message.[7] John Ashton posits that one thing that makes the Fourth Gospel so distinctive is the conscious borrowing from apocalyptic texts and apocalyptic thought—not that John wrote the Fourth Gospel as an apocalypse (see chap. 7), but simply that he draws apocalyptic elements into the document.[8] Martyn approaches the Fourth Gospel as a "two-level drama," fusing together two story horizons. John's community was struggling with a clash with the Jewish synagogue, and John tells his Jesus story in a way that—on another level—speaks to the social situation of his intended readers.[9] Maurice Casey boldly argues that John's Gospel is riddled with anti-Jewish bias and ought not to be associated with the historical life of Jesus at all.[10]

With these kinds of attitudes and challenges in mind in relation to the Fourth Gospel, many scholars in the last two hundred years have discounted this text as a useful source for the study of the historical Jesus. The Jesus Seminar, for example, came to this conclusion in their study of the canonical Gospels: "The Fellows of the Seminar were unable to find a single saying

5. J. Louis Martyn, *History and Theology in the Fourth Gospel*, 3rd ed. (Louisville: Westminster John Knox, 2003), 27.

6. See P. Gardner-Smith, *Saint John and the Synoptics* (Cambridge: Cambridge University Press, 1938).

7. Rudolf Bultmann, *The Gospel of John: A Commentary*, trans. G. R. Beasley-Murray (Oxford: Blackwell, 1941).

8. John Ashton, *Understanding the Fourth Gospel* (Oxford: Oxford University Press, 1991).

9. Martyn, *History and Theology in the Fourth Gospel*.

10. Maurice Casey, *Is John's Gospel True?* (London: Routledge, 1996).

[in the Fourth Gospel] they could with certainty trace back to the historical Jesus. They did identify one saying that might have originated with Jesus, but this saying (John 4:44) has synoptic parallels. There were no parables to consider. The words attributed to Jesus in the Fourth Gospel are the creation of the evangelist for the most part, and reflect the developed language of John's Christian community."[11] This statement from the Jesus Seminar seems resolute. But it is not the only perspective.

The Fourth Gospel Is Historical

No one would say that the Fourth Gospel records *nothing* historical about the life and words of Jesus. It is not pure myth or fiction. Rather, for most of the Enlightenment the prevailing attitude was that the Fourth Gospel was so heavily embellished with John's theology that, for all intents and purposes, it provided nothing useful beyond what was *already* found in the Synoptics; and when it deviates from the Synoptics its unique material cannot be trusted as historically reliable. Now, there have always been conservative voices in scholarship who have defended the historical usefulness of John's Gospel, but we have seen a major surge of interest and investment in these issues especially in the last twenty years.

Logic and History

Without discounting the ethereal nature of the Fourth Gospel, more and more scholars are identifying features of John's Gospel that can be confirmed by history or logic. For example, in the Synoptics, Jesus is represented as teaching in very short, pithy sayings—and then moving on to another town. But it makes more sense that he would have taught in long blocks, as we see in the Fourth Gospel. In John's story, Jesus makes regular visits to Jerusalem for holy days, something a devout Jew would be expected to do. Many scholars also recognize that John's portrayals of historical figures like Caiaphas resonate with other (nonbiblical) sources.

Alternative Tradition

Historically, the Fourth Gospel has been compared against the Synoptics, the latter considered more straightforwardly reliable. When you do the math, then, it appears as if John's Gospel loses out, three to one. But Paul N.

11. Robert W. Funk and Roy W. Hoover, eds., *The Five Gospels* (San Francisco: Harper-SanFrancisco, 1993), 10.

Anderson argues that this is not the best way to look at the Fourth Gospel and the Johannine tradition. If Matthew and Luke follow Markan tradition (see chap. 1), then what we really have in the New Testament is not three against one but a "Bi-Optic Gospels" perspective—two main traditions, the Markan tradition and the Johannine tradition. Anderson urges scholars to let the Fourth Gospel be heard and studied as a unique Jesus tradition alongside Mark, but not in competition with Mark per se.[12]

Genre

One of the biggest pieces of the Gospels puzzle is the matter of determining their genre. Scholars often put the Gospels to the test in respect to objective factual reporting of events and sayings of Jesus, but it is crucial to ask the question, What exactly were the evangelists' intentions? Most scholars have largely thrown out the facile categories of "history" (e.g., Mark's Gospel) and "myth" (e.g., John's Gospel). Thanks to the important work of Richard Burridge, there is a general consensus that all four Gospels fit broadly within the genre of Greco-Roman biography.[13] Such texts in the ancient world had the purpose of recounting the life of an important person especially to praise their achievements and honor and to inspire emulation in virtue. And it is also recognized that, while ancient Greco-Roman biographies were held to some general expectation of historical credibility, there was room for artistic license from the writer to carry certain thematic threads through the person's life or develop their narrative into a coherent and inspiring story. This has many important implications for studying the canonical Gospels in general, and the Fourth Gospel in particular. First, it has been widely recognized now that it is silly to assume that Mark's Gospel was written merely as fact, devoid of theological nuancing; and, alternatively, it is equally wrong to assume John ignored history altogether. All four Gospels appear to frame their works as biographies of Jesus, with theological agendas, and with varying degrees of "freedom" to narrate, theologize, and provide an interpretation or explanation of what appear to be parts of the source traditions.

The Fourth Gospel as Testimony

Today, we receive world news many steps removed from the actual events—something gets investigated and reported, and then passed on, and on, from

---

12. See Paul N. Anderson, *Riddles of the Fourth Gospel* (Minneapolis: Fortress, 2011).

13. Richard Burridge, *What Are the Gospels? A Comparison with Graeco-Roman Biography* (Cambridge: Cambridge University Press, 1992).

one publication to another, and we see it on our favorite news website or on TV. We often don't pay attention to who the journalist was that was *actually there*. This can trick us into thinking that the evangelists were basically editors who collected tradition materials, stitched them together or modified them, and produced a new text. Richard Bauckham, though, has argued that according to ancient standards, any text claiming association with history was expected to be generated from eyewitness testimony. And if one pays careful attention to the Fourth Gospel, "testimony," "witness," and "truth" are oft-repeated keywords. John seems to go to some length, then, to verify that truth is genuinely important to his project. But Bauckham is also quick to point out that ancient eyewitness testimony was not expected to be "objective" or "dispassionate." It is worth offering an extended section of his conclusion.

> The concurrence of historiographic and theological concepts of witness in John's Gospel is wholly appropriate to the historical uniqueness of the subject matter, which as historical requires historiographic rendering but in its disclosure of God also demands that the witness to it speak of God. In this Gospel we have the idiosyncratic testimony of a disciple whose relationship to the events, to Jesus, was distinctive and different. It is a view from outside the circles from which other Gospel traditions largely derive, and it is the perspective of a man who was deeply but distinctively formed by his own experience of the events.[14]

Reflections

One of the most important Jesus books of the twentieth century is N. T. Wright's *Jesus and the Victory of God* (1996). In 2010, I attended a conference at Wheaton College that reflected on the scholarship of Wright. One session that vividly stands out in my mind is a presentation by Marianne Meye Thompson called "*Jesus and the Victory of God* Meets the Gospel of John"—with Wright eagerly listening and afterward offering a response. Thompson observed that Wright does not engage with the Gospel of John as a source in his study of the historical Jesus, and Thompson argued, "I think John and *JVG* [*Jesus and the Victory of God*] would get along quite well."[15] By that, she meant that material in John would have supplemented and supported Wright's arguments. Wright gave a thoughtful response: the

---

14. Richard Bauckham, *Jesus and the Eyewitnesses: The Gospels as Eyewitness Testimony*, 2nd ed. (Grand Rapids: Eerdmans, 2017), 411.

15. The conference papers were later published. See Marianne Meye Thompson, "*Jesus and the Victory of God* Meets the Gospel of John," in *Jesus, Paul, and the People of God*, ed. Nicholas Perrin and Richard B. Hays (Downers Grove, IL: InterVarsity, 2011), 21–37, at 37.

Jesus scholarship in the middle of the twentieth century (when Wright was beginning his studies) was by nature skeptical about saying anything meaningful at all about Jesus's aims and intentions, even from the Synoptics, let alone the Fourth Gospel. He felt that he had to be cautious about John's Gospel, because it was not treated as a "fair" historical source in the context of Jesus scholarship. He did not want to jeopardize making his case about the historical Jesus due to scholars throwing out his book altogether because of his inclusion of the Fourth Gospel. Wright recognized that there has been a shift in the guild today, and though John's work is still treated as unique, it is being regularly included in Jesus studies. For example, a Society of Biblical Literature group formed in 2002 called "John, Jesus, and History." Widely respected Johannine scholars were brought together, representing a variety of theological stripes and persuasions. Several book projects have emerged from the work of this group, including three major collections titled *John, Jesus, and History*.[16] It is not too much to say, then, that the Fourth Gospel is receiving attention hitherto unprecedented, even in Jesus studies.

In the past, the nature of the discussion about John and history has largely revolved around authorship and sources. Because the exact origins of this Gospel remain unclear, that approach appears to be a dead end—we might be able to construct a hypothetical profile of the author(s), but what kind of results this would offer for this conversation is unclear. Much the same could be said of the issue of sources. Like the other canonical Gospel writers, John obviously utilized some historical tradition(s), but, also as with the other Gospels, we do not have any of those exact documents. Unsurprisingly, then, much of that discussion (source criticism) has dried up in relation to the Fourth Gospel.

For the present and future, what appears to be more promising is further engagement on genre and the communicative or rhetorical aims of the author. Johannine scholar Harold Attridge has made a strong case for seeing John as attentive to existing genres—whether on the microlevel of literary devices and tropes, or the broader level of reading the Fourth Gospel as a biography—but cleverly practicing "genre bending."[17] In a recent essay, Attridge argues that John was not dependent on the Synoptics. John appears to be aware of them, perhaps even borrows from them on occasion, but he writes his own story of Jesus "with a sovereign freedom."[18] John may have been attracted to the

---

16. See the John, Jesus, and History Group homepage at http://johannine.org/JJH.html.

17. Harold Attridge, "Genre Bending in the Fourth Gospel," *Journal of Biblical Literature* 121, no. 1 (2002): 3–21.

18. Harold Attridge, "The Gospel of John: Genre Matters?," in *The Gospel of John as Genre Mosaic*, ed. Kasper Bro Larsen (Göttingen: Vandenhoeck & Ruprecht, 2015), 27–46, at 32.

mysterious qualities of Mark or interpersonal encounters in Luke, but the Fourth Evangelist ultimately found these Gospels unsatisfactory.[19] Attridge positions John as intentionally pressing *against* the historical approach of Luke's Gospel. That is, if Luke had the intention of telling the Jesus story according to "just the facts," as it were, John believed this was the wrong way to go about it.[20] Attridge imagines genre-bending John to have intended something like this: "I am not going to offer you a simply historicizing account; historical recollection is not where you encounter God. I am going to offer you a dramatic encounter with the Divine Word itself; through my words you will be brought face to face with One who will change your life!"[21]

In terms of *genre*, Attridge does not think this special intention of John disqualifies it as a Greco-Roman biography; in line with the idea of genre bending, Attridge appeals to the inclusion in the Fourth Gospel of elements of drama. Ancient Greco-Roman drama had certain generic features, and Attridge argues that we see some of these in the Fourth Gospel. But ultimately what makes the Fourth Gospel special is this often-jarring element of dramatic encounter with God through Jesus. Thus, John has bent the Gospel and biography genre so as to produce a *dramatic* performance of the Jesus story.

Whether one agrees with Attridge's assessment or not, one can see we are far away from facilely labeling the Fourth Gospel as history or legend, truth or myth. Whether we call the Fourth Gospel "theological history," "testimony," or "drama," scholarship is becoming highly attentive to the dynamic nature of this work. Those who study the Johannine writings will continue to fall on a scale of treating it as *more* straightforwardly historical or less so, but its period of neglect or exile is apparently over.

Suggested Reading

Beginner

Anderson, Paul N. *Riddles of the Fourth Gospel*. Minneapolis: Fortress, 2011.

Edward, Ruth B. *Discovering John: Content, Interpretation, Reception*. Grand Rapids: Eerdmans, 2015.

Skinner, Christopher. *Reading John*. Eugene, OR: Wipf & Stock, 2015.

19. Attridge, "Gospel of John," 33.
20. Virtually all scholars agree that Luke (as Mark and Matthew) had a theological agenda, but Luke also seems to go out of his way to explain to his readers that he has written a historical and credible account.
21. Attridge, "Gospel of John," 34.

The Fourth Gospel Is Not Historical

Casey, Maurice. *Is John's Gospel True?* New York: Routledge, 1996.

Funk, Robert W., and Roy W. Hoover, eds. *The Five Gospels*. Sonoma, CA: Polebridge, 1993.

The Fourth Gospel Is Historical

Blomberg, Craig. *The Historical Reliability of John's Gospel*. Downers Grove, IL: InterVarsity, 2011.

Keener, Craig. *The Gospel of John*. 2 vols. Peabody, MA: Hendrickson, 2010.

Advanced

Anderson, Paul N., Felix Just, and Tom Thatcher, eds. *John, Jesus, and History*. 3 vols. Atlanta: SBL Press, 2007, 2009, 2016.

Bauckham, Richard. *Jesus and the Eyewitnesses: The Gospels as Eyewitness Testimony*. 2nd ed. Grand Rapids: Eerdmans, 2017.

Larsen, Kasper Bro, ed. *The Gospel of John as Genre Mosaic*. Göttingen: Vandenhoeck & Ruprecht, 2015.

Thatcher, Tom. *Why John Wrote a Gospel*. Louisville: Westminster John Knox, 2006.

Thompson, Marianne Meye. *John: A Commentary*. New Testament Library. Louisville: Westminster John Knox, 2015.

FOUR

Jesus and Paul

In 2008, a Christian book was published called *Jesus for President*.[1] The book argues that believers are called upon to embody Jesus's own attitude and values toward society. Despite the fact that the authors of this book were trying to demonstrate the countercultural leadership vision of Jesus, the book became a bestseller due in no small part to the fact that pretty much *everyone* likes Jesus. Generally speaking, the world has carried a favorable impression of Jesus, viewing him as a caring person who gave his life in love. What about the apostle Paul? There is no corresponding book called *Paul for President*! For many Christians, Paul comes across very differently than Jesus. Paul can seem cold, grumpy, overly doctrinaire, and bossy.[2] New Testament scholar Anthony Thiselton poignantly describes these ostensibly contrasting characters in this way: "Very many people, perhaps even millions, view Jesus of Nazareth with admiration and respect, but see Paul as the founder of a different system of doctrine and the inventor of established churches. They regard Jesus as a religious idealist, who taught a simple religion of love and tolerance; they regard Paul very differently, as one who imposed his ideas onto others, and who, unlike Jesus, undervalued women and the marginalized of society. This constitutes a first obstacle to understanding and appreciating Paul as he really was, and can be for us today."[3] This "Jesus versus Paul" mentality has a unique history in New Testament scholarship. Especially at the end of the nineteenth and beginning of the twentieth centuries, many scholars bought into a certain reconstruction of early Christian history whereby the "purity" of Jesus's Jewish message and movement was corrupted by the influence of Greek

1. Shane Claiborne and Chris Haw, *Jesus for President* (Grand Rapids: Zondervan, 2008).
2. See the recent book, E. Randolph Richards and Brandon J. O'Brien, *Paul Behaving Badly: Was the Apostle a Racist, Chauvinist Jerk?* (Downers Grove, IL: InterVarsity, 2016).
3. Anthony Thiselton, *The Living Paul* (Downers Grove, IL: InterVarsity, 2010), 1.

Gnosticism and pagan mystery cults. Ultimately, this means that scholars assumed when the followers of Jesus took their message into the wider Greek world, Hellenistic thought consumed that message and mutated it into something else entirely. Many scholars put Paul at the center of this mutation, since (a) he was the early church's most influential theologian, (b) he was "apostle to the gentiles," and (c) he was born a child of the Diaspora (i.e., born among the pagans). The classic proponent of this sort of historical reconstruction of Christianity is German scholar William Wrede (1859–1906), who argued that Paul was "the second founder of Christianity" who "exercised beyond all doubt the stronger—not the better—influence" (over and against Jesus).[4]

There are a number of arguments and assumptions behind Wrede's attitude that have now been debunked. Palestine (where Jesus lived) was not free from Greek influences; so also Jews living in or hailing from the Diaspora were not *less Jewish* than those in Judea per se. Perhaps most important, it is now commonly recognized, based on strong historical evidence and arguments, that Paul's theology bears the marks of central influence from his *Jewish* heritage.[5] Despite the fact that Paul was apostle to the gentiles, while he tried to express his gospel often in ways that could be understandable to gentiles, he did not co-opt pagan Greek deities or pagan religious practices. He was not a syncretist. He proclaimed and honored the one true God (1 Thess. 1:9), he praised the work of God in the life of Israel (Rom. 9), and he continued to identify with his Jewish fellow believers in Christ (see Col. 4:11).

Despite the fact, though, that many of Wrede's working assumptions have been demonstrated to be deeply erroneous, the kind of scholarship that draws a major rift between Jesus and Paul has not disappeared. James Tabor, for example, has written a recent work that questions the move toward bringing Paul and Jesus into alignment, as if Paul were simply the thirteenth apostle, who, as missionary to the gentiles, came into conformity with the wider unified apostolic mission of spreading the gospel of Jesus to the world.[6]

Tabor treats the new scholarly narrative (reading Paul as unified with Jesus and the Twelve) as nothing more than a myth that "serves theological dogma more than historical truth." "To defend such a portrait," Tabor adds, "requires one to ignore, downplay, or deny altogether the sharp tensions and the radically irreconcilable differences reflected within our New Testament documents,

4. William Wrede, *Paul*, trans. E. Lummis (Boston: Beacon, 1908), 180.
5. See the now classic work by Marvin R. Wilson, *Our Father Abraham: Jewish Roots of the Christian Faith* (Grand Rapids: Eerdmans, 1989); cf. N. T. Wright, *Paul: In Fresh Perspective* (Minneapolis: Fortress, 2009).
6. James Tabor, *Paul and Jesus: How the Apostle Transformed Christianity* (New York: Simon & Schuster, 2013).

particularly in Paul's own letters."[7] Tabor, taking up the mantle of Wrede, views Paul as the veritable "founder" of the Christianity we know. Paul broke with the first disciples and taught things they would have considered disgraceful.[8] I am reminded of the 1988 film *The Last Temptation of Christ*, directed by Martin Scorsese. The film, based on Nikos Kazantzakis's novel of the same title, portrays Jesus as listening to Paul preaching about the crucifixion and resurrection (obviously only loosely drawing from the New Testament). The following conversation between Jesus and Paul takes place in the movie:

> JESUS: I'm a man like everyone else. Why are you spreading these lies?
> PAUL: I'm glad I met you. Now I'm rid of you. . . . I've created truth out of longing and faith. . . . If it's necessary to crucify you, then I'll crucify you—and I'll resurrect you, like it or not. The enemy is death and I'll defeat death by resurrecting you—Jesus of Nazareth, Son of God, Messiah.[9]

I begin with these interesting and provocative illustrations of the Jesus and Paul discussion in order to draw attention to the importance of this long-standing debate, but in reality most scholars today eschew such stark contrasts and sensational portrayals of Paul's connection to, or divergence from, Jesus. Still, the point is that one ought to read the Gospels carefully alongside Paul's Letters and try to tune in to recognizable differences as well as similarities. This does not make one the antitype of the other, but it does raise important questions about how and why Paul came to write and think so differently from the Jesus we see and hear in the Gospels.

Just to give an example, I sometimes ask students what they think Paul's gospel was focused on. They tend to come up with the classic answer, "justification by faith." When it comes to Jesus, the answer is *never* "justification by faith" but is closer to something like "the kingdom of God" or "love of God and love of neighbor."

Another illustration comes from a famous statement by Alfred Loisy—he once remarked something to this effect: Jesus called for the kingdom to come, and instead the church showed up![10] This makes light of the fact that Jesus seemed to have spoken often of the "kingdom of God" and rarely of "the

---

7. Tabor, *Paul and Jesus*, 5.

8. Tabor, *Paul and Jesus*, 7.

9. As quoted in Paul Barnett, *Paul, Missionary of Jesus*, After Jesus 2 (Grand Rapids: Eerdmans, 2008), 14.

10. See Alfred Loisy, *The Gospel and the Church*, trans. C. Home (New York: Scribner's, 1908), 166.

church." On the other hand, Paul almost never talked about the "kingdom of God" but frequently about "the church(es)."

Today within the mainstream of New Testament scholarship there tends to be two views on the matter of Jesus and Paul—those who find a significant gap between Jesus and Paul, and those who find a strong cohesion there. I will refer to the first view as "Paul *beyond* Jesus" (especially underscoring *difference*) and to the second view as "Paul following *after* Jesus" (noting Paul's subsequent and unique ministry, but maintaining a strong sense of *continuity*). In the first view, Paul did not seek to subvert the work of Jesus, but neither do we sense a strong continuity; Paul built on the Christ event but clearly developed Pauline Christianity in a unique way. The second approach, Paul following after Jesus, is meant to be a bit of a double entendre. In a literal sense, Paul's ministry coming *later* than Jesus means that there are inevitable differences between them as early Christianity began to take shape. But "following" also carries that sense of discipleship, where Paul sought to carry on the work that Jesus inaugurated (thus, this view underscoring continuity).

Paul beyond Jesus

Obviously Paul's writings are saturated with the name of Jesus Christ, thus he is considered Christocentric. The word "Christ" (in Greek, *Christos*) appears literally hundreds of times in his letters. So much is not contested. But if we tried to use Paul's Letters as an exclusive resource for studying the historical Jesus, admittedly we would have only a meager amount of data for this portrait.

We would know that Jesus was "born" a Jew descended from David (Rom. 1:3; Gal. 4:4). We would incidentally learn that Jesus had a brother (Gal. 1:19). We would know that he had disciples (1 Cor. 15:5), that he had a "last supper" with his disciples (1 Cor. 11:23), and that he was crucified (and thus had offended the Roman state; Gal. 3:1; 1 Cor. 2:2). And of course we would know that the early Christians believed that he was raised from the dead (1 Cor. 15). This hardly makes for a detailed biography. As Victor Furnish points out, if all we had from early Christianity was Paul's Letters, Paul would not clue us in to what Jesus taught (in particular through his parables); we would not know that Jesus was a performer of nature miracles, healings, and exorcisms; we would not know who Jesus's disputants were (e.g., Pharisees, Sadducees, teachers of torah, chief priests); we would not know of a trial or words from the cross; we would not know about Mary and Joseph, John the Baptist, Judas, or Pilate.[11]

11. Victor Furnish, *Jesus according to Paul* (Cambridge: Cambridge University Press, 1993), 43.

Also, given that Paul likes to quote the Old Testament, one might expect him to quote Jesus, but he does so only on the rarest of occasions. A cursory reading of Paul's literature would tell us that the apostle was far more interested in the *Christ event* (Jesus's death and resurrection) than the *life and teachings of Jesus*. There appear to be only three places in Paul's Letters where we detect an overt quotation from the Jesus tradition: 1 Corinthians 7:10–11; 9:14; and 11:23–25.

> To the married I give this command—not I but the Lord—that the wife should not separate from her husband (but if she does separate, let her remain unmarried or else be reconciled to her husband), and that the husband should not divorce his wife. (1 Cor. 7:10–11)

> In the same way, the Lord commanded that those who proclaim the gospel should get their living by the gospel. (1 Cor. 9:14)

> For I received from the Lord what I also handed to you, that the Lord Jesus on the night when he was betrayed took a loaf of bread, and when he had given thanks, he broke it and said, "This is my body that is for you. Do this in remembrance of me." In the same way he took the cup also, after supper, saying, "This cup is the new covenant in my blood. Do this, as often as you drink it, in remembrance of me." (1 Cor. 11:23–25)

This number is remarkably small.[12] But beyond the expectation of quotations, many scholars urge that even certain core elements of the identity and message of Jesus are not present or apparent in Paul's Letters. For example, while disciples and discipleship are central concerns of Jesus, the relevant Greek words ("disciple," *mathētēs*; "to be a disciple," *mathēteuō*) are *entirely* absent from Paul's Letters. To be blunt, this is hardly an accidental omission. It is almost impossible that Paul preached and taught about discipleship but didn't happen to mention it in his letters. If it was terminologically important to Paul, it would have crept into the letters as typical vocabulary, in the same way Paul constantly uses the language of "holiness" or "brothers/sisters."

Another significant concept—not absent from Paul but noticeably underrepresented—is "kingdom of God." This is clearly favored language of Jesus,

---

12. Those who advocate for *more* influence from Jesus (tradition) to Paul appeal to indirect references to Jesus's teachings and life (see below), but some are very skeptical about what this adds; so S. G. Wilson writes, "Allusions to Jesus' meekness (2 Cor. 10:1) or humility (2 Cor. 13:12; Rom. 15:23) at best add an ounce of flesh to these otherwise bare bones [of Jesus quotations]." See "From Jesus to Paul: The Contours and Consequences of a Debate," in *From Jesus to Paul*, ed. Peter Richardson and J. C. Hurd (Waterloo, ON: Wilfrid Laurier University Press, 1984), 1–22, at 7.

but it is used only a smattering of times in Paul's Letters (Gal. 5:21; 1 Cor. 4:20; 6:9–10; 15:50; Rom. 14:17; Col. 4:11; cf. 1 Thess. 2:12; Col. 1:13). Why did Paul not latch onto Jesus's royal imagery?

We could note the ostensible differences between Jesus and Paul regarding the Old Testament law. Jesus affirmed torah, was himself torah obedient, and made it a point, according to Matthew, to say that he did not intend to put aside or abolish the law (Matt. 5:17).[13] Yet, Paul famously announced the "end of the law" with the coming of Christ (Rom. 10:4).[14]

Finally, while we have already noted that Paul's passion for Jesus is what linked the two in the first place, still many scholars have noted how Paul elevated Jesus far beyond what we see in the (Synoptic) Gospels. If we take the Gospel of Mark, we tend to see a Jesus who preaches about his Father in heaven but does not refer much to himself as the center of salvation, and never calls himself God.[15] For example, in Mark 10:17–18, when a man asks Jesus, "Good Teacher, what must I do to inherit eternal life?" Jesus responds, "Why do you call me good? No one is good but God alone." Thus, Jesus ostensibly points away from himself to the one God.[16] Compare this with the hymn of Colossians 1:15–20 (author's translation), which praises a cosmic Christ:

> He [Jesus Christ] is the image of the invisible God,
>> The firstborn over all creation;
> For in him all things were created,
>> In heaven and on earth,
>> Things visible and invisible,

13. According to Matthew, Jesus expected his followers to continue Jewish practices such as fasting and alms (Matt. 6:2–4, 17).

14. The word here for "end" is *telos* in Greek, and scholars and translators disagree on its nuance; it could be "end" in the sense of termination (of something negative, the end of the "reign" of a bad king, so to speak). Or some prefer to translate it as "goal" (CEB) or "culmination," which, while it does carry a sense of completion, has a more positive connotation. If the second interpretation is correct, then Paul's statement in Rom. 10:4 is not dismissive of the law. Still, there are other places where Christ and the law are clearly juxtaposed, as in Rom. 6:14, "Sin will have no dominion over you, since you are not under law [i.e., torah] but under grace."

15. There is some debate, though, about the meaning of the introductory words of Mark: "The beginning of the good news of Jesus Christ" (1:1). Is this "good news" preached *about* Jesus Christ (i.e., Jesus is the message), or is the "good news" preached *by* Jesus Christ (i.e., Jesus is the messenger)? Scholars are divided on the interpretation of this verse—the wording could mean either one.

16. There is an ongoing debate about whether Mark has a low Christology (Jesus is portrayed as human, not divine, or much closer to human than divine) or a high Christology (Jesus is divine, eternal, preexistent, omniscient, etc.).

> Whether thrones or dominions, principalities or powers—
>   All things were created through him and for him;
> And he is before all things,
>   And in him all things hold together.
> And he is the head of the body, the church.
> He is the beginning,
>   The firstborn from the dead,
>   In order that he might be preeminent in everything,
> For in him all the fullness was pleased to dwell,
> And through him to reconcile all things to him,
>   Whether things on earth or in heaven,
>   By making peace through his blood shed on the cross.

In Colossians we have come a long way from "Why do you call me good?" Here Jesus is Creator (or prime agent of creation) and supreme over all, all things were created "for him," and the fullness of deity dwells in him. Famously, Rudolf Bultmann argued that the Christian faith did not become "Christian" until Jesus Christ became the center of the gospel message, and the historical Jesus did not preach *himself* as the gospel of salvation—this was a later development especially worked out by Paul. A process took place whereby Jesus was brought to this center, and we see that unfold over time such that Jesus Christ *is* the gospel in Paul's Letters; thus, "he who formerly had been the *bearer* of the message was drawn into it and became its essential *content. The proclaimer became the proclaimed.*"[17] William Telford draws out how this has shaped the way some scholars view the difference between the historical Jesus and the apostolic ministry of Paul: "In the Gospels, Jesus is presented as the proclaimer of the coming kingdom of God. He directed his hearers to God and his imminent, supernatural intervention in history. The content of his message was the rapidly approaching advent of the Messianic age, God's coming rule. In Acts, as in Paul, the early church is found directing people, by contrast, to Jesus, not the coming kingdom. The content of the church's message, in other words, is Jesus himself."[18] While most scholars who find this statement apt do not think that the apostles were willfully (let alone manipulatively) divergent from the historical Jesus, still the discontinuities they detect merit this kind of label in the eyes of some scholars: Paul *beyond* Jesus. That is, while Paul was fixated on the person of Jesus, he clearly did not adopt some of the core language of Jesus's teachings, nor did he feel the need

---

17. Rudolf Bultmann, *Theology of the New Testament*, trans. K. Grobel (Waco: Baylor University Press, 2007; first published 1951–55 by Scribner's [New York] as 2 vols.), 33.

18. See William R. Telford, *The New Testament: A Beginner's Guide* (London: Oneworld, 2014), 42.

or desire to quote from the Jesus tradition at length. The person and message of Jesus became something more by the middle to end of the first century.

Paul Following after Jesus

No scholar legitimately argues that Paul and Jesus were just two peas in a pod. A quick comparison of the Letters of Paul and the Gospels will show significant differences, examples of which we have noted above.[19] But there are a number of scholars who have strongly resisted the perspective of Wrede and others who press for Paul being the so-called second founder of Christianity (which implies subversion, mutation, and usurpation).

The case for linking Paul and Jesus tends to be threefold: (1) identifying quotations and allusions, (2) identifying shared concepts and themes, and (3) offering a reasonable rebuttal to concerns about vocabulary and thematic differences between these two figures.

Quotations and Allusions

We already mentioned the few Jesus quotes that come from Paul. Beyond that meager evidence, many scholars advocate for a plethora of allusions— that is, moments when Paul draws from the Jesus tradition without citing Jesus verbatim. Scholars tend to list the sorts of parallel texts I offer in table 2.

While it was observed above that Paul did not quote teachings of Jesus word for word very often, this list of allusions demonstrates that there is more to the story, and just because Paul wasn't using full-sentence quotations does not mean he was not heavily influenced by the words of Jesus as they were passed on to him. Paul sometimes refers to Christian traditions taught to him and to traditions he has been entrusted with passing on (e.g., Rom. 6:17; 1 Cor. 11:2; Phil. 4:9), and these almost certainly would have included teachings from Jesus, as the list of allusions suggests.[20]

---

19. What about the Gospel of John? There are, indeed, many similarities between the Johannine Jesus and Paul, but many scholars tend to doubt that John represents the wording and actions of the historical Jesus; see chap. 3. For more on Paul and the Fourth Gospel, see Colin G. Kruse, "Paul and John: Two Witnesses, One Gospel," in *Paul and the Gospels*, ed. Michael F. Bird and Joel Willitts (London: T&T Clark, 2011), 197–219.

20. One factor in this matter involves the method of how allusions to the Jesus tradition are determined. Some scholars argue for as many as sixty connections from Paul to the words of Jesus; others are more strict on the criteria and argue for only a handful. For a helpful methodological discussion, see C. Blomberg, "Quotations, Allusions, and Echoes of Jesus in Paul," in *Studies in the Pauline Epistles: Essays in Honor of Douglas J. Moo*, ed. Matthew Harmon and Jay E. Smith (Grand Rapids: Zondervan, 2014), 129–43.

Table 2. Allusions in Paul to Jesus's Teaching

1 Thessalonians 5:1–7: Now concerning the times and the seasons, brothers and sisters, you do not need to have anything written to you. For you yourselves know very well that **the day of the Lord will come like a thief in the night.** When they say, "There is peace and security," then sudden destruction **will come upon** them, as labor pains come upon a pregnant woman, and there will be no escape! But you, beloved, are not in darkness, for that day to **surprise you like a thief;** for you are all children of light and children of the **day;** we are not of the night or of darkness. So then let us not fall asleep as others do, but let us keep awake and be sober; for those who sleep sleep at night, and **those who are drunk get drunk at night.**

Luke 12:39–40: But know this: if the owner of the house had known at what hour **the thief** was coming, he would not have let his house be broken into. You also must be **ready,** for the Son of Man is coming at **an unexpected hour.**

Luke 21:34–35: Be on guard so that your hearts are not weighed down with **dissipation and drunkenness** and the worries of this life, and that **day** does not catch you **unexpectedly,** like a trap. For it **will come upon** all who live on the face of the whole earth.

Romans 12:14: Bless those who persecute you; **bless** and do not **curse** them. (Cf. 1 Cor. 4:12–13.)

Luke 6:28: Bless those who **curse** you, pray for those who abuse you. (Cf. Matt. 5:44.)

Romans 13:7: Pay to all what is due them—taxes to whom taxes are due, revenue to whom revenue is due, respect to whom respect is due, honor to whom honor is due.

Mark 12:17: Jesus said to them, "Give to the emperor the things that are the emperor's, and to God the things that are God's."

Romans 13:8–10: Owe no one anything, except to **love** one another; for the one who loves another has fulfilled the law. The commandments, "You shall not commit adultery; You shall not murder; You shall not steal; You shall not covet"; and any other commandment, are summed up in this word, "**Love your neighbor as yourself.**" Love does no wrong to a neighbor; therefore, love is the fulfilling of the law.

Mark 12:28–34: One of the scribes came near and heard them disputing with one another, and seeing that he answered them well, he asked him, "Which commandment is the first of all?" Jesus answered, "The first is, 'Hear, O Israel: the Lord our God, the Lord is one; you shall love the Lord your God with all your heart, and with all your soul, and with all your mind, and with all your strength.' The second is this, '**You shall love your neighbor as yourself.**' There is no other commandment greater than these." Then the scribe said to him, "You are right, Teacher; you have truly said that 'he is one, and besides him there is no other'; and 'to love him with all the heart, and with all the understanding, and with all the strength,' and 'to love one's neighbor as oneself,'— this is much more important than all whole burnt offerings and sacrifices." When Jesus saw that he answered wisely, he said to him, "You are not far from the kingdom of God." After that no one dared to ask him any question.

Romans 14:14: I know and am persuaded in the Lord Jesus that **nothing** is **unclean** in itself; but it is **unclean** for anyone who thinks it **unclean.**

Mark 7:15: There is **nothing** outside a person that by going in can **defile,** but the things that come out are what **defile.**

Shared Concepts and Themes

Those who try to argue that Paul took a serious interest in the whole story of Jesus (from before his incarnate birth to beyond the tomb) point to Philippians 2:5–11 and the master narrative of Paul's Christology.

> Let the same mind be in you that was in Christ Jesus,
> who, though he was in the form of God,
>> did not regard equality with God
>> as something to be exploited,
> but emptied himself,
>> taking the form of a slave,
>> being born in human likeness.
> And being found in human form,
>> he humbled himself
>> and became obedient to the point of death—
>> even death on a cross.
>
> Therefore God also highly exalted him
>> and gave him the name
>> that is above every name,
> so that at the name of Jesus
>> every knee should bend,
>> in heaven and on earth and under the earth,
> and every tongue should confess
>> that Jesus Christ is Lord,
>> to the glory of God the Father.

This story from early Christian tradition presumes Jesus's divine preexistence, his incarnation, his death on a cross, and his subsequent exaltation. For those who argue that *all* Paul cared about was the Christ event, the Philippian hymn clearly demonstrates a longer narrative, though it obviously leaves out details related to his earthly ministry. Below I offer, furthermore, several shared themes and concepts that connect Paul to Jesus.[21]

Faith, Good News, and Salvation

Jesus, according to the Gospel tradition, went about preaching the impending kingdom of God and calling Israel to repent and believe in the good news. He commended "faith" (*pistis*; e.g., Mark 5:34). He brought a special kind

---

21. For these themes, I have depended on Todd Still, ed., *Jesus and Paul Reconnected: Fresh Pathways into an Old Debate* (Grand Rapids: Eerdmans, 2007), and James D. G. Dunn, *Jesus, Paul, and the Gospels* (Grand Rapids: Eerdmans, 2011).

of "good news" (*euangelion*; Mark 10:29) and showed followers how to be "saved" (Mark 13:13). Paul adopted remarkably similar vocabulary for his religious discourse—note the confluence of this same language in the famous passage Romans 1:16: "For I am not ashamed of the *gospel* [*euangelion*, good news]; it is the power of God for *salvation* to everyone who has *faith*, to the Jew first and also to the Greek" (emphasis added).

The Grace of God

Consider the use of the language of "grace" (*charis*) in the New Testament. One scholar shows the strong emphasis on grace in both Jesus and Paul by referring to the former's parable of the Pharisee and the tax collector (Luke 18:9–14) and the latter's understanding of the generous forgiveness and mercy shown to him by God (1 Cor. 15:1–10; cf. Eph. 3:8).[22] Thus, both Jesus and Paul make much of the power of God found in divine favor and clemency.

The Virtue of Love

One might think that ancient religious leaders and philosophers commonly talked about "love" (*agapē*); they, in fact, did not. This ethical theme, though, is indeed something shared by Paul and Jesus and stands at the core of both of their messages. For example, Jesus is remembered in the Gospels as someone who affirmed the torah commands to love neighbor (Lev. 19:18) and to love God (Deut. 6:4–5) with one's whole self (see Mark 12:31–33; Matt. 22:37–39; Luke 10:27). As for Paul, love of God is represented well in his letters (1 Cor. 2:9; 8:3; Rom. 8:28; cf. Phil. 1:16), as too is love of neighbor (Gal. 5:14; Rom. 13:9–10).

The Spirit-Flesh Battle

We might also look at the way "spirit" (*pneuma*) and "flesh" (*sarx*) are set in opposition or tension for both Paul and Jesus. Paul writes to the Roman Christians that setting the mind on "flesh" leads to death but setting the mind on the "Spirit" leads to life and peace (Rom. 8:6); to the Galatians he explains that flesh and Spirit stand against each other, the former serving to enslave and ensnare (Gal. 5:16–17).

As for Jesus, he famously chastises his disciples in the garden of Gethsemane for falling asleep while they are meant to be keeping watch with him. He teaches them, "The spirit indeed is willing, but the flesh is weak" (Mark

22. John M. G. Barclay, "'Offensive and Uncanny': Jesus and Paul on the Caustic Grace of God," in Still, *Jesus and Paul Reconnected*, 1–18.

14:38; Matt. 26:41). According to the Gospel of John, Jesus explains that the spirit gives life and the flesh is worthless (John 6:63). There are some questions about whether Jesus is referring to *pneuma* as the Holy Spirit or as the human spirit, but in either case the same tension is expressed.

Care for the Poor

This last point is not the most central theme either in the Gospels or in Paul's Letters, but its distinctiveness bears consideration: both persons, Jesus and Paul, apparently took a special interest in and concern for the poor. Jesus calls the poor "blessed" by God (Luke 6:20), and he defines his ministry in part by how God has brought good news to the poor (Luke 4:18; 7:22). Paul is known for requesting from the gentile churches that money be raised to serve the "poor among the saints at Jerusalem" (Rom. 15:26). Perhaps more important, when Paul recounts how the Jerusalem apostolic leadership first embraced his ministry, he notes that they impressed upon him the need to care for the poor, and Paul quickly adds that he had already been eager to do so (Gal. 2:10).

Rebuttals

One line of debate that comes from those who argue for Paul in *continuity* with Jesus regards rebuttals or responses to those who argue for *discontinuity*. Below I will simply refer to two common rebuttals.

Paul Was Not Jesus's Disciple

Those who argue that Paul and Jesus are remarkably similar often do acknowledge the notable *differences* between these two men. How can this be explained? While some have gone the route of considering Paul a *corruptor* of Jesus's message, there may be a simpler explanation. Paul was *not* a disciple of Jesus the way the other apostles were; he did not live with the earthly Jesus or follow him in his ministry. He did not hear Jesus's parables or see him do healings and nature miracles. That does not mean that Paul was not *influenced* by Jesus. Inevitably, some scholars argue, this leads to differences in expression and even thought.

What the Pauline Letters Assume

It is common to point out that Paul rarely *quotes* the Jesus tradition, and he does not give instruction that emphasizes the earthly life and ministry of Jesus. This is irrefutable. However, one rebuttal is that the letters do not tell the whole story. By and large Paul writes to churches that he himself planted, and he could presume that his epistolary teachings build on his previous instruction among them. Just because he does not quote Jesus and refer to the life of Jesus often in his letters does not mean they were not part of his original apostolic message and instruction. That is, absence of evidence does not amount to evidence of absence.

Reflections

As with all themes in this book, there is no clear winner in this debate. Both sides have worthwhile points to make, and many scholars fall somewhere between the opposing poles. On the side of those who argue for *discontinuity* are the obvious facts that the Pauline Letters simply do not place much interest in or emphasis on the teachings of Jesus and his earthly life and ministry; rather, his tendency is to focus on the Christ event, the saving and formational significance of the death, resurrection, and living lordship of Jesus. On the other hand, sympathizing with those who urge for *continuity*, we can presume that Paul would not have been embraced by the (Jewish) apostolic leadership in Jerusalem unless he was carrying on the vision and program of Jesus. In Galatians, for example, Paul is rather insistent that his gospel could pass muster with the Jerusalem "pillars" like Peter and James. He claimed an independent calling and authority, but he also received "the right hand of fellowship" from them (Gal. 2:9).

There are at least three factors worth mentioning here that help us to process the challenge of the differences between Jesus (of the Gospels) and Paul (of his letters).

The Early Christian Movement(s)

By "movement" here I don't simply mean "group." A movement is a collective that is *in motion*, growing and progressing toward some common purpose. We need to take seriously how Christianity did not simply develop into a full-blown religion the minute Jesus began to preach the kingdom of God in the early first century. Rather, we must think of Christian origins in terms of *stages*. Jesus, of course, came first and (to put it rather simply) launched a movement that was carried on by his followers after his death. Paul became an apostle of Jesus Christ *after* Jesus's death. Even then, the earliest letters of Paul that we have were written well over a decade after the death of Jesus. Scholars sometimes refer to a kind of *gap* between Jesus's and Paul's ministries, this space often referred to as the "tunnel period" (30–50 CE). Presumably much of what shaped earliest Christianity happened in that time, of which we have very little information. Scholars like Victor Furnish have pointed out the problem with trying to compare Jesus and Paul as *individuals* without taking into consideration what can be called "primitive Christianity"—that is, the factors that formed the leadership of the Jesus group in that tunnel period and that would have shaped Paul as well.[23]

Texts and Their Purposes

The tendency in the study of Jesus and Paul is to extract and compare or contrast selections from the Gospels (in relation to Jesus), and Acts and the Letters of Paul (in relation to Paul). Obviously these are the best sources for such a comparative project, but this cut-and-compare process can obscure the fact that Paul's Letters are well-crafted theological documents, as are the Gospels. Frank Matera makes the crucial observation that these documents (letters by Paul, Gospels by the evangelists) have their own unique perspectives and purposes. Matera notes that "the Pauline tradition focuses like a laser beam on Christ's death and resurrection as the decisive moment of God's salvific work," while the Synoptic Gospels "present their theologies in light of the inbreaking kingdom of God."[24] To pose these as contradictory runs the risk of oversimplifying and reducing their theological concerns, which may have served different Christian communities in different ways.

The Damascus Road Vision

This point has been made above, but it should be kept in mind that Paul's starting point for his relationship with Jesus was not being called by the earthly Jesus to serve as one of Jesus's disciples (i.e., students). Thus, Paul did not know Jesus as "teacher." Rather, Paul was accosted by the risen Jesus and commissioned to serve him as an apostle. Thus, the lord-slave relationship was Paul's dominant understanding of Jesus rather than the teacher-student one.

Conclusion

Every generation wrestles anew with the Jesus-Paul question, trying to make sense of the relationship and relative continuity between these massive fig-

---

23. See Victor P. Furnish, "The Jesus-Paul Debate: From Baur to Bultmann," in *Paul and Jesus: Collected Essays*, ed. A. J. M. Wedderburn (Sheffield: Sheffield Academic Press, 1989), 18–50, at 45.

24. Frank Matera, *New Testament Theology* (Louisville: Westminster John Knox, 2007), 99.

ures at the origins of Christianity. We can quite easily set aside the notion that Paul sought to undermine the vision of the earthly Jesus. On the other hand, a close inspection of the Gospels and the Letters of Paul (with insight from Acts) clearly demonstrates the inimitable quality of the apostle's message and perspective. Paul was neither opponent of Jesus nor "disciple." He was a one-of-a-kind apostle of Jesus, called to bring the good news of Jesus to the gentiles. The Jesus-Paul discussion should encourage readers of the New Testament to eschew simplistic harmonization and appreciate the varied voices and contributions that come from different people, communities, and texts that composed and shaped what we now consider formative Christianity.

Suggested Reading

Beginner

Murphy-O'Connor, Jerome. *Jesus and Paul: Parallel Lives*. Collegeville, MN: Liturgical Press, 2007.

Still, Todd D., ed. *Jesus and Paul Reconnected: Fresh Pathways into an Old Debate*. Grand Rapids: Eerdmans, 2007.

Wenham, David. *Paul and Jesus: The True Story*. Grand Rapids: Eerdmans, 2002.

Paul beyond Jesus

Furnish, Victor P. *Jesus according to Paul*. Cambridge: Cambridge University Press, 1993.

Lüdemann, Gerd. *Paul: The Founder of Christianity*. New York: Prometheus, 2002.

Paul Following after Jesus

Barnett, Paul. *Paul, Missionary of Jesus*. After Jesus 2. Grand Rapids: Eerdmans, 2008.

Wenham, David. *Did St Paul Get Jesus Right? The Gospel according to Paul*. Oxford: Lion Hudson, 2010.

Advanced

Allison, Dale C. "The Pauline Epistles and the Synoptic Gospels: The Pattern of the Parallels." *New Testament Studies* 28 (1982): 1–32.

Richardson, Peter, and J. C. Hurd. *From Jesus to Paul: Studies in Honour of Francis Wright Beare*. Waterloo, ON: Wilfrid Laurier University Press, 1984.

Wedderburn, A. J. M., ed. *Paul and Jesus: Collected Essays*. Sheffield: JSOT Press, 1989.

Wenham, David. *Paul: Follower of Jesus or Founder of Christianity?* Grand Rapids: Eerdmans, 1995.

FIVE

Paul's Theological Perspective

In 2012, *Christian Century* engaged in an insightful experiment. They asked fifteen theologians how they might summarize their understanding of the Christian gospel in only seven words.[1] The author of this article, David Heim, explains the inspiration for this project by recounting a story in the autobiography of Will Campbell. Campbell's friend P. D. East challenged Campbell to define Christianity succinctly, "in ten words or less." Obligingly, Campbell responded, "We're all bastards but God loved us anyway." East quickly replied, "If you want to try again, you have two words left."[2]

This anecdote led me to wonder how the apostle Paul would have summarized his own theology. In a Twitter age, succinctness is a virtue, but it would be a tall order indeed to get scholars to agree on a seven-word message for Paul. In 2 Peter 3:15–16, the author takes it for granted that Paul was a man full of wisdom but that some of the things he discussed were "hard to understand." Not much has changed on that score in two thousand years—Pauline scholars vigorously disagree on just about every area that Paul engages, except perhaps that his theology was focused on Jesus Christ.

Thus, you can imagine that much ink has been spilled regarding Paul's theological perspective: What is Paul's overarching approach to theology? Is there a center, or a driving concept or framework? If you had to summarize Pauline theology in only a sentence or two, what would you say? Terms have been put forward to articulate the heart of Paul's theology: for example, "grace," "love," "reconciliation," "peace," "justification by faith." But words like these are properly understood and interpreted only within theological

---

1. David Heim, "The Gospel in Seven Words," *Christian Century*, August 23, 2012, 20–25.
2. Will D. Campbell, *Brother to a Dragonfly* (1977; repr., Jackson: University Press of Mississippi, 2018), 187.

structures and frameworks, so it may be best to address the question of Paul's theology in terms of *approach* or *orientation*. With this in mind, we might say, then, that four approaches or orientations are most common in Pauline scholarship, though we will quickly see that they are not necessarily exclusive. For many scholars, the difference between the following approaches is a matter of emphasis, though almost all will agree that the distinctions introduced by each emphasis matter in the reading of Paul's Letters.

Justification by Faith[3]

The classic Protestant perspective on the theology of Paul concentrates on justification by faith, whereby sin is forgiven by God through the perfect righteousness of Christ, and redemption is received by the believer by faith alone and through the grace of God alone, not by earning favor with God through human works. Martin Luther, the Reformation father of the theology of justification by faith, was especially dependent on Galatians in his formulation of this doctrine; there Paul writes, "We know that a person is justified not by the works of the law but through faith in Jesus Christ. And we have come to believe in Christ Jesus, so that we might be justified by faith in Christ, and not by doing the works of the law, because no one will be justified by the works of the law" (Gal. 2:16).

From Luther's perspective, law and gospel were in conflict. The law places demands on mortals regarding what they owe to God, and humans are not able to meet God's holy and righteous standards because of sin. They stand condemned before God. For those who are redeemed by Jesus Christ, the law can no longer define their relationship with God, because it has been redefined through the righteousness of Christ.[4]

The evidence from Paul that would support this perspective comes primarily from Galatians and Romans, where the preponderance of words occur relating to justification/righteousness, boasting, law, and the work(s)/faith juxtaposition (see Gal. 2–3; Rom. 3). Prior to Christ was the age of the law (i.e., torah), but the purpose of the law was *not* that it could be perfectly obeyed—according to Luther it could not—but rather that humans would inevitably fail in their attempts to establish their own righteousness through the law and, thus, would be moved to turn to God through Jesus Christ for mercy.

3. Scholars who advocate for this approach emphasize words like "justification," "forgiveness," "substitution," "sacrifice," and "atonement."
4. For more on the classic Lutheran view of Paul's theology, particularly pertaining to law and grace, see chap. 6.

The image presented here of salvation, of the gospel, is one that is best imagined in terms of the law court. God is the judge, but he is also the one who sets the standard of human behavior. Humans are condemned for their failure to live up to God's standards and thus deserve punishment. Christ offers himself up to take the place of the sinner; his righteousness is imputed, carried over to the sinner, who receives a status of alien righteousness by faith and hope. Thus, believers can be justified, put right with God, by faith in Jesus Christ.

The most attractive features of this reading of Paul's theological orientation involve two elements: (1) Christology and (2) the works/faith juxtaposition. In the first place, this Lutheran reading places the focus on Jesus Christ: humans have no contribution to make to earn status before a holy God; only the perfect righteousness of Christ can satisfy the justice of God. Second, there is certainly some sort of tension between works and faith in Paul, and Luther defines this tension in terms of achievement and boasting. To be justified *by faith* means that the believer relies completely on the work of Christ for redemption, not on personal merits of any kind.

To help compare and contrast the perspectives on the four approaches to Paul's theology, we will use the text of Romans as the subject for analysis of each approach. When it comes to justification by faith, proponents of this view typically appeal to Romans 1–4. In 1:18–32, in particular, Paul acknowledges the sinfulness of those who have turned away from God and who have reveled in their wickedness. For such people, the wrath of God must stand against what is ungodly (1:18). In chapter 2, Paul highlights the guilt of Jews, the people of God, as well (see 2:17–23). Thus, it must be recognized that "all, both Jews and Greeks, are under the power of sin, as it is written: 'There is no one who is righteous, not even one'" (3:9–10). But, the good news is that, "apart from law, the righteousness of God has been disclosed" (3:21), which is "through faith in Jesus Christ for all who believe" (3:22). Though all have sinned, they can be justified by grace through the saving work of Jesus Christ (3:24).

While the sensibility of this approach has often been affirmed, the justification-by-faith view is not without critics. Those who have pointed to weak spots in this perspective note the following. First, the gospel/law tension tends to exalt the New Testament and the gospel at the expense of the Old Testament. Was there no good news in the Old Testament? Was the law simply meant to crush the mortal's attempt at earning favor before God? Second, Luther placed a significant emphasis on faith, such that some were left to wonder what to do with works. Were they necessary? In what framework? Finally, the justification-by-faith approach tends to be existential—where do I stand before a holy God? In that sense, there can be a self-centered focus on the nature of salvation. This has led to questions about the role and mission of the church. Is there a reason and mission for the community, or can one virtually exist as a believer by oneself?

Salvation History[5]

As noted above, for some critics of Luther's justification-by-faith approach, there is the sense that the New Testament is not tied closely enough to the Old Testament as one continuous story. Thus, some scholars have preferred an approach that focuses on "salvation history" (German: *Heilsgeschichte*), "the personal redemptive activity of God within human history to effect his eternal saving intentions."[6] Here a path of divine activity on behalf of humanity is tracked historically, usually in terms of *phases* of history—for example, from Adam, to Abraham, to Moses, to David, to the exile, to Jesus, and on through the Spirit in the age of the church.

The thrust of this theological perspective is that Paul plotted himself within a climactic stage of history where God had worked in a way anticipated by the Old Testament to enact his plan of redemption in Jesus Christ. According to the salvation-history approach, the Old Testament periods should not be viewed antithetically to the age of Jesus Christ, though they would have had limitations (such as the absence of the indwelling Holy Spirit), but each stage in history contained signposts pointing to final redemption in Christ.

A strong piece of evidence to support this approach is Paul's appeal to the fulfillment of Old Testament promises and prophecies. Perhaps most noteworthy is the appeal to the promise made to Abraham: "And the scripture, foreseeing that God would justify the Gentiles by faith, declared the gospel beforehand to Abraham, saying, 'All the Gentiles shall be blessed in you'" (Gal. 3:8). A bit later Paul summarizes again, "Christ redeemed us from the curse of the law by becoming a curse for us—for it is written, 'Cursed is everyone who hangs on a tree'—in order that in Christ Jesus the blessing of Abraham might come to the Gentiles, so that we might receive the promise of the Spirit through faith" (Gal. 3:13–14).

Again, this kind of approach seems to be in line with the more *narrative-driven* orientation to the gospel demonstrated by Stephen's speech in Acts, where he tells the story of Israel beginning with Abraham, and then he continues

---

5. Scholars who advocate for this approach emphasize words like "promise" and "fulfillment," "climax," and "good news" or "gospel."

6. Robert Yarbrough, "Paul and Salvation History," in *Justification and Variegated Nomism*, ed. D. A. Carson et al. (Grand Rapids: Baker Academic, 2004), 2:297–342, at 297.

with Jacob, Joseph, Moses, Joshua, David, Solomon, and the prophets, finally coming to a climax with Jesus (Acts 7:1–53). Also, a salvation-history approach reflects more closely the Jewish expectations of the language of *gospel*. According to Isaiah, for an Israel languishing in exile and helpless in sin, there would come a day for the herald to ascend the high mountain and announce "good tidings" that God has finally appeared and acted to revive and guide his people (Isa. 40:9); God will come to bring peace and salvation as he reestablishes his kingship among them and his benevolent reign extends to the ends of the earth (52:7–10).

If we again use Romans as our test case, scholars following this approach regularly appeal to Romans 9–11, where Paul takes up the subject of the fate of Israel and the faithfulness of God. Paul defends the righteousness and faithfulness of God toward Israel throughout history. Using the example of Elijah, Paul notes how the prophet questioned God for making him suffer alone; but, Paul points out, God reveals to Elijah that "I have kept for myself seven thousand who have not bowed the knee to Baal" (Rom. 11:4; see 1 Kings 19:18). Those who read Paul from a salvation-history perspective tend to make note of the *continuity* and *consistency* across the canon of God's acts and the overall *progress* of his plan of redemption.

In these chapters of Romans scholars also note how Paul's focus is not on the individual per se but on individuals following God within groups (such as Israel, or the church) and during successive stages of history. Romans 9–11 has to do with the blessing and acceptance of the gentiles (people traditionally ignorant of Israel's God) who have embraced the gospel of Jesus Christ, while the Jews (people who have been protectors of the covenant) have largely rejected the messiahship of Jesus. A salvation-history approach tries to widen the perspective of the gospel from the individual alone to the broader ways that God has worked out his will and sought to fulfill his promises through Israel and the Messiah Jesus, and, now, through the church.

The reason why many scholars are attracted to this approach is because it brings a sense of unity to the biblical canon, Old and New Testaments, especially through a story of God's progressive fulfillment of his promises and plans. Second, it takes seriously Paul's (and the other New Testament authors') interests in the fulfillment of Old Testament Scripture; somehow New is linked to Old, what Christ has done and is doing is connected to what God has done in the past, though now in a greater and more complete sense (though awaiting final consummation).

The pushback against this perspective tends to come from the proponents of the third view (see below, "The Apocalyptic Paul"), particularly that the salvation-history approach, while sensible on a very basic level, tends to overemphasize continuity between past and present. Some articulations of a salvation-history approach make it seem as if the coming of the Messiah, even his death on a cross, was simply the anticipated next step in God's plan, one that fits perfectly the trajectory of redemption in the Old Testament. The problem with this presumption, of course, is that the cross was anything but acceptable to most first-century Jews, and gentiles quickly became the majority in the early church precisely because a crucified Messiah was scandalous, even blasphemous. Can we then speak of *continuity* and *progress* when we see the early Christian writers working so hard to make sense of what looks like an unprecedented *twist* in the story?

A second concern that some have had with this position is that if it seems like the work of God can be plotted so neatly along a line of redemptive work, then we might think that we have God all figured out. One prominent New Testament theologian, Ernst Käsemann, especially showed outrage at this notion: "This would make the divine and the human interchangeable and would allow the church ultimately to triumph over its Lord, by organizing him instead of listening and obeying. The peace of God passes all understanding, and so does God's plan of salvation."[7] Käsemann was also concerned with the salvation-history perspective because it might make it appear as if life should get better and better for Christians, but there must always be something counterintuitive about the gospel: any sense of triumphalism must be shattered by the sign of the cross.[8]

The Apocalyptic Paul[9]

The third perspective we will survey is called "the apocalyptic Paul." Particularly in the centuries just before the appearance of Jesus Christ, some forms of Judaism became interested in the work of God whereby he would rend the heavens and break into history (e.g., Isa. 64:1) to bring salvation to his people in a powerful way, establishing a new creation. The change from the old epoch to the new epoch would be not slow or simple but catastrophic and comprehensive. Note what is written in Isaiah:

> All the host of heaven shall rot away,
> and the skies roll up like a scroll.

7. Ernst Käsemann, *Perspectives on Paul*, trans. M. Kohl (Philadelphia: Fortress, 1971), 63.
8. See Käsemann, *Perspectives*, 67–68.
9. Scholars who advocate for this approach emphasize words like "deliverance" or "rescue," "victory," and "new creation."

> All their host shall wither
>> like a leaf withering on a vine,
>> or fruit withering on a fig tree. (34:4)

Jesus expands on this same kind of vision and adds, "Then they will see 'the Son of Man coming in clouds' with great power and glory. Then he will send out the angels, and gather his elect from the four winds, from the ends of the earth to the ends of heaven" (Mark 13:26–27).

The word "apocalyptic" comes from the Greek word *apokalypsis*, which means "unveiling." In early Jewish literature this word often had to do with the revealing of divine mysteries, things previously kept hidden, but it came to be linked with the world-transforming work of God whereby he would vanquish the unrighteous and vindicate his own people. A Jewish apocalyptic perspective divided history into two periods: the "old age," marked by evil and sin, and the "age to come," in which God would usher in a new period of righteousness and peace. Such an expectation of a new age often depended, on the one hand, on extreme pessimism toward human goodness and efficacy and, on the other hand, the almighty work of God for the sake of helpless mortals. In no way could humans partner with God, or help him out in his plans. Humanity was viewed as spiritually bankrupt, incapable of goodness. They were not merely lost wanderers, needing to be turned back on the path. Rather, they were captives, prisoners in need of rescue.

An apocalyptic worldview, dependent as it was on seeing the failure of human progress, emphasized the power of cosmic entities: demons and the devil, angels and the will of God. Those with hope did not turn to one another with the expectation of a fresh commitment to obedience; they turned to the heavens and invoked the saving work of a liberating God.

Scholars who attribute an apocalyptic mind-set to Paul tend to reject a simplistic salvation-history approach, because the "apocalypse" of Jesus Christ was so utterly world shattering and unexpected that it put an end to the kind of world it left behind. James D. G. Dunn explains a Pauline apocalyptic perspective in this way: "For Paul the gospel meant not the extension forward in time of the ongoing line of salvation-history, but the breaking of the line, the irruption of a wholly new and different age upon the old; and the latter (the old age) now has to be seen not as the age of antecedent or proleptic grace, but as the age characterized by evil from which the gospel provides the means of rescue."[10] From this perspective, the gospel of the crucified and risen Christ was such a unique event that, instead of fitting into a present

---

10. James D. G. Dunn, *The New Perspective on Paul* (Grand Rapids: Eerdmans, 2008), 254.

pattern as its conclusion, it established a brand-new frame of reference that redefined everything before it.

To summarize, we may say that an apocalyptic perspective contains three key elements: (1) the unveiling of new and special revelation; (2) cosmic warfare between spiritual and supernatural powers that impinge upon human, earthly experience, especially focused on Christ's conquering of "Sin" and "Death" (as spiritual tyrants); and (3) an age of "new creation" that transforms the totality of existence, though with acknowledgment that the world awaits final redemption at the return of Christ. An apocalyptic approach to Paul underscores God and his Christ as victors (through the cross and resurrection) over Sin and Death, and over all evil. This does not deny the reality of present suffering; rather, suffering happens because evil continues to put up a fight despite its defeat. But the emphasis still falls on the battle won by the overwhelmingly superior salvific power of God.

If we look at Romans, the focus for an apocalyptic approach tends to be directed toward chapters 5–8. A key dimension of these chapters is the emphasis on sin and death. However, for Paul, "sin" is not simply wrongdoing, and "death" is not merely the end of life. Rather, Paul seems to use these terms ("sin" and "death") as ciphers for two cosmic entities or evil powers: Sin and Death. Thus, "death exercised dominion from Adam to Moses" (5:14). Death is viewed as the ultimate enemy of God, some*one* to be defeated (1 Cor. 15:26). Similarly, Sin, understood by Paul as some kind of partner to Death, also "reigned" until the coming of Christ (Rom. 5:21). Believers are called to recognize Sin and Death for who they are, the archenemies of God, and to resist the mastery of Sin (6:12–14). While humans were previously slaves to Sin, those who are in Christ have been "set free" and now belong to God (6:18–22). Despite this new freedom from captivity, the people of God must resist the flesh and the temptation of Sin until the final hope of glory, when all of creation will be set free (8:19–25).

The apocalyptic approach has much in its favor: it is able to account for some of the unique ways that Paul refers to sin and death as more than anthropological phenomena. There is also something larger than life about Paul's portrayal of the work of God, battling against the powers of evil and promising the intervention of Christ with his holy angels (2 Thess. 1:7). This approach is able to account for Pauline language of freedom, deliverance, and victory that marks his letters (1 Cor. 15:54–57; Rom. 8:37; Gal. 5:1; Col. 1:13).

But what about the sense of *discontinuity* that is part of this approach to Paul? Does an apocalyptic perspective necessarily clash with the salvation-history approach? This is a major criticism of the apocalyptic perspective.

We will explore this further below, but suffice it to say some have criticized this perspective for failing to acknowledge fulfillment language in Paul.[11]

Participation in Christ[12]

The fourth approach to Paul's theology we will examine is most commonly referred to as "participation in Christ" or "union with Christ." This perspective begins with the idea that Christology is at the heart of Paul's thought about history, salvation, and all of life. In terms of how this appears in Paul's Letters, the easiest place to begin is with Paul's language of "in Christ." Regularly in his writings, Paul refers to believers as living, being, or existing *en Christō* ("in Christ"), as in the well-known Pauline verse "If anyone is *in Christ*, there is a new creation: everything old has passed away; see, everything has become new!" (2 Cor. 5:17). Paul takes for granted that to be a Christian is not simply to be thought of as receiving divine benefits through Christ but somehow to actually be united with Christ himself (Rom. 16:7).

This idea of being united with Christ comes out clearly in 1 Corinthians 6, where Paul scolds certain Corinthian believers for senselessly sleeping with prostitutes: "Do you not know that your bodies are members of Christ? Should I therefore take the members of Christ and make them members of a prostitute? Never! Do you not know that whoever is united to a prostitute becomes one body with her? For it is said, 'The two shall be one flesh.' But anyone united to the Lord becomes one spirit with him" (1 Cor. 6:15–17).

For Paul, participating in Christ, however this can be explained conceptually (see below), is primarily relational but leads to transformation of the person—as Christ lives within, he changes the believer from the inside out. But this process happens through a sharing in not simply the resurrection life of Christ but also his suffering and death. Romans 6:1–14 is an important passage in this regard. On the matter of whether believers can continue in sin, Paul offers a negative answer precisely because of the transforming presence and power of being one with Christ. Paul uses the imagery of baptism to illustrate this union with Christ: "Do you not know that all of us who have been baptized into Christ Jesus were baptized into his death?" (6:3). Believers must enter into the suffering, burial, and death of Christ in order to experience the fullness of his new life (6:4). Again, for Paul, this is the mechanism of true

---

11. The matter of prophecy or Scripture and its fulfillment in Paul is a very complicated debate and is treated in chapter 12, on the Old Testament in the New.

12. Scholars who advocate for this approach emphasize terms like "union with Christ," "participation," "transformation," and "cruciformity," and any kind of "in Christ" language.

redemption—to be "united with him in a death like his" (6:5) in order to put to death the nature of the "old self" enslaved by sin (6:6). This participation in Christ's death has the capacity to set the believer free from the power of sin and death (6:7); "death no longer has dominion over [Christ]" (6:9), and those who share in the death of Christ experience that same freedom (6:11).

One scholar refers to this redemptive process not as *substitution* (which implies exchange) but as *interchange*; that is, the death and resurrection of Christ "work" for salvation not because the sinner and Christ change places but because the believer *enters into* this process and is affected *with* Christ, not apart from him.[13] This idea of interchange is often explained with reference to a pithy statement deriving from second-century theologian Irenaeus: Christ became what we are, so that we might become what he is.[14] Christ was innocent and obedient; humans, as sinners, are guilty and disobedient. In terms of interchange, what is required is not simply a verdict of "not guilty" but for real change to happen at the core of the sinner, the part infected and corrupted by sin. This is often understood by Paul in terms of severing the tie to the old Adam, the human race linked to the enslaving power of sin east of Eden. Insofar as Adam served as the representative of all humanity before Christ, Paul could refer to being "in Adam" (1 Cor. 15:22). What Christ came to do was establish a new way to be human, a new type of humanity after the pattern of a new Adam (or "last Adam"; 1 Cor. 15:45).

A new life "in Christ," then, requires the death of the old life "in Adam." This perspective (interchange) helps to explain Galatians 2:19–20: "I have been crucified with Christ; and it is no longer I who live, but it is Christ who lives in me. And the life I now live in the flesh I live by faith in the Son of God, who loved me and gave himself for me."

Many scholars believe this idea of union with Christ or participation in Christ has some undeniable explanatory power when it comes to Paul's understanding of salvation, but the question remains, What framework makes this approach sensible? Put another way, is there a context or paradigm that inspired this idea for Paul? In its actual expression, Paul either leaves it generic ("in Christ"), or he is given to using several different metaphors (baptism, burial, marriage, etc.). Is there a wider system that connects these smaller expressions? A popular idea of a bygone era, now largely debunked, treated Paul's union-with-Christ language as mystical, a kind of ethereal and spiritual participation presuming that Paul was influenced by (pagan) Greek religious notions. Noting

13. See Morna D. Hooker, "Interchange in Christ," in *From Adam to Christ: Essays on Paul* (Cambridge: Cambridge University Press, 1990), 13–25.
14. See Irenaeus, *Against Heresies* 5.preface.

Paul's Jewish heritage and commitments, scholars today have more of a desire to link his participation thought to *Jewish* categories like the covenantal bond. Still, there appears to be a feature of this union language and thought, as it relates to the death, resurrection, and new life of Christ, that is unprecedented.

The advantage of this view is that it is so readily demonstrable from Paul's Letters; the concept of being "in Christ" is almost literally on every page of his writings. The problem is that it is so all-consuming, with so little agreement among scholars about where this language comes from, that it becomes difficult to flesh out how it works (so to speak) in his theology. Thus, it can be combined with any of the other approaches. When a view is that wide, there is concern that it loses some of its substance as a distinctive approach to Paul's theology.

Reflections

Over the years, as I have put forward to students these four approaches to Paul's theology and recounted the serious debate and zealous passions that come with the discussion in scholarship, students are often left wondering why scholarly views tend to be so polarized. Why does it seem to scholars that there must be just one right answer? Some have advocated for a kaleidoscopic view[15] that tries to find ways to integrate different perspectives, but most scholars tend to lean heavily in favor of one or two of these approaches for a variety of reasons.

Those who have historically advocated for the justification-by-faith view are largely indebted to the theological influence of Luther and Reformation emphases, and there is a tendency to focus the discussion primarily on Romans and Galatians. When it comes to salvation history, there is strong advocacy from scholars in the Reformed (Calvinist) tradition with an interest in seeing Old and New Testaments together as one overarching story of salvation. As for the apocalyptic perspective, scholarly interest in this perspective especially developed during and in the aftermath of the horrors of the Holocaust and World War II, and with the recognition that too much emphasis has been placed on so-called human progress; what was needed in theological reflection was a fresh rethinking of divine power and transformation in light of the evils and atrocities of human sinfulness. Finally, with the participation approach, the influences are multiple and quite diverse, but some scholars have said that this kind of approach is more prominent in the Eastern Christian traditions (like Greek Orthodoxy), not least because Romans and Galatians did not have the superior status that they maintained in the Reformational

15. See Joel B. Green, "Kaleidoscopic View," in *The Nature of the Atonement: Four Views*, ed. James Beilby and Paul R. Eddy (Downers Grove, IL: InterVarsity, 2006), 157–201.

communities. If texts like 1–2 Corinthians and Philippians had been considered with equal attention and weight, some have said, a "union with Christ" theology might have developed more strongly and dominantly in Protestant Pauline scholarship than it did.

What we might learn from this brief reflection on influences and perspectives is that there is much richness in the Pauline corpus, and historical influences and personal and ecclesial commitments have guided theologians in their study of Paul. It is now widely acknowledged that we all come to the text of Scripture with presuppositions—it does no good to deny this. Stripping ourselves of assumptions and commitments is not only impossible but would also be detrimental. Rather, the best thing is to be aware of *undue* bias and to approach reading as a learner and not master of the text.

When we look at the cutting-edge discussions of this issue, there are a cluster of three dynamics that set the terms of how the debate takes shape.

Contingency and Coherence

How do we hold together both the fact that Paul's Letters are contextualized correspondences to particular churches, often to answer problems or deal with false teaching or misunderstandings, and the reality that behind these letters is one Pauline theology (or at least one coherent way of thinking)? How do we discover the theology or theologizing that can be gleaned (if possible) through such correspondences, especially when we have only Paul's voice (and not the original questions or concerns from the Corinthians or the problematic teachings that were given to the Galatians from opponents of Paul)?

Human and Divine Agency

When we look at Paul's theology, what roles do human will, effort, and obedience play in the relationship with God, particularly in view of salvation and final judgment? What role does God play? Is this a zero-sum dynamic—God offers a certain percentage of agency, and humans another? Is it all God? If so, then do humans do anything at all? If human obedience is obligatory, does grace cease to be grace? How active is faith? What kind of agency does participation assume? Does the nature of human agency change from the people of God in the Old Testament to the people of God in the New Testament?

Old and New, or Continuity and Discontinuity

A major point of debate involves the relationship between the New Testament and the Old Testament (or the period[s] before Christ and the period[s] after). Is the Bible a continuous story? Does the twist of Jesus frustrate this? Is the Old Testament law (torah), so central to divine grace in the Old Testament, preparatory for the gospel of Jesus Christ or at odds with it, or something else? These are questions that have been asked since the time of the earliest Christians, and yet they are still very much in play in modern discussions and debates as well.

Suggested Reading

Beginner

Bassler, Jouette. *Navigating Paul*. Louisville: Westminster John Knox, 2006.

Bird, Michael F., ed. *Four Views on the Apostle Paul*. Grand Rapids: Zondervan, 2012.

Gombis, Timothy. *Paul: A Guide for the Perplexed*. London: T&T Clark, 2010.

Justification by Faith

Seifrid, Mark. *Christ, Our Righteousness: Paul's Theology of Justification*. Downers Grove, IL: InterVarsity, 2001.

Westerholm, Stephen. *Perspectives Old and New on Paul*. Grand Rapids: Eerdmans, 2003.

Salvation History

Yarbrough, Robert. *The Salvation Historical Fallacy? Reassessing the History of New Testament Theology*. Leiden: Deo, 2004.

The Apocalyptic Paul

Beker, J. Christaan. *Paul's Apocalyptic Gospel: The Coming Triumph of God*. Philadelphia: Fortress, 1982.

Blackwell, Ben C., John K. Goodrich, and Jason Maston, eds. *Paul and the Apocalyptic Imagination*. Minneapolis: Fortress, 2016.

Martyn, J. Louis. *Theological Issues in the Letters of Paul*. Nashville: Abingdon, 1997.

Participation in Christ

Gorman, Michael J. *Participating in Christ: Explorations in Paul's Theology and Spirituality*. Grand Rapids: Eerdmans, 2019.

Hooker, Morna D. *From Adam to Christ: Essays on Paul*. Cambridge: Cambridge University Press, 1990.

Advanced

Campbell, Douglas A. *The Quest for Paul's Gospel*. London: T&T Clark, 2005.

Wright, N. T. *Paul and His Recent Interpreters*. Minneapolis: Fortress, 2013.

Zetterholm, Magnus. *Approaches to Paul: A Student's Guide to Recent Scholarship*. Minneapolis: Fortress, 2009.

SIX

Paul and the Jewish Law

Several years back I happened to be visiting a friend's church on a Sunday when the pastor was preaching on grace in the New Testament. On the screen above his head, he had these equations:

Old Testament = Law
New Testament = Grace

He spent a large portion of his preaching time assuring his congregation that we can be relieved that we are not beholden to the Old Testament law, and that now we live according to God's graciousness and mercy. I can see how some have come to this understanding—after all, "the law indeed was given through Moses; grace and truth came through Jesus Christ" (John 1:17). However, I was concerned that this sermon would convey a problematic assumption that if the New Testament gospel is "good news," then the Old Testament teaching is basically "bad news." No wonder many Christians neglect the Old Testament! Who wants to spend time reading about law when you could read about grace?

The kind of teaching described above raises important questions about the relationship between the Old and New Testaments, and particularly about the role of the Old Testament law. When the New Testament is portrayed as rivaling the Old Testament theologically, then how can one help but want to put the Old Testament at a distance. This problematizes the role of the Old Testament in Christian formation and theology.

Much of the discussion around these issues focuses on the Letters of Paul in particular, especially because of certain statements Paul makes in Galatians and Romans, and how those texts have shaped Christian thinking throughout the years. Just to give an example, recently I happened upon a short self-published book on Galatians that had, on its cover, a photograph of a SWAT team officer with his eyes looking through the scope of some kind of large assault-style weapon. The title of the book was *Galatians: Step Away from the Law*. It would be a serious understatement to say that the author of this book saw the Old Testament law as an enemy of the Christian believer!

Undoubtedly the above examples are extreme perspectives, but they do represent a wider recognition that Paul has some negative things to say about the Old Testament law. Before we look at some sample texts, it is helpful to define what we mean by the "Old Testament law."

We think of laws today in particularly political terms—traffic laws, avoiding criminal activity, paying taxes, and so on. In most cases, though, Paul was referring to the *covenantal* commitment that bound Israel to God, especially the regulations and expectations given to the people through Moses on Mount Sinai. Thus, this is sometimes referred to as the Mosaic law. The Hebrew word for this covenantal law is *torah*. It is a mistake to think of torah, from a Jewish perspective, as simply a bunch of oppressive laws. When we read all of the rules and laws stipulated in the Pentateuch, our tendency is to presume the Israelites saw this as a burden. However, it behooves us to read texts like Psalm 19, which exalts torah as a divine gift and treasure: "The law of the LORD is perfect, reviving the soul" (19:7). Torah gives joy to the heart and light to the eyes (19:8). "More to be desired are [the commandments of God] than gold, even much fine gold; sweeter also than honey, and drippings of the honeycomb" (19:10). In modern terms, the psalmist would say, "To gain the law I would sell my laptop, smartphone, and car, tear up my winning lottery ticket, and swear off chocolate and ice cream forever!"

How could Israelites believe that? Who likes following rules and laws? Think of it this way: Pretend you are a good swimmer, but you want to be better. Imagine an Olympic swimming coach graciously selects you to be one of her primary trainees. Her only stipulation is that you have to follow meticulously the training regimen of the Olympic athletes. Would you say, "Ho-hum, sounds too involved, and I can't bother"? No! You would jump at the privilege and opportunity to receive that kind of first-class training. No matter how *hard* the rules are, it would all be worth it because *the coach knows best*. It is not drudgery; it is an honor and privilege. And so it is with Israel and the torah's commandments: "By them is your servant warned; in keeping them there is great reward" (Ps. 19:11). Nevertheless, despite this Davidic praise of torah, we are left with some less-than-glowing statements from Paul.

> Yet we know that a person is justified not by the works of the law but through faith in Jesus Christ. (Gal. 2:16; cf. Rom. 3:28)

For all who rely on the works of the law are under a curse; for it is written, "Cursed is everyone who does not observe and obey all the things written in the book of the law." (Gal. 3:10)

But if you are led by the Spirit, you are not subject to the law. (Gal. 5:18)

For sin will have no dominion over you, since you are not under law but under grace. (Rom. 6:14)

For God has done what the law, weakened by the flesh, could not do: by sending his own Son in the likeness of sinful flesh, and to deal with sin, he condemned sin in the flesh. (Rom. 8:3)

For Christ is the end of the law so that there may be righteousness for everyone who believes. (Rom. 10:4)

The sting of death is sin, and the power of sin is the law. (1 Cor. 15:56)

How could Paul, a good Jew, write such things? What was the problem with the law? A dominant perspective, inherited especially from the Protestant Reformation and Martin Luther in particular, is that the primary problem is one of trying to earn justification through one's works, rather than trusting in Jesus Christ for justification by grace through faith. About forty years ago, however, this faith-versus-works perspective on Paul's problem with the law was challenged by a number of scholars and led to a New Perspective on Paul that has changed the landscape of the discussion of this topic.[1]

The New Perspective on Paul

The New Perspective on Paul (NPP) opposes the attitude that the Judaism of Paul's day was legalistic and driven by works righteousness. Proponents of the NPP argue that it is problematic when modern interpreters import a legalistic framework of Judaism into the reading of Paul's Letters, assuming Paul's grand vision becomes justification by faith and a movement away from the merit-based justification of Judaism. In contrast, the NPP posits that Second Temple Judaism was based on a covenant that recognized and valued as foundational the grace and mercy of God.

1. Some of the material from this chapter comes from Nijay K. Gupta, "Paul, New Perspective on," in *The Lexham Bible Dictionary*, ed. John D. Barry, David Bomar, et al. (Bellingham, WA: Lexham Press, 2016). Used by permission.

The NPP argues that when Paul criticizes works, he is referring in particular to the Jewish law (torah). Thus, Paul was not arguing against doing good things for God, nor was he prioritizing inner faith over outward deeds. The NPP sees Paul as opposing that form of Jewish Christianity that would require gentiles to adhere to the requirements of the torah in order to be part of the people of God. From this angle, Paul was not against works per se but against the idea that gentiles were required to obey torah in order to be welcomed into the church (as the one people of God). Thus, the NPP has always had a strong sociological and ecclesiological dimension, viewing Paul's contribution to an understanding of salvation and faith as not only a vertical doctrine (about the individual and God) but a horizontal one as well (welcoming gentiles into the covenantal community *as* gentiles and not as converts to a Jewish religion). In the history of the development of the NPP, four key founders or proponents have been identified.

Krister Stendahl: No Guilty Conscience for Paul the Jew

Swedish New Testament scholar Krister Stendahl wrote a watershed article in the 1960s called "The Apostle Paul and the Introspective Conscience of the West," in which he pressed scholars to read and interpret Paul in terms of Paul's own religious environment—reacting to the problems of his own day and not to ours.[2] Stendahl discourages Pauline interpreters from reading the experience and rhetoric of Paul through the lens of Martin Luther's introspective struggle. Stendahl argues that neither the religious environment of Paul's Jewish context nor the evidence of his letters suggests that Paul should be treated as someone who sought God's justification as a hopeless sinner. To put it bluntly, Christians have established a narrative where a guilty Paul sought hopelessly for a forgiving and loving God—only to eventually find him in Jesus Christ (thereby discarding and rejecting legalistic Judaism). The problem here, Stendahl argues, is that Paul seemed confident in his Jewish religiosity until Christ confronted him and turned his world upside down.

E. P. Sanders: Rethinking Judaism

In his 1977 work, *Paul and Palestinian Judaism*, Ed Parish Sanders argues that the pattern of the Judaism of Paul's time was not indicative of a legalistic religion based on the accumulation of good works.[3] Rather, Sanders pro-

2. Krister Stendahl, "The Apostle Paul and the Introspective Conscience of the West," *Harvard Theological Review* 56 (1963): 199–215.
3. E. P. Sanders, *Paul and Palestinian Judaism* (Philadelphia: Fortress, 1977).

poses that Palestinian Judaism relied on God's election of Israel and his grace toward his people. While torah obedience had its place, Jews of that period demonstrated a religious attitude and practice that assumed divine mercy as well as human responsibility and action. Sanders coins an important phrase for this religious dynamic or pattern: "covenantal nomism"—a relationship with God founded on divine grace and mercy ("covenantal"), but also driven by the expectation of torah obedience ("nomism").[4] He emphasizes that the sacrificial system presumed that the covenantal people would fall short of the high expectations of the torah and provided a means for restoration and atonement when such transgressions occurred.

Even though Sanders's covenantal nomism model has been criticized, his findings have greatly affected New Testament scholarship, because they have brought about a renewed interest in the Jewish roots of and influence on the New Testament. Sanders argues that the texts of early Judaism must be treated with more care and a keener interpretive eye.

Sanders also proposes that Paul did not follow the covenantal nomism model after his encounter with Christ, but this view is less accepted even by many of those who identify with the NPP. Sanders himself believes that Paul was so focused on participation in Christ that his own religious approach could not be reasonably compared to common Judaism.

For Paul, Christ was the unique solution to humanity's problem with sin. Sanders argues that Paul was not desperately in search of a solution to the problem of sin prior to encountering Christ. Rather, texts like Philippians 3:6 ("As to righteousness under the law, [I was] blameless") show that the Pharisee Paul would have considered himself acceptable to God within the parameters of the Jewish covenant. Once Paul was confronted by Christ, however, his reflections on sin and salvation worked from "solution to plight"[5]—that is, only after meeting the crucified and risen Christ did he realize that he and his Jewish people were in need of rescue from a desperate situation.

James D. G. Dunn: Works of the Law as Jewish Identity Markers

The phrase "New Perspective on Paul" was first coined by James D. G. Dunn during a university lecture in 1983.[6] While crediting Sanders for aiding biblical scholars in their understanding of the pattern and nature of early Judaism, especially the model of covenantal nomism, Dunn has shown concern

---

4. From the Greek word *nomos*, which means "law."

5. Sanders, *Paul and Palestinian Judaism*, 475.

6. Subsequently published as James D. G. Dunn, "The New Perspective on Paul," *Bulletin of the John Rylands Library* 65 (1983): 95–122.

with the distinction Sanders draws between the Judaism of Paul's time and Paul's new pattern of religion "in Christ."

Using Sanders's model of covenantal nomism, Dunn notes that the Mosaic law functioned *socially* as an ethnic boundary marker or badge, marking out those who were Jewish and thus fell within God's elect covenantal family. He reasons that Paul was not arguing in Galatians that it was wrong to perform works in general; rather, he was concerned that a Jewish focus on torah obedience had become a barrier between Jews and gentiles—one that Christ had abolished so that humankind could be unified by faith in him. Certain troublemaking teachers were proposing that gentile Galatians can be acceptable to God only by honoring Christ *and* becoming Jewish; and in that time and culture one demonstrated Jewish identity through in-group badges such as circumcision, proper practice of food laws, and keeping the Jewish holy days. What Paul argued against was not works *as works* but these specific kinds of works that compelled gentiles to become Jewish in order to be justified.

N. T. Wright: A New People of Abraham in the Messiah

In addition to his substantial scholarly work on Paul, N. T. Wright has brought this discussion to a broader audience through his international lectures, popular works, and commentaries. He has responded favorably to Sanders's covenantal nomism pattern for Judaism and Dunn's argument that Paul's terminology of "works of the law" was especially focused on the social dimension of torah dividing Jews from gentiles. Wright focuses on drawing implications from the work of Sanders and Dunn with a view toward biblical theology. He emphasizes that Jesus as the Jewish Messiah has summed up in himself the role of Israel in Yahweh's plan of redemption and salvation, especially in fulfillment of the promise covenant to Abraham.[7]

In the last several decades, many New Testament scholars have endorsed and supported this New Perspective, especially in view of these three arguments:

1. Paul must be studied within the religious and social milieu of his own time. The terms and expressions he uses need to be examined in respect to the closest texts of his environment—namely, texts of early Judaism (e.g., the writings of Josephus and Philo, the Old Testament Pseudepigrapha and Apocrypha, and the Dead Sea scrolls).

7. See especially his early work, N. T. Wright, *What Saint Paul Really Said: Was Paul of Tarsus the Real Founder of Christianity?* (Grand Rapids: Eerdmans, 1997).

2. Those studying Paul must not make hasty presumptions about what he was arguing against, as if his Jewish opponents were tallying up merit points in view of final judgment. Jewish texts must be read closely and judiciously. The NPP has brought about a greater awareness that many early Jewish texts contain a strong element of the mercy and committed love Yahweh shows for his people.

3. Paul was a social advocate and agent as well as a theologian; he was concerned for the unity of God's people, both Jews and gentiles. This was not a secondary concern but a primary one. It does not supplant the matter of salvation but is intricately bound up in the divine plan of redemption.

Against the New Perspective on Paul

While the NPP was the hot topic of Pauline studies in the last quarter of the twentieth century, there has been much criticism and pushback from a variety of sectors. It is worth noting four key criticisms of the work of Stendahl, Sanders, Dunn, and Wright on their approaches to Paul.

From Plight to Solution

Frank Thielman questions Sanders's attitude that Jews did not see themselves as stuck in a "plight."[8] By analyzing early Jewish texts, and also Galatians, Romans, and the torah, Thielman argues that Jews *did* see themselves as "tainted with sin" and in need of God's eschatological rescue. He argues that Paul's language of the law fulfilled in Christ offers the kind of climactic hope that Jews had been anticipating.

The Problem of Jewish Boasting

Simon Gathercole challenges the NPP, focusing on the language of Jewish boasting in Romans 1–5.[9] He argues that when Paul treats Jewish boasting as inappropriate, he is confronting the idea that a person could rely on torah obedience for "final vindication at the eschaton."[10] Gathercole insists that Paul was criticizing both ethnic pride and the faulty soteriological perspective that seemed to depend heavily on one's own works.

8. Frank Thielman, *From Plight to Solution: A Jewish Framework for Understanding Paul's View of the Law in Romans and Galatians* (Leiden: Brill, 1989).

9. Simon J. Gathercole, *Where Is Boasting? Early Jewish Soteriology and Paul's Response in Romans 1–5* (Grand Rapids: Eerdmans, 2002).

10. Gathercole, *Where Is Boasting?*, 37.

Rehabilitating Luther as Pauline Theologian

Stephen Westerholm defends a Lutheran reading of Paul, arguing that the apostle concentrated on Christ's unique ability to deal with sin beyond what was possible before.[11] He seeks to bring a soteriological component back to the center of the discussion of Paul's language of "righteousness"/"justification" and to rehabilitate the scholarly treatment of Luther's reading of Paul.

Justification and Variegated Nomism: Not Covenantal Nomism

In the first volume of *Justification and Variegated Nomism*, a two-volume project edited by D. A. Carson, Peter O'Brien, and Mark Seifrid, a group of biblical scholars tests Sanders's theory of Jewish covenantal nomism to see if this pattern of grace and obligation holds up under close scrutiny of the evidence from early Jewish texts.[12] The editors conclude that these Jewish texts were diverse enough with respect to torah obedience, salvation, and judgment that it is difficult to draw them all together under one rubric. This diversity casts suspicion, in the editors' views, on an attempt to develop a singular, broad pattern of Judaism called "covenantal nomism."

The debate is ongoing in scholarship regarding the nature of Judaism in Paul's time and why Paul was so critical regarding the Jewish law in texts like Galatians. Two key questions, when one looks carefully at Paul's Letters, stand at the forefront of this discussion: *Why was torah given to Israel?* and *What is Paul's problem with works of the law?*

Debated Topic 1: Why Was Torah Given to Israel?

As noted above, Paul seems to interpret the Mosaic law, torah, as no longer having a dominating role in the life of the people of God (so Rom. 6:14). In fact, "all who rely on the works of the law are under a curse" because they do not fully obey the law (Gal. 3:10; cf. Deut. 27:26). But if there is such a problem with following torah, why was it even given? What purpose did it serve? In Galatians 3:19, Paul addresses this question: "Why then the law? It was added because of transgressions, until the offspring would come to whom

11. Stephen Westerholm, *Perspectives Old and New on Paul: The "Lutheran" Paul and His Critics* (Grand Rapids: Eerdmans, 2004).

12. D. A. Carson, Peter T. O'Brien, and Mark A. Seifrid, eds., *Justification and Variegated Nomism*, vol. 1, *The Complexities of Second Temple Judaism* (Grand Rapids: Baker Academic, 2001).

the promise had been made; and it was ordained through angels by a media-
tor." So, Paul explains that the law was given "because of transgressions."
Although this is his answer, it is not clear how this should be interpreted.
Scholars tend to fall into three camps in their readings of this statement.[13]

Causative: "To Cause Transgressions"

It is possible to read "because of transgressions" in a causative way: the
law was added to cause sins and transgressions. Scholars who support this
reading appeal to Romans 5:20 (translated literally): "The law came in [such]
that the trespass might increase." Many translations understand this to mean
that the purpose of the giving of the law was to *increase* sin. So, for example,
the Common English Bible translates Romans 5:20 in this way: "The Law
stepped in to amplify the failure, but where sin increased, grace multiplied
even more." One scholar, who takes this reading, explains that the law, for
Paul, is a "power that provokes and, as it were, calls forth sin (in the sinner).
The law does not restrain sin, but causes it to awaken; it does not reduce sin,
but rather makes it to increase."[14] But why would God want sin to increase?
The common answer from this perspective is that when sinners spiral out of
control in their own sinfulness, this can "accentuate the more clearly the grace
of Christ in its all-transcending significance."[15]

Cognitive: "To Identify Transgressions"

A second view of Galatians 3:19 ("because of transgressions") also views
the purpose of the law as to increase sins, but not in the sense that the law
provokes the sinner to sin more. Rather, the law is viewed as increasing sin
(Rom. 5:20) in the sense that the law categorizes sin and establishes a code
of penalty. In this sense, the sinner does not sin *more* because of the law but
is rather *more fully aware* of the sin, its problem, and its consequences; sin
is "given a new dimension as rebellion against the revealed, detailed will of
God."[16] As support for this view, proponents tend to draw in Romans 4:15b,
where Paul writes that "where there is no law, neither is there violation."
Thus, only law can bring the sinner to recognition that he or she has violated

13. It is difficult to label these approaches as NPP or anti-NPP; but painting with broad
brushstrokes, we can say that NPP advocates tend to argue *against* the causative view, because
it offers such a dark portrayal of the purpose of torah.
14. Herman Ridderbos, *Paul: An Outline of His Theology* (Grand Rapids: Eerdmans, 1975),
144.
15. Ridderbos, *Paul*, 150, in his interpretation of Romans 5:21.
16. Douglas J. Moo, *The Epistle to the Romans* (Grand Rapids: Eerdmans, 1996), 348.

God's command directly. It should be pointed out that views 1 (causative) and 2 (cognitive) are not mutually exclusive, and some scholars indeed combine the two views.[17]

Corrective: "To Curtail Transgressions"

The third view is notably different from the first two by taking a more positive view of the Jewish law. One way to take Paul's "because of transgressions" (Gal. 3:19) answer is to simply read it as *preventing* transgressions. The law was given to curtail or correct disobedience. But what about Romans 5:20? Proponents of the corrective interpretation contest traditional translations of this verse. The Greek word *hina* in Romans 5:20 *can* indicate causation—the law came in *in order to* (*hina*) increase transgression. But, *hina* can also indicate *result*—the law came in *resulting in* (*hina*) the increase of transgression. Sometimes it is difficult for those who have not studied Greek to understand how one word can make such a difference for translations, but it is instructive to note the English translation difference between the Revised Standard Version (RSV) and the New Revised Standard Version (NRSV).

RSV: "Law came in, to increase the trespass" (causative or cognitive reading of *hina*)

NRSV: "But law came in, with the result that the trespass multiplied" (resultative reading of *hina*)

Both of these are legitimate translations of the word *hina*, and only context can determine the right meaning. The corrective reading of Paul's view of the giving of the law proposes that the law was considered by Paul holy and good (Rom. 7:12), but a good thing that was abused and misused by sinners. The greatest advantage of this reading is the key element of how laws are perceived in general; laws are given to prevent and punish sin. Also, some of the laws of the Old Testament are carried on into the New Testament (e.g., love of God and neighbor) such that one cannot imagine *these* laws provoking an increase in sin.

However, the drawback of this view is that Paul would have to be saying something very positive about the law in Galatians (i.e., that it corrects sin) in the context of very negative statements about works of the law. Also, if the law offers something so profitable, what is the value of the "faith in Christ" alternative that Paul sets forth? One answer a corrective view offers to this

17. So Thomas R. Schreiner, *Romans* (Grand Rapids: Baker, 1998), 296.

question is that while the law has a good purpose and can curtail or restrain sin, it does not actually *solve* the human sin problem—Christ alone does.

Debated Topic 2: What Is Paul's Problem with Works of the Law?

That leads us directly into the whole matter of Paul's negative statements about works of the law in Romans and especially Galatians. What was Paul's problem with works of the law? This is, perhaps, the most heavily debated question in the study of Paul's theology today! Similar to the several views of Galatians 3:19 above, so perspectives abound regarding a text like Galatians 2:16, where Paul claims that justification is not by "works of the law" but by "faith in Jesus Christ."

The Problem of Meritorious Works

A helpful place to begin with influential interpretations of Paul's works/ faith dichotomy is Luther's writings. Luther stands against any view that urges that one needs to be pious in order to be saved. Rather, he vigorously argues that Galatians especially centers God's salvation on the work of Christ, not anything humans can do. Thus, all that is needed is faith in Christ, and by performing works of the law no one can be saved.

Luther observes all kinds of pious people around him thinking highly of themselves for their works for God. He compares this to Israel trying to be justified by boasting in the achievements of law obedience. But Luther argues that the law brings "sin, death, and the wrath of God to light" so that the sinner might know his or her utter fallenness and rely only on the grace of Christ through faith.[18] So, "God accordingly uses the Law for a hammer to break up the illusion of self-righteousness, that we should despair of our own strength and efforts at self-justification."[19]

This is, perhaps, the dominant view in Western Christianity on Paul's faith/ works dichotomy insofar as it places the emphasis on the problem of human self-righteousness and hopeless sinfulness and establishes "faith alone" as the motto of Pauline salvation. The works of sinners cannot please God or meet his divine standard. Only Christ's work can save sinners, and each must place their faith in him and rely on his righteousness. This view is associated with an "Old Perspective on Paul," a Protestant reading of Paul that the NPP rejects.

18. Martin Luther, *A Commentary on St. Paul's Epistle to the Galatians* (Grand Rapids: Zondervan, 1939), 71.
19. Luther, *Galatians*, 76.

The Problem of Jewish Exclusivity

The NPP offers a different reading of Paul's "faith in Christ" and "works of the law" texts. Dunn has forcefully argued that when Paul refers to "works of the law," he is not talking about good works in a general sense. Rather, he is specifically referring to "the conduct prescribed by the Torah."[20] Among the whole covenantal set of obligations and commandments expected by torah, three had special prominence in the time of Paul: circumcision, food laws, and Sabbath/holy days. These particular practices or commitments became central to how Jews distinguished themselves over and against the other nations.

In Paul's Letter to the Galatians, we learn that some Galatian believers were tempted to become circumcised by the influence of certain interloping teachers. Paul takes it upon himself to step in and demand that the Galatians reject this pressure. According to the NPP, these teachers were trying to convince gentile Galatian believers that merely believing in Jesus was not enough to be justified by God. Rather, they had to fully enter the Jewish covenant with God, which required taking on a Jewish covenantal identity—and that identification required circumcision as a formal indication of no longer being a gentile, no longer identifying with the pagan nations. Paul resists this thinking because it seeks to add something to the gospel of Jesus Christ; it seeks to require conversion to *Jewishness* for gentiles in order to become acceptable to God. Put another way, the NPP argues that Paul warned the Galatians not to seek to be justified by works of the law, because they did not need to take on a national *Jewish* identity to be saved.

While most NPP proponents do not boil Paul's faith/works dichotomy down to ethnic and social matters per se, they tend to highlight this as the key problem in Galatians. Paul saw doing the law, torah, not as a problem of achievement but rather as a problem specifically when it was used to force gentiles to identify with the ethnic Jewish people in order to be acceptable to God.

The Problem of Torah's Limits

Yet another view of the problem of the works of the law for Paul sees torah overall as something that had a positive role to play in some ways but eventually had to be set aside because it was not the *permanent* solution to the problem of sin. Those who take this view point to Galatians 3:24, where Paul describes the law as a *paidagōgos*. A *paidagōgos* was a slave in

---

20. James D. G. Dunn, *The New Perspective on Paul* (Grand Rapids: Eerdmans, 2008), 22.

the Roman world who had the responsibility of looking after children until they could take care of themselves. Paul depicts the law as a *paidagōgos* that tends to the people until the coming of Christ. Some scholars have interpreted this *paidagōgos* as a negative figure, because sometimes these slaves were nasty to the children under their care. However, because Paul does not elaborate on the demeanor of the law as *paidagōgos*, it is prudent to read this metaphor at face value. Torah played the role of caretaker, guardian, child minder until Christ. In one sense, the law is insufficient because it is temporary and the human is in need of something more. On the other hand, for its time and occasion, it had an important function. This view is more popular among those who take a salvation-history view of Paul's theology (see chap. 5) and could be integrated into either a NPP approach or an anti-NPP approach.

Reflections

Given the complexity and history of debate on this subject, no doubt I could not include all the important facets of this topic in this chapter. However, it is appropriate now to dwell on a few implications of the nature of this debate.

Context

It is critical to examine the Pauline texts carefully in their own sociohistorical context. The temptation to use the text as a springboard for personal beliefs can sometimes be overwhelming, but we must resist that inclination and patiently listen to Paul and understand him on his own terms. This will require careful (re)examination of the words he uses and what they meant in his own environment. It requires sensitivity to how Jews discussed and debated political and religious matters in their own time as well.

Continuity and Discontinuity

At the beginning of the chapter, I noted the folly of setting Paul and the New Testament at too far a distance from the Old Testament. We dare not reject the Old Testament (actively or in effect), which Paul held so dear! What we must wrestle with is how Paul can sometimes refer to the Jewish law so positively (e.g., Rom. 7:12) and, at other times, appear to set it aside or reject it. In what sense is the Old Testament law "Scripture"? How is it authoritative for Paul and for Christians of all times and places? Furthermore, what is completed or fulfilled? Clearly the New Testament writers did not think believers needed to observe Jewish food restrictions (Mark 7:19) or become circumcised (1 Cor. 7:19). And yet Paul saw the Old Testament, even Old Testament regulations, as eminently relevant (2 Tim. 3:16; cf. 1 Cor. 9:9).

Faith and Works

On the one hand, Paul is very clear that one should not dwell on self-achievement, and yet works are critically important. Thus, "for by grace you have been saved through faith, and this is not your own doing; it is the gift of God—not the result of works, so that no one may boast. For we are what he has made us, created in Christ Jesus for good works, which God prepared beforehand to be our way of life" (Eph. 2:8–10). Works do not earn salvation, and yet humans were created to work.

When it comes to "faith," we also need to be careful how we understand the Greek term behind this—*pistis*. *Pistis* was a very rich and nuanced word in early Judaism. While it can have a strong cognitive component, which relates to believing, *pistis* was also a key word chosen by Jews of Paul's time to represent Jewish loyalty to the covenant. Because of the richness of its usage in Jewish texts, it ought to signal a warning to us not to differentiate so casually "faith" and "works" as two entirely separate things. While Paul can sometimes juxtapose them, he does not mean that "faith" is the opposite of "works" or that "faith" does not include a component of activity. *Pistis* is best understood as a representative term for the ideal Christian response to God, as a whole-person devotion to and dependence on Christ that is as inclusive of activity as our English word "commitment."

Conclusion

Scholars today often make the observation that the "New Perspective on Paul" is now a misnomer—it is no longer "new" (it's at least forty years old now), and in some ways it is more about early Judaism than it is about Paul. Still, scholars today tend to either accept it or reject it, and certain lines of interpretation and the theology of Paul are defined by this debate. Pauline scholarship in general has come away from this discussion with a deeper sense of appreciation for how certain figures have shaped the study of Paul, like Luther, and the importance of studying Paul as a man of his own time. Truth be told, many scholars pick and choose aspects of old and new perspectives that seem correct; this is probably because Paul lived in a watershed period of history, and he himself was an extraordinary person and writer.

Suggested Reading

Beginner

Gombis, Timothy G. *Paul: A Guide for the Perplexed*. New York: T&T Clark, 2010.

The Paul Page. http://www.thepaulpage.com/.[21]

Yinger, Kent L. *The New Perspective on Paul: An Introduction*. Eugene, OR: Cascade, 2011.

The New Perspective on Paul

Dunn, James D. G. *The New Perspective on Paul*. Grand Rapids: Eerdmans, 2008.

Sanders, E. P. *Paul and Palestinian Judaism: A Comparison of Patterns of Religion*. Philadelphia: Fortress, 1977.

Wright, N. T. *What Saint Paul Really Said: Was Paul of Tarsus the Real Founder of Christianity?* Grand Rapids: Eerdmans, 1997.

Against the New Perspective on Paul

Kim, Seyoon. *Paul and the New Perspective: Second Thoughts on the Origin of Paul's Gospel*. Grand Rapids: Eerdmans, 2001.

Schreiner, Thomas. *Faith Alone—The Doctrine of Justification: What the Reformers Taught and Why It Still Matters*. Grand Rapids: Zondervan, 2015.

Waters, Guy P. *Justification and the New Perspectives on Paul: A Review and Response*. Phillipsburg, NJ: P&R, 2004.

Advanced

Anderson, Garwood. *Paul's New Perspective: Charting a Soteriological Journey*. Downers Grove, IL: InterVarsity, 2016.

Barclay, John M. G. *Paul and the Gift*. Grand Rapids: Eerdmans, 2015.

Bird, Michael F. *The Saving Righteousness of God: Studies on Paul, Justification, and the New Perspective*. Paternoster Biblical Monographs. Eugene, OR: Wipf & Stock, 2007.

Carson, D. A., Peter T. O'Brien, and Mark A. Seifrid, eds. *Justification and Variegated Nomism*. 2 vols. Grand Rapids: Baker Academic, 2001, 2004.

---

21. The Paul Page, operated by Faithlife / Logos Bible Software, offers a number of free essays that relate to the NPP (for, against, and "neutral").

Fredriksen, Paula. *Paul: The Pagans' Apostle*. New Haven: Yale University Press, 2017.

Gathercole, Simon J. *Where Is Boasting? Early Jewish Soteriology and Paul's Response in Romans 1–5*. Grand Rapids: Eerdmans, 2010.

Westerholm, Stephen. *Perspectives Old and New on Paul: The "Lutheran" Paul and His Critics*. Grand Rapids: Eerdmans, 2004.

Wright, N. T. *Paul and the Faithfulness of God*. 2 vols. Christian Origins and the Question of God 4. Minneapolis: Fortress, 2013.

SEVEN

Interpreting the Book of Revelation

When I was a teenager, I was practically terrified of the book of Revelation—as far as I had heard (since I had never read it), it was a book of horrible damnations and prophecies about doom for unbelievers. I recall a Sunday school teacher trying to explain to me a very complex New Testament eschatology chart of dates, years, and unusual terms and figures (such as the "Beast" and the "Bema Seat"). Some people I knew found all of this fascinating, but I treated it as an unusual hobby that I never developed a taste for. Fast-forward almost twenty years, and I was teaching "Introduction to the New Testament" to freshman undergraduate students. At that time Christian radio personality Harold Camping had been in the news for predicting the end of the world and imminent judgment—he calculated the precise timing (May 21, 2011) according to his unique ability to crack the code of the Bible (especially prophetic texts like Daniel and Revelation). Many students came to me and asked me if this was legitimate. Was Camping right? How did he crack the Bible's apocalyptic code? Can we confirm his work? Should we prepare for the apocalypse? Suffice it to say, Camping was wrong. Eventually, when May 21 came and went, he admitted that the final judgment did *not* happen as he predicted. Nor was he right about the later date (in October 2011) he switched to when the first one didn't work out.

The reason why many today will have forgotten Camping's predictions from 2011 is probably because he was not the only person who believed he held the keys to unlocking the Bible's eschatological puzzle. Countless "scholars" and "prophets" believed they had come to true revelatory insight about the end. The Millerites, followers of William Miller, set the second coming of Jesus to October 22, 1844—as many as one hundred thousand Millerites purged their worldly possessions and moved into the mountains awaiting the end that never came. Over a century later, Edgar C. Whisenant published his cleverly titled book *88 Reasons Why the Rapture Will Be in 1988* (selling

4.5 million copies, by the way). After his prediction failed, he changed his timetable to 1989 with his book *The Final Shout: Rapture Report 1989*. There are many stories of this kind in the history of Christianity, demonstrating the widespread fascination with how Scripture refers to time and the true nature and meaning of eschatological and apocalyptic texts. And, of course, Revelation often lies at the center of these inquiries with its provocative symbolism and seemingly inscrutable numerology. In this chapter I will break down several ways that scholars approach the book of Revelation. Before I address these perspectives, though, it is necessary for the uninitiated to get a handle on the academic terminology that is often found in the discussion of ancient apocalypticism, biblical prophecy and eschatology, and Revelation studies.

How Can I Understand Unless Someone Explains It to Me?

When I first dipped my toes into debates related to eschatology and apocalypticism, it felt like another language. Here I will try to break down the jargon and offer simple definitions. If the material in this section feels too technical or academic, I encourage you to skip ahead to the next section ("What Kind of Text Is Revelation?").

Eschatology

Eschatology is the theological discipline that pertains to last things (the Greek word *eschatos* means "last, final"). This discipline covers all matters pertaining to *later* stages in Christian history (which can include, for example, the incarnation and Christ event), but it tends to focus on the second coming of Jesus and the final judgment.

Apocalypses and Apocalypticism

Let's start with the most concrete and agreed-upon term, "apocalypse," which is a type of literature. The Society of Biblical Literature has constructed a careful definition of an apocalypse: "Apocalypse is a genre of revelatory literature with a narrative framework, in which a revelation is mediated by an otherworldly being to a human recipient, disclosing a transcendent reality which is both temporal, insofar as it envisages eschatological salvation, and spatial, insofar as it involves another, supernatural world."[1] If Revelation

---

1. John J. Collins, "Introduction: Towards the Morphology of a Genre," in *Apocalypse: The Morphology of a Genre* (Chico, CA: Scholars Press, 1979), 1–19, at 9.

is classified as an "apocalypse" (see below), we must recognize it fits into a particular literary genre that is shared with many other ancient works, including *1 Enoch*, *2 Baruch*, and the *Apocalypse of Abraham*. It is also clear that a certain way of thinking about God, the world, and time is presented in these apocalypses; and many other religious texts (Jewish and Christian) demonstrate apocalyptic sensibilities or interests even if they are not officially labeled as apocalypses (e.g., Daniel, *Jubilees*, *Testaments of the Twelve Patriarchs*, *Sibylline Oracles*). Furthermore, religious texts that do not bear resemblance to the literary features of an apocalypse can sometimes demonstrate "apocalyptic" thought—for example, interest in the end of the world, heavy cosmic dualism, or special revelations from a heavenly figure. Therefore, we can distinguish an "apocalypse" (a particular genre) from "apocalypticism," a specific worldview or perspective shared by a group of people that demonstrate some or all of the following characteristics:

Supernatural Cosmology: Spiritual entities wage war in the battle of good and evil in such a way that the realm humans inhabit is deeply affected.

Special Revelation: God's people sometimes receive special messages and insight from heaven about mysterious, salvific, and/or eschatological matters.

Eschatology: The faithful live in a state of urgency and vigilance as the end draws near.

Dualism/Conflict: The world is at war—good and evil, righteous and unrighteous, light and darkness—driving toward a consummating final showdown.

Divine Sovereignty: Mortals cannot win the battle on their own strength or resolve, but the righteous rely on God to vanquish the wicked and rescue his people.

Radical Transformation: The present state of the world is marked by sin, death, chaos, and slavery; but when God ushers in the new (and final) age, the world will flourish with holiness, righteousness, wisdom, and new life.[2]

Apocalypses, such as Revelation, display many of these features, and an apocalyptic mind-set can be found in several early Jewish and early Christian texts. Many apocalypses emerged in the Common Era, but one of the oldest

---

2. Some of this material is adapted from Nijay K. Gupta, *1–2 Thessalonians* (Eugene, OR: Cascade, 2016), 94–95.

works to demonstrate apocalyptic discourse is *1 Enoch*.[3] The figure "Enoch" is portrayed as receiving a vision and writing this: "It was shown to me, and I heard the holy messengers, and as I heard from them everything and understood I saw [. . . and spoke]" (1.2). The apostle Paul, while he did not write an "apocalypse," as far as we know, easily demonstrates apocalyptic thought. He does not shy away from making reference to the nefarious activity of Satan (1 Thess. 2:18; 2 Cor. 2:11; Rom. 16:20). He mentions receiving revelations and visions from God (Gal. 1:12; 2 Cor. 12:1). Cosmic dualism is pervasive in his letters; for example: "For what the flesh desires is opposed to the Spirit, and what the Spirit desires is opposed to the flesh; for these are opposed to each other, to prevent you from doing what you want. But if you are led by the Spirit, you are not subject to the law" (Gal. 5:17–18). And, obviously, Paul was interested in the end of the ages, referring to this current period as "the present evil age" (Gal. 1:4) and the impending final period of the consummation as "new creation" (see Rom. 8:18–25). Many other New Testament writings (like Mark and 1 Peter) are considered to have apocalyptic textures, while again not technically qualifying as apocalypses.

What Kind of Text Is Revelation?

Scholars often point to Revelation as demonstrative of features of Jewish-style apocalypses. But Revelation *also* contains literary and formal features of other genres, such as that of a prophecy and a letter. Prophecy texts, contrary to popular belief, do not serve the exclusive purpose of making future predictions. Rather, prophecy involves "speaking words of comfort and/or challenge, on behalf of God, to the people of God in their concrete historical situation."[4] Revelation actually identifies itself as a *prophecy* (1:3) offering warning to those tempted to assimilate to cultural pressures and comfort to those attempting to survive and overcome persecution. And Revelation also bears features of a letter. Beginning at Revelation 1:9, the author, "John," mentions his situation (exile on the island of Patmos) and his intentions in this writing. He received a vision ("I was in the spirit on the Lord's day, and I heard behind me a loud voice . . ."; 1:10) and was instructed to write to seven churches seven letters that are found in 2:1–3:22.

An important takeaway from the analysis of Revelation's genre is that this text was not sui generis—a brand new way of writing—for its time. While

3. According to scholarship, some portions of *1 Enoch* date back to as early as the third century BCE.
4. Michael J. Gorman, *Reading Revelation Responsibly* (Eugene, OR: Cascade, 2011), 23.

it combines different styles of communication, early Jewish and Christian readers would have recognized what the writer was trying to accomplish and would *not* have been bewildered by the symbolism or vivid language (certainly not as befuddled as my teenage self). At the same time, there is much that *is* mysterious about the book of Revelation. Understanding Revelation as an apocalypse puts the text into a familiar framework in a way, but scholars continue to debate how the coded language relates to the past and the future—and even the present. We will survey four main views related to the interpretation of Revelation: preterist, historicist, futurist, and idealist. Before we jump into these views, it is helpful to have a quick rundown of the book of Revelation as a whole.

A Thumbnail Sketch of Revelation

Before diving into the various approaches to interpreting Revelation, I will offer a brief outline of the book of Revelation—but don't take this as a substitute for reading the text of Revelation yourself!

Prologue (1:1–8)

The prologue sets the scene for the prophecies offered in Revelation. Here we are told that the revelation is first and foremost about Jesus Christ (1:1), transmitted through John (1:1–2). And the initial audience of this text is seven persecuted churches in Asia (1:4).

John's Inaugural Vision (1:9–20) and Jesus's Messages to the Seven Churches (2:1–3:22)

John testifies that he shares their suffering as he lives in exile on the island of Patmos, punished for his ministry. He is given a special vision and message to dispatch to churches in Ephesus, Smyrna, Pergamum, Thyatira, Sardis, Philadelphia, and Laodicea (1:11). From the beginning, the vision is laden with evocative symbolism: seven stars, which represent the angels of the seven churches, and seven lampstands, which represent the churches themselves. One by one John is given individualized messages to relay, mostly a mixture of encouragement and admonishment. These churches of Asia, some of them probably embroiled in persecution and hostile resistance, many tempted by various vices, are called upon to be steadfast and vigilant. Several times the warning is given: Jesus Christ will return soon, and he will judge the works of these churches for their good or downfall: "I reprove and discipline those whom I love. Be earnest, therefore, and repent" (3:19).

Inaugural Vision of Heaven (4:1–5:14)

The letters to the seven churches, then, set up the stakes for what remains in Revelation. The world is the stage for a great showdown, and followers of Jesus Christ must ready themselves for war. But before getting into the trenches of the battle, John presents a vivid depiction of the heavenly throne room. John is transported into the presence of God. He witnesses the majesty of the Ruler and the glorious continual worship by the heavenly hosts. In chapter 5, the spotlight, so to speak, shines on a slaughtered Lamb who is also the object of worship and homage: "You were slaughtered and by your blood you ransomed for God saints from every tribe and language and people and nation; you have made them to be a kingdom and priests serving our God, and they will reign on earth" (5:9b–10). This Lamb is especially praised for his ability to open a secret scroll locked by seven seals.

The Seven Seals (6:1–8:5) and Seven Trumpets (8:6–11:19)

When the Lamb opens the seals, this unleashes horses of different colors, symbolizing judgment and destruction. The drama escalates in anticipation of a climax—the seventh seal. But before any sense of resolution, John transitions to the blowing of seven trumpets.

The trumpet blasts in turn usher in fire scorching the earth, a toppled mountain, a poisoned sea, a burning fallen star that ruins the waters, the corruption of heavenly lights, the unleashing of a plague of locusts that wreak havoc on earth, and devastation caused by the triple plagues of fire, smoke, and sulfur. Finally, when the seventh trumpet is allowed to sound, we hear the proclamation: "The kingdom of the world has become the kingdom of our Lord and of his Messiah, and he will reign forever and ever" (11:15). The saints and martyrs are promised vindication and reward, and the wicked are punished and vanquished (11:18).

The Story of God's People in Conflict with Evil (12:1–15:4)

In this next section, John retells the cosmic gospel story in apocalyptic terms. A pregnant woman battles a terrible dragon (Satan). A war is waged in the heavens between the angel Michael and the dragon, who is eventually defeated. Despite the devil's downfall, with his remaining breath he hunts the woman down, as well as her other children, followers of Jesus. The dragon is supported by two beasts. Mortals fall into false worship and allegiance through the first beast from the sea. The second beast comes from the land. This leads to divided allegiances—Will mortals worship the beast or the Lamb?

The Seven Bowls (15:5–16:21)

Next we are introduced to another sequence of seven—this time representing bowls of divine wrath. Curses are poured out on earth, such as sores on the worshipers of the beast, poisoning of the sea, flesh-scorching flames from the sun, and maddening darkness. When the final bowl is poured out, it leads to cosmic tumult of lightning flashes and earthquakes, such devastation that the inhabitants of earth cry out in fear and dread.

Babylon the Harlot (17:1–19:10)

These chapters focus on the punishment of a terrible prostitute, who has led many leaders into sin. She is called "Babylon the great, mother of whores and of earth's abominations" (17:5). She has also consumed many witnesses of Jesus. Ultimately Babylon is destroyed. God's people are warned not to trust her, lest they face wrath along with her.

Transition from Babylon to the New Jerusalem (19:11–21:8)

Finally, the cyclical depictions of judgment (chaps. 6–18) give way to an extended vision of the new Jerusalem. This section parallels chapters 4–5 of Revelation with its emphasis on jubilant worship of the Lamb. But here the heavenly host prepare for a great "marriage supper of the Lamb" (19:9). Here too Satan is sent to eternal punishment, and the book of life is opened. The final era of a "new heaven and a new earth" dawns. A heavenly voice proclaims: "See, the home of God is among mortals. He will dwell with them; they will be his peoples, and God himself will be with them; he will wipe every tear from their eyes. Death will be no more; mourning and crying and pain will be no more, for the first things have passed away" (21:3–4).

The New Jerusalem, the Bride (21:9–22:21)

The final part of Revelation concentrates on the holy city of Jerusalem, the bride of the Lamb. It radiates with glorious beauty and power: "The nations will walk by its light, and the kings of the earth will bring their glory into it. . . . Nothing unclean will enter it, nor anyone who practices abomination or falsehood, but only those who are written in the Lamb's book of life" (21:24, 27). Revelation concludes with a statement that this vision is trustworthy and true. John recounts how he was told that the Lord is soon to return. So, those servants of this master must continue to be faithful and then be rewarded.

Four Approaches to Interpreting Revelation

If you have read Revelation, or even if you just read the above summary, it is clear to you that this text uses vivid imagery and symbolism to paint a picture of conflict, warfare, and—ultimately—resolution and victory. But how does any of it correspond to the "real world"? There are a few pieces of the puzzle that are pretty easy to figure out, whether it be references to Mary (the pregnant woman; Rev. 12) or Rome (Babylon; Rev. 14:8, etc.). But by and large we are given little in the text that identifies other human figures, real places, or historical events. Thus, it is no surprise there are several different ways to analyze Revelation when it comes to past, present, and future. Here I offer four classic approaches to Revelation.

Preterist ("In the Past")

The word "preterist" comes from the Latin word *praeter*, which refers to "time beforehand."[5] Scholars who subscribe to this approach to Revelation argue that the symbolism and messages of this book are oriented to the world of its composition—the earliest Christians in the Roman Empire. This view opposes the notion that John wrote Revelation to speak to Christians in *later* generations or centuries. Rather, it was written with prophecies and teachings that were directly applicable to the original readers. For example, when it comes to the famous "mark of the beast" (666; see Rev. 13:18), preterists connect this numerology to the despotic emperor Nero. Using a Hebrew math-code tool called "gematria" (where letters of the Hebrew alphabet correspond to numbers), the name Neron Caesar adds up to 666.[6]

The point that preterists wish to make is that the book of Revelation is not some ethereal, free-floating text that can be unlocked by an "enlightened" person like Harold Camping. The key that unlocks the language of Revelation is the cultural encyclopedia of Jewish and Christian discourse and thought in the ancient Greco-Roman world. Revelation's unusual language can be decoded by

5. We get the English prefix "pre-" from this Latin word.
6. See this example in Ben Witherington III, *Revelation*, New Cambridge Bible Commentary (Cambridge: Cambridge University Press, 2003), 177.

anyone who understands how these symbols relate to people, events, places, familiar ideas, and objects of its time, and not a later time. Preterists wish to contextualize Revelation into its world of composition, rather than see it as launching off from the first century only to be relevant later on to people of future ages. An extreme form of the preterist view argues that the author of Revelation believed that all the prophecies he was communicating were fulfilled, or in the process of being fulfilled, in his own lifetime. Put another way, by the end of the second century CE, all the prophecies of Revelation were completely fulfilled. Other preterists are open to the prophecies of Revelation relating to the future, but all of the imagery and symbolism of the book would have been understood (or understandable) by the original readers based on their first-century cultural knowledge.

Perhaps the biggest obstacle for those who are not persuaded by the strict preterist viewpoint is the "end of the world" kind of events and language in Revelation. For example, Revelation 20:11–15 refers to the final judgment of the dead.

Historicist ("Throughout Time")

Another approach to the interpretation of Revelation is called the "historicist" view. This refers to the perspective that the prophecies of Revelation pertain to various figures and events throughout history from Revelation's time until today. Famously, Nicholas of Lyra (fourteenth century CE) tried to make the following links:[7]

Angel with the "seal of the living God" (Rev. 7:2)	Constantinian era
Trumpet plagues (Rev. 8:6–9:21)	Heretics Arius and Eutyches
Angel of the "little scroll" (Rev. 10)	Era of Emperors Justin and Justinian (sixth century CE)
Angel Michael (Rev. 12)	Emperor Heraclius

While this kind of approach to Revelation is unpopular today (for reasons we will see below), it was common especially in the medieval and Reformation periods. For example, while Luther had originally dismissed Revelation as unimportant, he later came to appreciate more its theological and prophetic potential. In his 1530 (revised) preface to Revelation, he explains that one helpful way to study this mysterious book is to "take from the histories the

7. See Craig Koester, *Revelation*, Anchor Yale Bible 38A (New Haven: Yale University Press, 2014), 47.

past events and misfortunes that have happened to Christendom up to now and hold them up to these images [in Revelation], comparing them word for word. If, then, the two perfectly match and coincide with one another, one could maintain that it is a certain or at least unobjectionable interpretation."[8]

Luther goes on to give his own take on the events and figures discussed in Revelation. The seven angels of the early chapters correspond to bishops and teachers in Christendom. He relates the tribulations of Revelation 7–8 to various heresies in history. They are held at bay and conquered by holy angels that are, in fact, holy fathers such as Athanasius, the Council of Nicea, and so on. The heretics are Tatian, Marcion, the Manicheans, the Montanists, Pelagius, and so forth. Some scholars believe that one of the main reasons why Luther came to take this historicist view of Revelation is because he became convinced that the pope of his time was the antichrist associated with unholy Babylon and the evil beast of Revelation 14.

The historicist view no doubt was highly attractive because it seemed to many throughout history that this book resonated with *their* era. This is certainly clear in Luther. "Here, now, the devil's final wrath gets to work: there in the East is the second woe, Mohammed and the Saracens; here in the West are papacy and empire, with the third woe. . . . Thus, Christendom is plagued most terribly and miserably, everywhere and on all sides, with false doctrines and with wars, with scroll and with swords."[9] But that is not just a sentiment of theologians of the past. In 1983, following his grief over a marine killed in Beirut, Ronald Reagan made this comment: "You know, I turn back to your ancient prophets in the Old Testament and the signs foretelling Armageddon, and I find myself wondering if—if we're the generation that is going to see that come about. . . . I don't know if you've noted any of those prophecies lately, but, believe me, they certainly describe the times we're going through."[10]

Despite these sorts of impressions and feelings about the present relevance of Revelation historically (represented here by Luther), the reason why this approach has fallen out of favor is because it operates with a heavily subjective bias. Each interpreter, regardless of *where* they are (Germany or America), or *when* they are (the 1530s or the 1980s), can develop a scheme that fits the pieces of Revelation into their timeline. On the one hand, Revelation's imagery

---

8. Martin Luther, "Preface to the Revelation of St. John (1530 and 1546)," in *Luther's Spirituality*, ed. and trans. Philip D. W. Krey and Peter D. S. Krey, Classics of Western Spirituality (Mahweh, NJ: Paulist Press, 2007), 50.

9. Martin Luther, *Prefaces to the New Testament*, trans. C. M. Jacobs (Cabin John, MD: Wildside Press, 2010), 53.

10. See John Herbers, "Religious Leaders Tell of Worry on Armageddon View Ascribed to Reagan," *New York Times*, October 21, 1984, https://www.nytimes.com/1984/10/21/us/religious-leaders-tell-of-worry-on-armageddon-view-ascribed-to-reagan.html.

is so generic that the pieces are easily placed into many seemingly relevant situations. On the other hand, they are gripping and extreme in such a way as to inspire a feeling of urgency. So—is Revelation *really* about the distant past (preterist), or the not-so-distant past and present (historicist)? Or, could it *actually* be about the future?

Futurist ("Not Yet")

A futurist approach operates under the assumption that the prophecies in Revelation largely pertain to events that will unfold around the time of the eschaton (i.e., the "end of the world" happenings). Some believe many such events will happen before the end, and others believe they will be wrapped up in the end. Nevertheless, futurists differ from preterists and historicists insofar as they believe Revelation focuses on the end of the world and the majority of its prophecies have not been fulfilled in past events or eras (ancient or recent).

As mentioned above, the historicist position dominated thought on Revelation until the nineteenth century. A new era of scholarship on Revelation then corresponded to the emergence of dispensationalism—the view that the Bible points to the world operating according to discrete time periods, or dispensations, with Revelation prophesying events of the last era. This view, associated especially with John Nelson Darby (1800–1882), was popularized through the Scofield Reference Bible, which interpreted Scripture with the help of dispensationalist study notes (1909).

Scholars who subscribe to a dispensational approach to eschatology and biblical chronology split into two main views on the nature and placement of the millennium (thousand-year reign of Christ) according to Revelation 20:1–7. Those who argue in favor of *premillennialism* conceive of a thousand-year reign of Christ that follows Christ's second coming (i.e., the second coming precedes the millennial reign of Christ). Others believe that the millennial kingdom (not necessarily a literal number) is an age of the flourishing of the church on earth, and the second coming of Christ follows this—hence this is called a *postmillennial* view.

In 1995, Christian writers Tim LaHaye and Jerry B. Jenkins wrote a fictional portrayal of the end times with special interest in the rapture—a view that the second coming will be preceded by a "snatching up" of Christians from the earth. The book was called *Left Behind* because unbelievers who were "left behind" had another chance to repent and be saved. The Left Behind book series became massively popular in America and embedded the rapture doctrine further into popular American evangelicalism. Many scholars today, though, reject the rapture doctrine for the following reasons:

1. It is a synthetic doctrine that misinterprets portions of books like Matthew, 1–2 Thessalonians, and Revelation (the word "rapture" does not appear in the Bible).
2. There is no clear reason to conclude that the New Testament writers pointed to *both* a "snatching up" event *and* a separate second coming of Christ.
3. The rapture doctrine was developed in the nineteenth century; before that, there were no churches or theologians who articulated such a position.
4. The New Testament does not seem to function with a theology that there will be an era when unbelievers can turn to the Lord *without* the presence and ministry of the church.

There are many churches, especially in America, and theologians who identify with premillennial dispensationalism (including the rapture doctrine). Their view of Revelation is distinctly *futurist*—that is, this apocalyptic book pertains, by and large, to events that surround the end times. Both preterists and historicists find a futurist position problematic because it pushes Revelation's relevance off to a later time. Futurists take Revelation as a preview of events yet to come, to help believers to be prepared, to warn them of the temptation of apostasy, and to encourage them to stand firm in the face of hostility and even martyrdom.

Idealist ("Timeless")

The three views we have briefly surveyed above carry different attitudes toward the matter of Revelation's events or prophecies and *time*. Are they tied to the ancient past (preterist)? The ages of history (historicist)? Or the future we have yet to experience (futurist)? Some scholars believe that these are the wrong questions. What if Revelation is not about one period of time or about particular events? One way to read Revelation is to conceive of it as a series of messages that are theological in nature and are *timeless*. This perspective views the events and images of Revelation like parables—the point is not to link these to historical or concrete referents but to understand the theological message. The prophecies are not designed to predict the future (whenever that "future" is determined to be). Rather, they portray the world in conflict as a battle between good and evil, and believers are meant to be equipped with certain spiritual weapons and a certain mind-set to be prepared for this battle.

One way to think about this approach is that it is timeless, but perhaps it is better to refer to it as *perennial*. It is not that Revelation does not correspond to *any* time; it clearly has links to events that went on in the early church in the Roman world. But, perhaps it should be understood to be relevant to every generation (so, in a sense, Luther and Reagan could both be right!). For example, the early Christian theologian Origen took the seven-headed beast of Revelation 13 to refer to evil itself and the seven deadly sins, and these could plague the church at any time.[11]

One version of this kind of timeless or perennial reading of Revelation takes on a distinctly political character.[12] Some scholars urge that ancient apocalypses (like Revelation and portions of the book of Daniel) play a role in opposing or challenging the abuses of empires (like the Roman Empire). One scholar sees Revelation as offering a "scathing critique of political idolatry in the first-century Roman Empire."[13] In every generation and place, Revelation repeats a message that is meant to "illuminate our theological and political landscape."[14]

The timeless approach to Revelation can serve as a kind of catchall that allows Revelation to speak to past, present, and future. But when taken to the extreme, Revelation becomes a generic teaching about faith that loses its connection to its world of composition. And the future. Was Revelation not written to critique evil leaders and powers of John's time? And was it not also intended to function as a prophecy, pointing to an anticipated future? But this simply reinforces the key interpretive question: What relationship does Revelation have to concrete events of the past and the future?

Reflections

When I was in seminary, debates about the meaning and interpretation of Revelation were common in the lecture hall and the late-night dorm. Obviously this biblical book continues to fascinate, frustrate, inspire, and confuse. And there are no signs of a consensus view emerging anytime soon. Craig Koester, though, rightly observes that certain interpretive habits and attitudes have emerged that lead to best practices in interpretation, and it is worth mentioning those here because almost all scholars can agree on these.[15]

11. See M. Eugene Boring, *Revelation*, Interpretation (Louisville: Westminster John Knox, 2011), 47.
12. By "political" here I do not mean "Republican" or "Democratic"; rather, this can have a more general meaning related to civic life and the interrelationships of individual, society, and government/empire.
13. J. Nelson Kraybill, *Apocalypse and Allegiance: Worship, Politics, and Devotion in the Book of Revelation* (Grand Rapids: Brazos, 2010), 22.
14. Kraybill, *Apocalypse and Allegiance*, 22.
15. Koester, *Revelation*, 38.

First, Revelation's meaning and message should be read on its own terms. There is the temptation to piece together early Christian eschatology by drawing together bits from different portions of the Bible (or the New Testament). There may be a theological or historical reason to attempt a whole-Bible study of eschatology, but the danger is creating a Frankenstein-like monster that brings disparate elements together in a haphazard way. Revelation ought to be studied, first and foremost, as a self-contained literary unit with a coherent message. That message was of the utmost importance to the author, and that should take priority.

Second, Koester argues that Revelation, even as an apocalypse, should be taken seriously *as a collection of historical letters*. That means that this text had a very specific audience and, presumably, very specific purposes and authorial intentions related to its own time and circumstances. That does not mean it loses its power and impact for today; it just means that its original purposes should be determined first, and these establish its overall meaning, which can then be applied today.[16]

We can add another important starting point: studying other apocalypses of the time helps to make sense of the nature and style of this genre. Why does Revelation communicate in this way? How did the earliest readers break down these symbols and images? Michael Gorman rightly urges modern readers to focus less on fascinating and perplexing details, such as the number 666 or the "true identity" of the antichrist, and concentrate more on the master themes of Revelation. Along these lines, Gorman identifies seven master themes in Revelation that I think are worth quoting.[17]

1. The throne: the reign of God and the Lamb (Jesus)
2. The reality of evil and of empire
3. The temptation to idolatry and immorality
4. The call to covenant faithfulness and resistance
5. Worship and an alternative vision
6. Faithful witness: the pattern of Christ
7. The imminent judgment and salvation/new creation of God

Neither Koester nor Gorman denies the importance of Revelation for thinking about the end of the ages. Rather, the danger comes with obsessing over concrete predictive identification, as if Revelation were some kind of road

---

16. See Koester, *Revelation*, 40.
17. Gorman, *Reading Revelation Responsibly*, 75–77 (original emphasis and capitalization omitted).

map to the Apocalypse. In fact, its fantastic imagery clearly defies such a process. David deSilva helpfully sketches the very basic way Revelation portrays last things with these emphases: "Christ's return to reinforce God's claims on creation, holding God's enemies to account and vindicating the faithful; the resurrection of the dead and the judgment of all people before the throne of God and of the Lamb; the destruction of all that has opposed God's rule; God's provision of a cosmos where righteousness is at home, where God and God's order are fully and perfectly experienced."[18]

Despite the way that Revelation has historically had a tendency to bewilder and disorient the reader, it appears that this text is enjoying a period of widespread interest in academic scholarship. This is partly because of the way that Revelation is being studied generically alongside ancient Jewish and Christian apocalypses. Also, there is fresh interest in Revelation as a politically oriented document of its time (see chap. 9 in this book). This does not mean Revelation supported the agenda of a political party at the time—it didn't quite work that way in the Roman world! Rather, Revelation speaks clearly about how life should be lived in society. It inspires the imagination to consider what faithfulness to the Lord Jesus Christ would look like in an age of resistance and hostility.

Suggested Reading

Beginner and Multiple Views

It is difficult to find individual books on Revelation that represent well the different views discussed above. For a layout of different views, see the books listed below by Gorman and by Pate (ed.).

Collins, John J. *The Apocalyptic Imagination: An Introduction to Jewish Apocalyptic Literature*. Grand Rapids: Eerdmans, 2016.

Gorman, Michael J. *Reading Revelation Responsibly*. Eugene, OR: Wipf & Stock, 2011.

Koester, Craig. *Revelation and the End of All Things*. Grand Rapids: Eerdmans, 2001.

Mangina, Joseph L. *Revelation*. Brazos Theological Commentary. Grand Rapids: Brazos, 2010.

Pate, Marvin C., ed. *Four Views on the Book of Revelation*. Grand Rapids: Zondervan, 2010.[19]

18. See David deSilva, *An Introduction to the New Testament* (Downers Grove, IL: InterVarsity, 2011), 926.
19. This book includes preterist, idealist, classic dispensationalist, and progressive dispensationalist views.

Rossing, Barbara R. *The Rapture Exposed: The Message of Hope in the Book of Revelation*. Boulder, CO: Westview, 2004.

Advanced

Bauckham, Richard. *The Theology of the Book of Revelation*. New Testament Theology. Cambridge: Cambridge University Press, 1993.

Beale, G. K. *The Book of Revelation*. New International Greek Testament Commentary. Grand Rapids: Eerdmans, 1999.

Hays, Richard B., and Stefan Alkier, eds. *Revelation and the Politics of Apocalyptic Interpretation*. Waco: Baylor University Press, 2015.

Kovacs, Judith, and Christopher Rowland. *Revelation: The Apocalypse of Jesus Christ*. Blackwell Bible Commentaries. Malden, MA: Blackwell, 2004.

Portier-Young, Anathea. *Apocalypse against Empire: Theologies of Resistance in Early Judaism*. Grand Rapids: Eerdmans, 2014.

EIGHT

Pseudonymity and the New Testament Letters

"Preach the gospel at all times; when necessary, use words." These oft-repeated words come from the twelfth-century monk St. Francis of Assisi. Or do they? While St. Francis is the name most often associated with this quote, there is no historical evidence that it came from him. That is, it doesn't appear in any of his writings, and none of his disciples or biographers attach this statement to his teachings. One could easily argue that the sentiment of the quote can be found in the teaching of the order of Franciscans that he founded, but biographers tell us that there is a strong focus on verbal proclamation in his own writings and that he was preaching and teaching the gospel constantly.

Now, learning that perhaps (probably?) St. Francis did not say this might be a bit of a letdown. But some have argued that if the quote is theologically true (i.e., deeds "preach" the gospel effectively), who cares who wrote it? On the other hand, there does seem to be a kind of special credibility given to quotable quotes that come from famous people like Aristotle, Abraham Lincoln, and Mother Teresa.

This simple case study helps us to consider important questions pertaining to authorship and authority. Such matters are rather hotly contested when it comes to the study of the letters of the New Testament. In the same way that some historians doubt that St. Francis of Assisi actually said or wrote the quote above, so also some biblical interpreters question whether some of the letters in the New Testament were actually written by the authors named in those letters. I stumbled upon this academic discussion through a book with (what I thought at the time was) a peculiar title: *Letters That Paul*

Did Not Write.[1] (I had thought, then, Wouldn't that be *all* the other letters ever written in the world?) But the subtitle was meant to be an important clue: *The Epistle to the Hebrews and the Pauline Pseudepigrapha.* I knew that Hebrews did not have an authorial name in the book, so it made sense that there was no strong support for Pauline authorship. But what were the "Pauline Pseudepigrapha"?

A "pseudepigraphon" is a text written by someone other than the person named as the author in the document. It comes from the Greek words *pseudo* ("false") and *epigraphon* ("inscription, writing"). An important related term is "pseudonymity"—writing under a false (pseudonymous) name. Some scholars argue that several New Testament letters show evidence of *not* being written by the purported author. We can categorize the New Testament letters into "disputed" (many scholars dispute their ascribed authorship, finding strong evidence to the contrary), "somewhat disputed" (some scholars dispute their ascribed authorship, finding some evidence to the contrary), and "undisputed" (scholars almost universally consider the traditional designations of authorship to be authentic).[2]

Disputed: 1–2 Timothy, Titus, 1 Peter, 2 Peter, James, Jude

Somewhat Disputed: 2 Thessalonians, Colossians, Ephesians

Undisputed: Romans, 1–2 Corinthians, Galatians, Philippians, 1 Thessalonians, Philemon[3]

Why Doubt Authorship?

For almost seventeen centuries of church history, nearly all readers of the Bible simply assumed that the New Testament letters were written by the named author. In the eighteenth century, scholars began to question certain

1. Raymond F. Collins, *Letters That Paul Did Not Write: The Epistle to the Hebrews and the Pauline Pseudepigrapha* (Wilmington, DE: Michael Glazier, 1988).

2. The list below reflects the view of many scholars. But there is variety among scholars in terms of which letters belong in which categories. For example, a scholar may view all of the New Testament letters as genuine except 2 Peter and the Pastoral Epistles. Also, one might view most New Testament letters as genuine, some as allonymous, and some as forgeries.

3. Hebrews we can leave out of the discussion because it did not have author names attached to it. As for Revelation, while it does belong in this discussion as it names an author (John), in this chapter we will focus our attention on letters. Revelation mixes three genres: letter, prophecy, and apocalypse (see chap. 7). As it should be treated in a category of its own, it will not be discussed here. When it comes to 1–3 John, 1 John is technically anonymous, while 2–3 John are purportedly written by the "elder," and this figure is ambiguous enough for pseudonymity not to be a central concern.

texts (listed above), finding them incompatible with the attributed apostolic figure. The reasons for such suspicions vary according to the text, though there are some clear methodological tendencies. There appear to be five factors that play into decisions related to authenticity or pseudonymity: style, personality, theological development, historical implausibility, and pseudonymity tells.

The first two factors are related: *style* and *personality*. When it comes to Ephesians, for example, the epistle uses some turns of phrase and expressions that do not seem consistent with undisputed letters from Paul like Romans and 1 Corinthians. What is to account for this? As for personality, sometimes scholars detect not only a different style of writing but what seems like a different *personality* behind the letter. For example, while the undisputed letter 1 Thessalonians has a very warm and personal tone, the (somewhat) disputed letter 2 Thessalonians has a more austere and authoritarian tone. Again, some scholars question whether the same "Paul" could be responsible for both of these letters.

A third factor, perhaps one of the most important, is *theological development*. In the Pastoral Epistles (1–2 Timothy, Titus) there seems to be a shift in the way the word "faith" (*pistis*) is used by the author, in contrast to letters like Galatians and Philippians. In Galatians, "faith" is more of a relational term, focusing on Jesus as someone whom believers should trust. In the Pastoral Epistles, "faith" comes across more like a technical term for a body of teachings or beliefs. The use of this terminology seems to some to be overdeveloped for Paul's own time. Those who consider the Pastoral Epistles pseudonymous point to theological phenomena such as this.

Fourth, pseudonymity is sometimes predicated upon statements in or features of the text that seem *historically implausible*. For instance, the Greek style of 1 Peter seems to some scholars to reflect a well-educated author, and therefore they consider this letter unlikely to have been written by the historical apostle Peter, who was a Galilean fisherman with presumably a very basic education. In 2 Peter, the author refers to the apostle Paul's letters in such a general way (assuming wide knowledge of his work) that it seems like his writings had been in circulation for a long time, long enough to establish a reputation among churches broadly distributed.

Finally, there are sometimes features of texts that appear to be *tells* that reveal a pseudonymous author. Second Thessalonians replicates the structure and flow of 1 Thessalonians quite closely, in such a way that it looks to some as if the writer is *trying* to look like Paul. Also, Ephesians repeats much of Colossians in content, so much so that it is suggested by some that the author of Ephesians reworked the material of Colossians for his own context and purposes.[4] Why would Paul copy his own work in such a rigid manner?

Scholars who argue for pseudonymity for certain New Testament texts differ on which factors are at play and where to place the weight. They also do not always agree on how many problems should amount to a decision of labeling a text as pseudonymous. In some cases, especially those labeled "somewhat disputed" above, scholars hold to their view rather lightly or come to their judgment not on the strength of one or two obvious problems but rather on the basis of the cumulative weight of several smaller concerns.

Again, while each text is judged in its own right, there are important broader questions pertaining to the phenomenon of pseudepigraphy or pseudonymity in antiquity, and scholars debate whether writing in someone else's name was legitimate and innocent or devious and sinister. Though it appears writing in someone else's name was not uncommon in the ancient world, was it common in all kinds of communities or just certain ones? What about the early Christians in particular?

While delineating a clearly distinguishable set of views can be artificial in such a constantly evolving academic subject as this one, for heuristic reasons I will refer to three different approaches to pseudonymity: allonymity (innocent continuation of apostolic tradition), forgery (deliberate deception, pious or not), and authenticity (genuine authorship from named sender).

Allonymity

The language of "pseudonymity" (literally "false-name" authorship) is, perhaps, unfortunate in an academic discussion of the matter because it presupposes a kind of devious activity associated with lying and stealing. Certainly we have stories from the ancient world where writers produced works as if they were a particularly famous figure and they did so with greedy motives. However, some scholars have made the case that not all pseudepigraphers had sinister motives and not all pseudonymous writings were understood by the readers to be dishonest.

If we turn particularly to the writing of Jewish texts, especially in the Second Temple period, it is notable how often works were penned and attrib-

---

4. This perspective creates a bit of a problem for those who think both Ephesians and Colossians are pseudonymous. Why would a pseudepigrapher (of Ephesians) copy another pseudonymous text? Some scholars suggest that the author of Ephesians copied from Colossians, presuming it was genuinely from Paul, but in reality (unbeknown to him) it was actually another pseudonymous document. Others find it more reasonable to think that, if Ephesians is pseudonymous and heavily reliant on Colossians, then Colossians is most likely genuine.

uted to the name or identity of a key figure of Israel's past such as Abraham, Moses, Joseph, or Enoch. We see this with works such as *1 Enoch*, in which the biblical figure Enoch himself supposedly recounts the revelation of divine mysteries. Is it legitimate to refer to *1 Enoch* as a "forgery"?

It is appropriate to introduce at this juncture the question of *motive*—why would a writer, who is not Enoch, write a first-person account of the experiences and revelations of Enoch? Scholars have attached an insightful German word to this type of situation: *Vergegenwärtigung*. According to James D. G. Dunn, this word means something like "reimagining," and, in the context of this discussion, refers to "actualizing or contemporizing a particular stream of tradition."[5] A writer might rework or contemporize authoritative traditions from esteemed leaders as an attempt to rethink their thoughts after them in light of new contexts and challenges. The use of the name of tradition figureheads was not, it seems in these cases, meant as a co-opting of their personal authority as much as a literary device or convention that allowed people of a later time to attend to key foundational voices. Thus, Dunn argues, "Canonical pseudepigraphy is best seen as an example of the Jewish understanding and practice of tradition as a living force."[6]

From this perspective, a Christian writer using the name of Peter would not be attempting to fool the readers into thinking he was Peter. Rather, out of reverence for Peter, he was writing in a way that channeled the Petrine tradition toward the problems of a new day. This bearing of the apostolic name would not have been understood by early Christians as lying but would ideally be interpreted as a form of respect, esteem, and even humility.

Given the negative connotations often linked to language of *pseudo-*, one scholar proposes that we use a different word for this kind of *Vergegenwärtigung* phenomenon: *allonymity*. "*Allonymity*" refers to *another* writer, not a false writer. In such a case, the intent was not to trick or deceive, and neither were the first recipients duped. It would be a kind of transparent fiction, with the audience knowing that the named apostle was dead, and that this work (by a faithful disciple) was continuing the influence of the apostle or leader, trying to reexpress his concerns and actualize his teaching in light of a fresh set of concerns and circumstances.[7]

Let's look at an example: 2 Peter. While 2 Peter is clearly a letter (with, e.g., greetings and a closing), themes and structural elements of this letter have some overlap with Jewish literary documents that fit into the genre category

5. James D. G. Dunn, *The Living Word* (Minneapolis: Fortress, 2009), 66.
6. Dunn, *Living Word*, 68.
7. I. Howard Marshall, *A Critical and Exegetical Commentary on the Pastoral Epistles*, International Critical Commentary (Edinburgh: T&T Clark, 2004), 84.

of "testamentary literature." In such Jewish testaments, a noble patriarch gives some kind of farewell speech where he shares about his impending death and offers moral advice to his children or followers regarding steadfastness and righteousness in light of future events. Scholars agree that early Jewish testament writings are fictional and, when written from a first-person perspective, are not autobiographical but pseudepigraphical. Examples of early Jewish testaments include *Testament of Moses*, *Testament of the Twelve Patriarchs*, *Testament of Job*, and *Testament of Solomon*. The popularity of this literary genre in the Second Temple period attests to the fact that Jewish readers were not tricked into thinking these texts were real statements from the named patriarch.

Richard Bauckham has argued extensively that 2 Peter combines an epistolary form with the testamentary genre and this means of communication was employed by a writer to allow the voice of Peter to be active beyond the grave to a generation of believers who needed instruction.[8] Again, in a case such as this, naming Peter as the letter sender of 2 Peter would have been not deceptive but honorific, attesting to the importance of Peter's legacy and his teaching after his death.

The strength of this perspective (allonymity) is seen when the interpreter finds strong reasons to doubt authenticity and notes the relationship between New Testament literature and a particular set of early Jewish texts. There was a strong literary tradition alive in the first century that attempted to extend the voice of key patriarchs, prophets, and leaders in order to teach and form new generations.

Forgery

While there is some evidence that leans in favor of the allonymity perspective, a number of scholars are not convinced that pseudonymous activity was so transparent. There is common concern among both those who advocate a forgery position as well as those who defend authenticity that the allonymity view falls short in two key areas. The first deals with concerns about authorship legitimacy in the second and third centuries, especially in regard to canonization. The second concern pertains to personal details in the New Testament letters.

As for the first matter, there is some evidence that early Christian leaders (after the first century) were sensitive to the possibility of forgery and spurned

8. Richard Bauckham, *2 Peter, Jude*, Word Biblical Commentary (Waco: Word, 1983), 131–35.

pseudoapostolic writings. The Muratorian Canon[9] refers to the *Epistle to the Laodiceans* as well as a letter to the Alexandrians as "forged in Paul's name." The example regarding the pseudonymous *3 Corinthians* is even more telling. This ancient letter was discovered to be a forgery. Tertullian records that this (unnamed) church elder was removed from office, despite the fact that he claimed he wrote it out of "love for Paul."[10] We might also add the story told by Eusebius regarding Serapion, bishop of Antioch, who deemed a document called the *Gospel of Peter* false. Serapion wrote, "For we, brethren, receive both Peter and the other apostles as Christ; but we reject intelligently the writings falsely ascribed to them, knowing that such were not handed down to us."[11]

These anecdotes give a small glimpse of how at least some of the early Christians were concerned with legitimate authorship and were protective of genuine apostolic authority. Perhaps these examples are more restrictive than the norm, but the fact of the matter is that we have no explicit early Jewish or Christian discussion of allonymity as a bona fide form of legitimate authorship. No Christian community, as far as we can tell, recognized a pseudonymous writing as falsely attributed and then accepted it as authoritative.[12]

A second issue that can be raised against allonymity is the presence of very personal details in some of the New Testament letters. For example, Titus (considered by many scholars to be pseudonymous) ends with "Paul" informing Titus that he is sending Artemas or Tychicus, and that Titus is meant to meet Paul at Nicopolis in winter (3:12). Titus is supposed to send Zenas and Apollos (3:13). If the letter was meant to be a rather transparent fiction, why add these details? What purpose would they serve, if not to make the letter seem more authentic, when it was in fact not written by Paul? In 2 Timothy (also considered by many to be pseudonymous), why would "Paul" tell Timothy to bring his cloak, books, and parchments (2 Tim. 4:13)? It is difficult to see these details, if simply made up by another writer, as anything other than literary tactics to reinforce the fiction in order to make it appear more believable as a letter by the apostle Paul himself. Compare this to, for example, Ephesians (a disputed letter), which lacks such personal commands and simply concludes: "Peace be to the whole community, and love with faith,

9. The Muratorian Canon is an ancient list of New Testament books dating back to the late second century CE.

10. See Tertullian, *On Baptism* 17.

11. Eusebius, *Ecclesiastical History* 6.12.3, in *Nicene and Post-Nicene Fathers*, second series, ed. Philip Schaff and Henry Wace (1890; repr., Grand Rapids: Eerdmans, 1982), 1:258.

12. The absence of evidence is not decisive, but if we were privy to such a discussion, the case of allonymity would be that much stronger.

from God the Father and the Lord Jesus Christ. Grace be with all who have an undying love for our Lord Jesus Christ" (6:23–24).

If some of the authors of the New Testament letters were not the named apostles of the prescript, and if they added little personal details to make the deception more believable (i.e., less transparent), then would this not amount to a serious ethical problem? How could a Christian author, someone who wrote about holiness and righteousness in the tradition of Peter, Paul, or James, consider it right to deceive the readers with a forgery? Those who advocate a position of forgery for texts like Titus or 2 Timothy point to the logic of the "noble lie" that would have been recognized in Greek philosophical circles in the first century. Plato urged that this sometimes means deception would need to be employed for a greater good, to support an important truth.[13] In the case of the early Christians, forgers would have dared to be deceptive for a pious end, that is, the articulation of proper doctrine in the light of false teachers, for example.

The greatest challenge with this position of forgery regards the ethical implications for the canonization of these texts. If certain New Testament letters were forged (albeit with good intentions), and if those responsible for canonizing these texts accepted them as Christian Scripture at least partly on the basis of apostolicity (authored, authorized, or informed by a recognized Christian leader), then one might wonder whether such documents truly belong in the Christian canon. While there is no easy resolution for this quandary, if forgery is recognized, some scholars are compelled to at least expose the forgery for the sake of proper historical study.

The strength of this perspective (forgery) is seen when the interpreter has strong reason to doubt authenticity and recognizes that genuine authorship was a concern to people in that time. Those who argue in favor of forgery for some New Testament letters appeal strongly to the commonness of this practice, with a variety of motives ranging from pious to sinister, though involving deception in any case.

Authenticity

The last position that will occupy our attention is that of authenticity—namely, that the disputed New Testament letters were neither allonymous nor forged. This perspective usually begins with the disposition of *in dubio pro reo* ("when in doubt, side with the accused")—or one might say "innocent

---

13. See Plato, *Republic* 2.376E–3.392C; 3.414C–414E; 5.459D; cf. Cicero, *Brutus* 9.42; Clement of Alexandria, *Miscellanies* 7.9; Origen, *Against Celsus* 4.18–19.

until proven guilty." The argument for seeing the disputed New Testament letters as genuine starts with the notion that authorial personality, style, and communication are all too often more complicated and nuanced than historical study sometimes allows. Moreover, many scholars believe that we are not working with a large enough control sample of the work of Paul (for example) in the undisputed letters to be able to detect whether or not Ephesians or 2 Thessalonians is written by someone else.

Because authenticity is the default position (insofar as it takes the text at face value), the arguments that support authenticity tend to be *defensive*; that is, proponents of authenticity tend to find the arguments for allonymity or forgery too weak or flimsy to create sufficient doubt regarding genuine apostolic authorship. Let us briefly look at how defenders of authenticity approach the five areas of concern around pseudonymity: style, personality, theological development, historical implausibility, and pseudonymity tells.

Most people acknowledge that minor variations in style are normal. Often enough I end an email with "Blessings" or "Thanks," but once in a while I write "Peace," and sometimes I have no closing at all. When style concerns are raised by those proposing pseudonymity, a common rebuttal is that there are no clear rules for when a variation in style becomes *atypical* for the purported author. How different does the style have to appear to cast sufficient doubt on authorship? The same can be said with the nature of personality and the mood of the author. Does Paul always have to express himself in the same way and have the same mood? Do we not sometimes apologize and tell someone, "I am not myself today"?

However, even though there are no hard-and-fast rules for detecting variance in style or personality, there are enough unique features of wording and turns of phrases in texts like Colossians and 1 Timothy that have given most scholars pause. In that case, those who are inclined toward authenticity have introduced the possible contributions of an amanuensis (a letter secretary). There are two important features of Paul's Letters that inform us that he used such an agent. First, the amanuensis actually addresses Paul's Roman readers: "I Tertius, the writer of this letter, greet you in the Lord" (Rom. 16:22; cf. 1 Pet. 5:12). Second, on several occasions, Paul notes that he has stepped in to write with his own hand (e.g., 1 Cor. 16:21; Gal. 6:11; Philem. 19; cf. 2 Thess. 3:17; Col. 4:18). But what exactly did an amanuensis do? The presumption sometimes is that they acted as scribes, writing the letter while the author dictated the wording. In that case, they would have no input. However, we know that amanuenses of that period occasionally did take on a more formative role, such that the author might give an outline of points and the amanuensis would actually produce the finished form. This is generally *not* considered pseudonymity, because the work would have been authorized and, perhaps, even checked by the letter initiator after composition.

Another option under consideration that could explain style and personality variance is the way other associates are written into the letters. Interestingly, while the Letter of James mentions only "James" as the sender (also 1 Peter, 2 Peter), Paul tends to include people like Sosthenes (1 Cor. 1:1), Timothy (2 Cor. 1:1; Phil. 1:1; cf. Col. 1:1), and Silvanus (1 Thess. 1:1; cf. 2 Thess. 1:1). Could Timothy, for example, have anything to do with the actual *writing* (style, content, argumentation) of Colossians? Many interpreters have considered this possibility, though there is no easy way to prove such a literary influence. Nevertheless, if Timothy planned and wrote Colossians on Paul's behalf and with his permission, this could account for style differences between Colossians and the undisputed letters of Paul, but few would consider this to be pseudonymity, because, again, Paul would have personally authorized Timothy.

The matter of theological development overall tends to be downplayed by those who prefer authenticity, usually on two accounts. First, theological variance can possibly be accounted for by the various unique situations of Paul and his addressees. Second, few would deny that Paul (or Peter) simply *had* to develop in thought. After all, these apostles were only human. However, the real problem is with texts that seem to develop too quickly for Paul's own short time of ministry.

What about pseudonymous tells—those features of a letter where it seems like a pseudepigrapher has done something to bring attention to himself? For example, some believe we have a tell in 2 Thessalonians when the writer notes, "I, Paul, write this greeting with my own hand. This is the mark in every letter of mine; it is the way I write" (2 Thess. 3:17). To some this looks like a pseudepigrapher working hard to convince the readers of the genuineness of the letter. However, those who advocate for authenticity point out that the detection of such tells is highly subjective; as long as it is not historically implausible, such tells cannot provide concrete evidence regarding pseudonymous authorship.

Perhaps the greatest challenge to advocates of authenticity is the matter of historical plausibility. Some New Testament letters seem to be addressing problems and circumstances that are too far beyond the earliest generation of Christians. For instance, the formality of texts like Ephesians and the Pastoral Epistles seems like a more settled and institutionalized form of Christianity. Doctrine appears to some to be more detailed and concrete in such cases. Church governance and the nature of community life also appear more hierarchical. Admittedly, such concerns are worthy of consideration, but there has been some pushback that recognizes leadership positions already in undisputed texts (e.g., Phil. 1:1).

Beyond these rebuttals given in defense of authenticity, two other arguments are employed especially directed against allonymity. First, while few deny that allonymity was common in all manner of early Jewish literature, and almost certainly not considered underhanded, there is very little evidence that pseudonymity was a transparent literary convention for personal letters. Typically, a pseudonymous Jewish work, such as a testament or apocalypse, was written long after the death of the patriarch (sometimes hundreds of years later). In the case of Peter or James, pseudonymous works would have appeared merely decades after their demise. How could you distinguish a real letter from an allonymous one?

The second point has to do with verisimilitudes, those personal details about the author's circumstances and relationships that would be superfluous if the authorship was not genuine. There is an ethical concern that such little details would have been fabricated with the intent to make the letter *look* real. How could the early church have accepted such dubious activity as avenues of divine communication?

A final concern for defenders of authenticity puts the burden of argumentation back on the critics: for Colossians, why would a pseudepigrapher, many decades after Paul's death, write to Colossae (a city wrecked by an earthquake)? In the case of the Pastoral Epistles, if a pseudepigrapher wrote 1 Timothy, why would he also write the very similar text of Titus (if these texts were for neither Timothy nor Titus)?

The strongest point in favor of the defense of authenticity is simply the lack of clear and concrete evidence. While many scholars find the clues and hints for pseudonymity cumulatively convincing, there does appear to be a need for clearer methodological tools to study things like development and stylistic variance.

Reflections

Clearly there are no easy answers when it comes to the matter of the pseudonymity and the New Testament letters where authorship is disputed. Nevertheless, this discussion offers the opportunity to consider the implications of this matter for the study of the New Testament and early Christianity. Five issues seem to stand at the center of the debate and require further clarification, study, and reflection.

Context

Those who advocate for studying the issue of pseudonymity with the Greco-Roman context in view tend to observe the questionable motives behind forgery and the co-opting of the fame and authority of an important figure. However, those who read the disputed New Testament letters alongside early Jewish writings tend to claim a sense of innocence and do not label pseudonymity as deceptive but consider it a common literary practice. Indeed, it is seen as almost deferential for a disciple (of Paul or James, for example) to write in the spirit of an apostle and give that figurehead the honor and credit thanks to the importance and vitality of his legacy. We are left with the question of what literary context and tradition the New Testament authorship practices fall within.

Canon

Much discussion and debate revolves around how and why certain books were admitted into the canon (or recognized as canonical), while others were rejected. What role did apostolicity and authorship play in this? How important was it that a letter was written by Paul himself? If we also consider that orthodoxy was a key feature of canonical acceptance or recognition, could an orthodox text make the cut despite unknowns or concerns about authorship? We have texts where authorship is unknown (Gospels) or underdetermined (Hebrews), so this may shed light on the canonizing process. On the other hand, early Christians after the first century were apparently eager to attach an authorial name to all the New Testament texts, such as the presumption that Paul wrote Hebrews. Perhaps we could introduce the hypothetical scenario about canonization—if the early church came to realize something like 2 Corinthians was a forgery, would they have overturned its canonical status?

Composition

As noted above regarding defenses in favor of authenticity, determining authorship is messy business indeed. It is overly simplistic to think Paul sat down in splendid isolation with pen and paper and wrote Romans in one day. On all accounts, serious writing in the ancient world was not usually a quick and solitary undertaking. As for Paul, to some degree he sent texts as part of a team (with Timothy, for example, on some occasions), even if most of his letters have a personal feel. What if Timothy "wrote" a letter? What if Paul composed the outline, and Timothy filled it out? Or edited it or added information? What kinds of limitations did amanuenses have?

Another area where composition gets convoluted is the possible inclusion of genuine apostolic fragments into pseudonymous works. For example, perhaps James did not write the Epistle of James, but is it possible there are portions of this text that originate with James or derive from his teaching? The inclusion of genuine fragments could be relevant to several of the disputed New Testament letters. In that case, how should we talk about authorship? How would this affect matters related to a text's authority?

Genres and Styles

Another area that requires further discussion pertains to the particular genres and styles of individual documents. How is a text deemed inauthentic? In the case of the study of Paul's Letters, it is by comparison to the undisputed letters. The general mentality is that letters like Romans, Galatians, and 1 Corinthians establish a Pauline personality and style, and when disputed texts deviate (or deviate *too far*) from these texts, suspicions arise. But sometimes this is presuming a kind of monolithic quality to the way a person writes. What accounting should there be for changes in style that are intentional? For example, some scholars believe that Paul wrote Ephesians to the Ephesian believers (in Asia Minor) in a particularly Asiatic style that could account for the unusual turns of phrases and more poetical quality. In other texts, the tone is more formal, and could intentional aspects of style account for this?

Early Reception of the New Testament Letters

Much of the debate and the analysis of evidence relating to pseudonymity centers on the interpretation of the texts themselves, particularly study of clues that lead to one conclusion or another. Sometimes underappreciated is the earliest reception of these disputed letters. It is helpful to bear in mind that, in some ways, the earliest church was in a better position to detect pseudonymity than we who look at these matters thousands of years later. It should be noted that the earliest editions of the Pauline corpus, for example, contained Ephesians, Colossians, and 2 Thessalonians, and some collections explicitly note that these were written by Paul. One historian states, "Thus all ten of these letters [minus the Pastoral Epistles] were from the outset universally received and recognized as authentically Pauline. There is no evidence that anyone in the ancient church called into question the authorship of any of the Pauline community letters."[14]

14. Harry Gamble, "Pseudonymity and the New Testament Canon," in *Pseudepigraphy and Author Fiction in Early Christian Letters*, ed. J. Frey et al., Wissenschaftliche Untersuchungen zum Neuen Testament 246 (Tübingen: Mohr Siebeck, 2009), 333–62.

The matter is quite different, by contrast, with the early reception of 2 Peter and James. In the early fourth century, Eusebius referred to these (along with Jude and 2–3 John) as *antilegomena* ("disputed [in terms of authenticity]"; *Ecclesiastical History* 3.25.3). For James, Dale Allison presents evidence that (a) there is little reason to think James was known before the end of the second century, (b) it is absent from many canonical lists through the fourth century (including the Canon Mommsenianus, the Cheltenham Canon, and the Muratorian Canon), and (c) its authenticity was disputed in the patristic period. On this last point, Jerome wrote, "James, who is called the Lord's brother . . . wrote only one epistle, which is one of the seven catholic epistles, which, it is asserted, was published under his name by another, although little by little as time went on it obtained authority."[15] Having such evidence from reception is obviously not conclusive, but it gives extra weight to arguments concerning pseudonymity.

Conclusion

On the subject of pseudonymity and the New Testament letters, the ongoing debate in scholarship is quite lively and far from reaching a consensus. Those who advocate for an allonymity position for many of the disputed letters tend to read such letters in line with a popular Jewish literary tradition of honoring a revered leader and his legacy for a new generation. From this perspective, deception is not involved, and the first-century readers would have recognized this as such.

Those who think that several of the disputed letters were forged insist that there is ample evidence for these texts not being genuine and that there is reason to believe that the pseudonymous authors were attempting to convince readers that Paul or Peter or James were the "authors" of the text. The case for forgery in the New Testament is often made on the basis of (a) the commonness of this activity in the Greco-Roman world; (b) clues in the New Testament texts that seem like the forgers were hiding their tracks, so to speak (2 Thess. 2:2; 3:17); and (c) the writing of many apocryphal apostolic letters in the second and third centuries and clear rejection of forgeries by church leaders.[16]

---

15. On the reception of James, see Dale Allison Jr., *A Critical and Exegetical Commentary on the Epistle of James*, International Critical Commentary (London: Bloomsbury T&T Clark, 2013), 13–28.

16. Some scholars have tried to argue that the rejection of apocryphal apostolic texts had more to do with their bad theology (heterodoxy) and not the source of the material as of first importance.

The argument for authenticity of the disputed letters is usually maintained by scholars concerned especially with an author-driven focus of textual meaning. There is also usually the concern that pseudonymity (as forgery in particular) was a deceptive practice, something that interpreters concerned with orthodoxy consider highly unlikely given the emphasis on truth, holiness, and righteousness in all of the New Testament letters. Finally, proponents of authenticity usually approach the New Testament texts from a position of innocent until proven guilty, though they may have an ideological bias toward minimizing evidence that might point to pseudonymity due to concerns that such documents should not have or could have become canonized.

Suggested Reading

Beginner

Dunn, James D. G. "Pseudepigraphy." In *Dictionary of the Later New Testament and Its Developments*, edited by Ralph P. Martin and Peter H. Davids, 977–87. Downers Grove, IL: InterVarsity, 1997.

McDonald, Lee Martin. "Pseudonymous Writings and the New Testament." In *The World of the New Testament*, edited by Joel B. Green and Lee M. MacDonald, 367–78. Grand Rapids: Baker Academic, 2013.

Allonymity

Dunn, James D. G. *The Living Word*. Minneapolis: Fortress, 2009.

Marshall, I. Howard. *A Critical and Exegetical Commentary on the Pastoral Epistles*. International Critical Commentary. Edinburgh: T&T Clark, 2004.

Forgery

Ehrman, Bart. *Forged: Writing in the Name of God—Why the Bible's Authors Are Not Who We Think They Are*. New York: HarperOne, 2011.

Authenticity

Porter, Stanley E. "Pauline Authorship and the Pastoral Epistles: Implications for Canon." *Bulletin for Biblical Research* 5 (1995): 105–23. See the response by Robert W. Wall, "Pauline Authorship and the Pastoral Epistles: A Response to S. E. Porter," *Bulletin for Biblical Research* 5 (1995): 125–28; and the rejoinder by Porter, "A Response to R. W. Wall's Response," *Bulletin for Biblical Research* 6 (1996): 133–38.

Advanced

Bauckham, Richard. "Pseudo-Apostolic Letters." *Journal of Biblical Literature* 107 (1988): 469–94.

Ehrman, Bart. *Forgery and Counterforgery: The Use of Literary Deceit in Early Christian Polemics*. Oxford: Oxford University Press, 2013.

Gamble, Harry. "Pseudonymity and the New Testament Canon." In *Pseudepigraphy and Author Fiction in Early Christian Letters*, edited by J. Frey, J. Herzer, M. Janssen, and C. K. Rothschild, 336–62. Wissenschaftliche Untersuchungen zum Neuen Testament 246. Tübingen: Mohr Siebeck, 2009.

Meade, D. G. *Pseudonymity and Canon: An Investigation in the Relationship of Authorship and Authority in Jewish and Earliest Christian Tradition*. Grand Rapids: Eerdmans, 1987.

Metzger, Bruce. "Literary Forgeries and Canonical Pseudepigrapha." *Journal of Biblical Literature* 91 (1972): 3–24.

Porter, Stanley E., and Gregory P. Fewster, eds. *Paul and Pseudepigraphy*. Pauline Studies. Boston: Brill, 2013.

Wilder, Terry L. *Pseudonymity, the New Testament, and Deception: An Inquiry into Intention and Reception*. Lanham, MD: University Press of America, 2004.

NINE

The New Testament
and the Roman Empire

Not long ago I came across a religious group based in Ohio called the "Embassy of Heaven." This movement believes that Christians should not be beholden to worldly governments because true believers are citizens of heaven according to Philippians 3:20 ("Our citizenship is in heaven"). This group issues its own identification documents (like passports and driver's licenses) and protests the requirement to pay taxes. As you can imagine, this community is rather small and idiosyncratic, but this raises an interesting question about how the earliest Christians in the Roman world conceived of their individual and social identity vis-à-vis the government. One might presume that their Christian religion was a private matter, a spiritual preference, and thus none of the government's business. But we have to remember that while modern Americans (like myself) have a particular cultural and political background of the separation of church and state, it is not that way in many parts of the world today, and a religion-free government was certainly not an assumption or reality in the Roman Empire of the first century CE. Religion was an integral part of life for everyone in the Roman Empire, and worship of Roman gods played a central role in political events and the imperial consciousness at large. (For example, from the time of Julius Caesar, the Roman emperor could hold the role of Pontifex Maximus, "High Priest," over the pagan priests of Rome.) This did not mean that *only* Roman gods were worshiped in the Roman Empire. The Romans allowed various conquered peoples and immigrants within their borders to continue to revere and honor their ancestral gods as a general rule. The point, though, is that cult (religious practices and piety) and good citizenship went hand in hand—if the state was in the care of the gods, the gods deserved homage to inspire their blessings and to curtail their wrath. Every member of society was expected to contribute to the divine blessing of the empire through respectful devotion to the gods.

Again, this can be very difficult for us to understand today. Over time, there has developed a certain attitude toward religion in the Western world that it is a personal choice that one adopts as a preference, philosophy, or lifestyle. And it can seem that religion contributes to personal fulfillment without necessarily becoming entangled in social or political matters. I recall that once upon a time this seemed to be reinforced for me when I read John 18:36, where Jesus tells Pilate, "My kingdom is not of this world" (NIV). As this conversation goes, Pilate is interrogating Jesus and asks him directly, "Are you the king of the Jews?" (18:33). The bigger picture here is that Pilate wants to know whether Jesus and his followers are a political threat to the leadership system that Rome has established over the Jewish people (i.e., was Jesus leading an uprising?). Jesus's response can seem rather dismissive, especially as articulated by some English translations—"My kingdom is not of this world." One *could* hear this to mean: "Don't worry about me, I am trying to save souls for heaven, not to meddle with worldly empires." Perhaps with some irony Jesus *is* crucified after all for political sedition, and the known insurgent Barabbas is set free (18:40).

One could get the impression, then, that Jesus had no interest in directly threatening or subverting earthly kingdoms. His aim was salvation and new birth. Over the years, nevertheless, Christians have disagreed about the proper attitude and posture that believers ought to have toward government and politics. Martin Luther talked about "two governments" and how the Christian lives in these simultaneously. There is the spiritual government, where one abides by spiritual laws (such as turn the other cheek). But there is also the secular world, where certain procedures and rules can exist that preserve physical life (e.g., punishment and use of force against criminals). Worldly governments can rule over mundane matters, Luther argued, but cannot govern human souls, such as through mandated beliefs. While it was never Luther's intention to support the notion that the worldly and spiritual never mix, the attitude did become prevalent over time that spirituality is a personal matter and can be separated from politics and worldly affairs.

But there are other stories and passages in the New Testament that seem to communicate that the gospel involves active political engagement and transformation. Consider Luke 1:46–55, where Mary the mother of Jesus sings a song of praise as she ponders the coming of the Messiah through her womb. Recounting the glorious works of Israel's God in former times, she remembers how "he has brought down the powerful from their thrones, and lifted up the lowly" (1:52). We might also point to Luke's sequel, the book of Acts, where the accusations are made against the apostles in Thessalonica (in front of the city authorities), "These people . . . have been turning the world upside down," and "They are all acting contrary to the decrees of the emperor, saying that there is another king named Jesus" (Acts 17:6–7).

All of this raises questions: How did the earliest Christians conceive of their relationship with and responsibilities toward the Roman Empire? Were they explicitly and directly critical of Rome? Did they teach and practice support of Roman imperial politics? Were they seen as a direct threat to Roman ideals and power?

Conversations in Christian theology about the church's stance toward the government have been around for a long time, but New Testament studies has experienced a major surge of interest and discussion along these lines in the last twenty years thanks to the recent debate about New Testament and empire. Looking in particular at the first-century Roman world, scholars have vigorously engaged in the matter of whether or not the New Testament writers intentionally and directly sought to criticize the Roman Empire and the emperor. Before getting to the two sides of the debate, it behooves us to consider *how* this particular discussion has intensified in recent history.

What Is Empire Studies?

Empire studies, or empire criticism, has become one of the hottest topics in biblical studies, but just thirty years ago no one would have used or understood such terms in the guild. So where did this come from? It appears that it developed especially in the 1990s—in America in particular—as a result of a confluence of several academic trends and cultural concerns. First, for a variety of reasons, New Testament scholars began to take more active interest in politics and religion in the Roman world of antiquity. As this world was inspected more closely and brought into comparison with the language and ideas of the New Testament, there were clear resonances that demanded explanation. Just to offer one example, scholars have noted the titles attributed to Roman emperors.[1] In the first century BCE, Augustus was hailed by oath as "god of gods." The emperor Domitian self-professed the title "lord and god" (cf. John 20:28). On Roman coins, it was not uncommon for emperors to bear the title *divi filius*—"son of (a) god." And, of course, a very common

---

1. See Helen Rhee, *Early Christian Literature* (London: Routledge, 2005), 161.

honorific title for the emperor was "lord" (*dominus*). If such titles were part of the fabric of the political reality of the Roman world, what did it mean, then, for Christians to attribute these same titles to the crucified Jew, Jesus Christ? How could they *not* be making a political statement via these carefully selected titles for Jesus?

Another factor that inspired empire studies is the ongoing impact of postcolonial criticism on biblical studies. Postcolonial criticism examines texts with a concern for power dynamics present in and behind the situation, especially how political platforms are established that support the colonizer and oppress the colonized. The controlling power of an empire can exist in the background of a text, and it can often be hidden to cultural outsiders (like those of us who read the New Testament removed in time and space from the first-century Roman world), and thus readers today can be ignorant of such a pervasive and powerful force in the real lives of the earliest Jews and Christians.

Part of postcolonial criticism is paying attention to how those who are colonized respond to the colonizers. From this perspective, biblical scholars have taken interest in whether, or to what degree, early Christian writers express—in subtle or more overt ways—protest or criticism of imperial power. And, it could be the case that subjects of empire show a mixture of critique, accommodation, and even appreciation.

A final consideration involves the political climate in America in the 1990s. Often American presidents have presented their nation both as a superpower (like an empire) and as a nation that follows the ideals of the Christian Bible. But scholars like Richard Horsley have argued that Scripture often portrays the people of God as *resisting* the evils of power-hungry empires.[2]

We turn now to look at essentially two different views on the New Testament and the Roman Empire. On one side, there are those who argue that, by and large, the early Christians and Jesus were critical of the empire. A second view urges that anti-imperial statements or ideas in the New Testament are potentially present, but the evidence for a thoroughgoing, pervasive, and consistent anti-imperial sentiment is absent or ambiguous. Furthermore, there are also signs of a more positive attitude toward Rome, the emperor, and empires in some New Testament texts. This appears to demonstrate that the early Christians had to carefully navigate through difficult political terrain, showing a mixture of accommodation and resistance.

---

2. See especially Richard A. Horsley, ed., *In the Shadow of Empire: Reclaiming the Bible as a History of Faithful Resistance* (Louisville: Westminster John Knox, 2008).

New Testament Opposing Empire

We have already mentioned above that there appears to be evidence that the New Testament writers borrowed political language to talk about the one God and Jesus Christ (as Lord, Son of God, Savior, etc.). And there is much more material along these lines. For example, one of the most important theological terms in the New Testament—"gospel" (Greek: *euangelion*)—had currency as a political term in the Roman world as well. We know of a calendar (9 BCE) from Asia Minor that refers to the birthday of Emperor Octavian (Augustus) as "the beginning of good news" (Priene Inscription, 105, 40; cf. Mark 1:1).[3] Now, one could use the language of "good news" for anything from the news of a work promotion to the news of a friend coming to visit. But is it merely a coincidence that Christians celebrated the incarnation and lordship of Jesus as "good news," while politically the emperor's reign was also recognized as "good news"?

Or consider the word "savior" (Greek: *sōtēr*). Both Julius Caesar and Augustus were granted the title of "savior and benefactor." These men were hailed for their agency not in spiritual salvation but rather in political leadership. Along these lines, emperors promised "peace" (Latin: *pax*; e.g., the Pax Romana), just as Jesus promised "peace."

But the argument for detecting anti-imperial attitudes in the early Christian writings does not amount to simply collecting and comparing terms. That was merely the tip of the iceberg for the emergence of empire studies. The broader argument has to do with the world of the biblical writers and the concerns and subject matter of their texts as a whole. The case is often made that politics in general is of prime interest in both the Old and New Testaments. Israel was a real political entity fighting for its existence, survival, and autonomy in the ancient world. God promised Israel land, a thriving national monarchy, and later a geographic return from exile to their homeland. In the first chapter of the book of Acts, when the risen Jesus gives his disciples instructions about events to come just before his ascension, his followers do not ask about spiritual salvation or the end of the world. The one question they present to Jesus is a *political* one: "Lord, is this the time when you will restore the kingdom to Israel?" (Acts 1:6).

Those who advocate for this (anti-imperial) reading also point out that Jesus's condemnation and crucifixion are a political affair. The Jewish leaders who reject Jesus's ministry send him through the required Roman channels

3. For more information on the Priene Inscription see "Iasos Honours Herokrates of Priene," trans. C. Crowther, Translations of Hellenistic Instriptions, Attalus, accessed May 23, 2019, http://www.attalus.org/docs/other/inscr_133.html.

to be executed in the most shameful way possible. Pilate is not necessarily concerned that Jesus is a religious leader, nor is he concerned that Jesus has made grandiose religious claims about himself. Rather, Jesus is crucified for claiming to be king of the Jews (Mark 15:26), a political leader who would be a rival to the client-king of Judea who was implemented by Rome (Herod Antipas). This Roman concern is not illusory. After all, John the Baptist, Jesus's friend and ally, opposes Herod rather directly (Matt. 14:3–4). And Jesus calls Herod a slanderous term ("fox") in front of the Pharisees and tells them to relay to him Jesus's unhindered, powerful ministry (Luke 13:32).

I have also mentioned above the natural assumption by Roman inhabitants that early Christians were politically deviant by nature. As already noted, Christians were considered seditious by following "another king named Jesus" (Acts 17:7). And there are some New Testament books that are *directly* critical of Rome. The book of Revelation addresses the suffering of the righteous and the impending apocalyptic triumph of God that will destroy the wicked and restore the faithful. Several times John mentions the ills of "Babylon" and its inevitable destruction. Here "Babylon" is a (rather transparent) code word for Rome; the whore of Babylon is probably evocative of the statue of the goddess Roma, the symbolic representative and protector of the great city that sits on seven hills (Rev. 17:9). In Revelation 18 the demise of Babylon is prophesied. As one scholar explains, "God responds to Rome's abuses with a series of destructions. . . . A catalogue of Rome's crimes as the political and economic hub of the 'earth' follows. Imperial triumphalistic theology and power is pitted directly against the power, sovereignty, and victory of God in Christ. They are competing kingdoms with conflicting aims."[4]

When these kinds of themes are brought to the forefront of readers' minds as they encounter the New Testament, it creates a new lens through which to view these texts. And this can lead to new questions and observations. Rome promised "peace and security" (Latin: *pax et securitas*), and Paul explicitly warns believers not to be wooed by promises of "peace and security" (1 Thess. 5:3). Is this a subversion of Roman-style peace? Is it more than a coincidence that the demons in Mark 5:9 are named Legion, the title for the largest Roman military unit? And what about these demons being sent by Jesus into a herd of pigs—since we know that the Roman legion in Palestine had a boar as its mascot?

---

4. Cynthia Long Westfall, "Running the Gamut: The Varied Responses to Empire in Jewish Christianity," in *Empire in the New Testament*, ed. Stanley E. Porter and Cynthia L. Westfall (Eugene, OR: Wipf & Stock, 2011), 230–58, at 254.

At the end of the day, though, one of the most important questions confronting this discussion of the New Testament and empire is how *much* the early Christians would have been concerned with imperial power and politics. N. T. Wright makes the claim that this would have been a top priority because "the emperor cult itself was the fastest growing religion" in the first century.[5] The emperor was not merely a nuisance to the early church, but the empire promoted a dominant ideology (revolving around the ultimate power of the sovereign) that was in direct conflict with Christian beliefs and values about the supremacy and salvation of Father, Son, and Spirit, one God and one Lord. If Caesar was both a ruling figure and also a recipient of homage (or divine honors), then Christians were forced to choose between worshiping the one God and worshiping an imperial idol. Their choice to give exclusive worship to Father, Christ, and Spirit was inevitably a political choice *not* to worship or submit fully to the supremacy of Caesar. So Wright claims about early Christian thought: "Jesus is lord and saviour, and by strong implication, easily audible to residents in a Roman colony, Caesar is not."[6] Put another way, given the world-shattering nature of the salvific work and lordship of Jesus Christ, and the world-dominating ideology of the Roman emperor, the Christian good news could not help but be politically subversive.

New Testament Negotiating Empire

But there is another take on this matter. Indeed, while anti-imperial readings of the New Testament have quickly become popular in the last few decades, we are seeing strong pushback or, to be more accurate, counterbalancing. It is not that opposing scholarship argues for the complete irrelevance of empire and politics. It is a given that Jesus and the earliest Christians lived out their lives and their faith in the Roman Empire and could not help but figure out ways to navigate and negotiate their social, religious, and political identities in that context. Rather, it can be viewed as a pendulum of scholarly interest. When a new theory or idea emerges, a segment of scholarship attempts to bring attention to that notion by giving it prominence and assembling the strongest evidence in its favor. After a period of time, the pendulum is bound to move again in the other direction (usually as a corrective). The details of those early arguments are put to the test, and often the matter of methodology is brought to the forefront of the discussion. Furthermore, scholars begin to

5. N. T. Wright, *Paul: In Fresh Perspective* (Minneapolis: Fortress, 2009), 64.
6. N. T. Wright, *The Resurrection of the Son of God*, Christian Origins and the Question of God 3 (Minneapolis: Fortress, 2003), 225.

ask, Have we left anything out? Where are the blind spots? How do we account for interpretive bias? This happens in many areas of scholarship, and this is certainly the case with empire studies and the New Testament.

Perhaps the most obvious place to begin is with instances where the early Christians appeared to be supportive of imperial systems. For example, in Romans 13 Paul writes,

> Let every person be subject to the governing authorities; for there is no authority except from God, and those authorities that exist have been instituted by God. Therefore whoever resists authority resists what God has appointed, and those who resist will incur judgment. For rulers are not a terror to good conduct, but to bad. Do you wish to have no fear of the authority? Then do what is good, and you will receive its approval; for it is God's servant for your good. But if you do what is wrong, you should be afraid, for the authority does not bear the sword in vain! It is the servant of God to execute wrath on the wrongdoer. Therefore one must be subject, not only because of wrath but also because of conscience. (13:1–5)[7]

Paul then goes on to justify the paying of taxes, again repeating the idea that political authorities serve the purposes of God (see Rom. 13:7). With relation to Rome, it is also noteworthy how Jesus interacts with Roman soldiers according to the canonical Gospels (especially as they are key agents of imperial power). They are often portrayed as interested in Jesus, and he tends to respond to them in positive ways (see Matt. 5:41; 8:5–13; cf. Mark 15:39). At no point does Jesus reject or shame a Roman soldier for his allegiances or political agency.

In the book of Acts, while it is true that many accusations of a legal nature are made against the followers of Jesus, Luke also makes a point to show how leaders like Paul speak publicly in their own defense and attempt to demonstrate civil respect rather than subversion. In Philippi, when Paul and Silas feel they are wrongly punished, after being miraculously freed from prison, instead of fleeing they file a public complaint: "They have beaten us in public, uncondemned, men who are Roman citizens, and have thrown us in prison; and now are they going to discharge us in secret?" (Acts 16:37). This results in an apology from the city magistrates.

Anti-imperial readings of the New Testament tend to portray imperial leaders, and specifically the emperor, as direct enemies of the church. But

---

7. Seyoon Kim refers to Romans 13:1–7 as the "Achilles' heel for all anti-imperial readings of Paul"; see *Christ and Caesar: The Gospel and the Roman Empire in the Writings of Paul and Luke* (Grand Rapids: Eerdmans, 2008), 36. A similar statement is made in 1 Peter (2:11–17).

many scholars are quick to point out that the New Testament writers do not *name* any emperor explicitly (i.e., Tiberius, Caligula, Claudius, Nero, Galba, Otho, Vitellius, Vespasian, Titus, or Domitian). The great enemies are not named human imperial or political figures but spiritual entities such as Satan, Death, and Sin.[8]

What about the way the early Christians used political language? While it *could* be seen as subversive to call Jesus "lord" or "savior," it might also be treated as a conceptual platform to understand the nature of Christian identity. Andy Crouch represents the attitude of many when he says that for the early Christians to say "Jesus is Lord" does not mean "Caesar is not"; "Rather, it entails *not saying* 'Caesar is Lord.' . . . The affirmation 'Jesus is Lord' requires not so much a strident denunciation of earthly lords as a studied silence concerning their pretensions."[9]

This camp, then, does not reject the real way in which the first Christians co-opted overtly political language. They also recognize the intimate relationship between religion and politics in the ancient world. What is up for debate is the degree to which the New Testament demonstrates direct and overt criticism of the emperor and the government. Was it of *first priority* for the New Testament writers to critique and denounce Roman rulers, laws, and politics? There is certainly room for New Testament texts (like Revelation) that are rather incisive about the demise of evil, whether political, spiritual, or otherwise. But there are many other places in the New Testament where it is difficult to sustain an anti-imperial sentiment or detect subversive language.

Reflections

At present, this matter is still a rather lively discussion in biblical studies. While there is a lot of sympathy for the anti-imperial reading, we are seeing more and more critical responses. Perhaps the most pressing concern is the desire for a clear and convincing methodology for demonstrating anti-imperial sentiments in a New Testament text. Wright has attempted to provide such a methodology by adapting a respected approach to detecting echoes of the Old Testament in the New Testament developed by Richard B. Hays.[10]

8. See John M. G. Barclay, "Why the Roman Empire Was Insignificant to Paul," in *Pauline Churches and Diaspora Jews* (Grand Rapids: Eerdmans, 2016), 363–88.

9. See Andy Crouch, foreword to *Jesus Is Lord, Caesar Is Not*, ed. Scot McKnight and Joseph B. Modica (Downers Grove, IL: InterVarsity, 2013), 7–14, at 13.

10. See Wright, *Paul*, 61–62; drawing from Richard B. Hays, *Echoes of Scripture in the Letters of Paul* (New Haven: Yale University Press, 1989), 29–32. For an overview of the academic discussion of the use of the Old Testament in the New, see chap. 12 in this book.

Wright's method has seven features. (As a sample case study, let us consider the language of "peace and security" as a Roman imperial slogan as it is mentioned by Paul in 1 Thessalonians 5:3. I will explain each test and then relate it to this text.)

1. **Availability:** *Was the (imperial) material readily available and knowable in the culture at the time?* Does the Roman slogan "peace and security" predate Paul's use, and was it widely available? (Implication: if a term/phrase is not historically available, then it cannot be a legitimate [anti-] imperial reference in Paul.)

2. **Volume:** *How significant or prominent is this material?* Would readers of Paul's letter readily recognize the slogan "peace and security"? How prominent was it in Roman culture? (Implication: if a term/phrase was not widely known or prominent, it is less likely Paul would have used it without clearer referencing.)

3. **Recurrence:** *Does the word or theme recur elsewhere in the Pauline corpus, sufficient for us to be able to establish a broader base of meaning?* Does Paul mention the slogan "peace and security" anywhere else in his letters? (Implication: if a term/phrase is repeated in the Pauline material, and those other occurrences fit an imperial reference, there is a strong case to make for its identification and importance as a political or [anti-]imperial reference.)

4. **Thematic Coherence:** *Does the theme cohere well with other aspects of what Paul is saying?* In 1 Thessalonians 5:3, does a reference to the Roman slogan "peace and security" fit into the letter's argumentation and serve its rhetorical purposes? (Implication: if it does not, the reference would seem superfluous.)

5. **Historical Plausibility:** *Could Paul have intended this meaning, or is it anachronistic or out of context when we predicate it of him?* Are there any sociohistorical or cultural factors that make a reference to "peace and security" in 1 Thessalonians 5:3 impossible or unlikely? (Implication: detecting "echoes of Caesar" is more than matching up wording—a wider perspective on empire, history, and culture must be taken into account.)[11]

---

11. I find "availability" and "historical plausibility" similar in the sense that they are both watching out for anachronism; the former, in my understanding, focuses more narrowly on whether the specific wording/phrase is historically identifiable as *prior to* the Pauline text that references it; I take "historical plausibility" as something broader in terms of Paul's motives, and the wider relationship between the early Christians and government/empire, and so on.

6. **History of Interpretation:** *Have other interpreters from other ages (and from around the world) read the text in any way like this?* Is there evidence that others have also detected a Roman slogan ("peace and security") in 1 Thessalonians 5:3 in the past? (Implication: the discovery of others who have spotted the same echoes strengthens the case for detecting imperial references. But Wright is quick to say that this factor is not a deal breaker, since new insights often lead to more accurate readings of a text.)

7. **Satisfaction:** *Does this reading enable the text to speak with new coherence and clarity? Does it lead to a fresh and better understanding of the Pauline text?* Does recognition of the Roman slogan "peace and security" in 1 Thessalonians 5:3 present a clearer and more satisfying understanding of the passage and the letter in the context of Paul's life and ministry? (Implication: detecting echoes of empire and politics ought to be not just an interesting exercise but one that leads to a better understanding of the text and context. The assumption is that if Paul purposely included a reference to imperial terminology or ideas, it must have served some purpose.)

The limiters and tests in this kind of methodological reflection help to sharpen the enterprise of relating early Christian discourse to ostensible imperial terms, concepts, values, propaganda, and thought. But Wright's approach is not without its critics. John Barclay finds Wright's appropriation of Hays's "echoes of Scripture" method problematic. When Hays devised his method, his starting point was bits and phrases that match up between Paul's wording and specific Old Testament texts, and then Hays related the wider wording of the Old Testament texts to Paul's rhetorical and theological interests in that given Pauline letter. Wright, Barclay argues, has difficulty establishing specific imperial material that Paul would be referencing, so he commences from a less secure launching point. Barclay explains, "From the massive evidence of citation, no-one could doubt that Paul's theology is closely engaged with his Scriptures; to posit a similar engagement with the Roman Empire would require a similar evidential base."[12] Despite Barclay's concerns here, many scholars appreciate that Wright has drawn attention to the importance of establishing a clear way to demonstrate early Christian appropriation of imperial or political language.

Another key consideration in this discussion is determining the *intent* of references to imperial terms and ideas. In much of the literature on this subject,

12. Barclay, "Why the Roman Empire Was Insignificant to Paul," 380.

it is assumed that if a New Testament writer reappropriated imperial terms and applied them to Jesus, God, church, and so on, then this must amount to *anti-imperialism* (opposition, parody, replacement, etc.). Of course, this is possible, but it is not the only option. Again, Barclay argues that various clubs and societies in the ancient world adopted political terminology for their groups without the assumption that this was a threat or challenge to Rome.[13] One can imagine a variety of reasons why one might borrow language from another context. Perhaps it seemed parallel or fitting. It *may* have been critical without being subversive. Wright is fond of using the language of *parody*—Paul and other New Testament writers exposed the counterfeit nature of imperial forms and that Christian ones were the real ones. But, at the end of the day, how does one know, even if an imperial echo can be demonstrated, exactly *why* it was included? This continues to be a bone of contention in empire studies.

The whole matter of attending to the imperial context of early Christianity and the apostolic writings has been an important revolution in biblical studies. This has brought fresh readings to all kinds of texts (e.g., Matthew, John, Acts, Romans, Philippians, 1 Peter, Revelation), and it has helped to fit these works into a wider sociopolitical context. Furthermore, scholars are more attentive to the relevance of political elements such as coins, monuments and statues, government buildings, and political records as part of the material culture that shaped life and society in the world of the first Christians. It has also become clearer that early Christians like Paul consciously adopted political language to talk about Jesus, God the Father, the gospel, salvation, and the church; but what is currently contested is the extent of this political discourse and its purposes. These questions and considerations have not only piqued historical curiosity but also invigorated churches today to think anew about the relationship between church and government, and the interconnection of the spiritual and the political.

Suggested Reading

Beginner

Carter, Warren. *The Roman Empire and the New Testament: An Essential Reader.* Nashville: Abingdon, 2010.

Horrell, David. *An Introduction to the Study of Paul.* 3rd ed. London: Bloomsbury T&T Clark, 2015.

13. Barclay, "Why the Roman Empire Was Insignificant to Paul," 376.

Oakes, Peter S., ed. *Rome in the Bible and the Early Church*. Grand Rapids: Baker Academic, 2002.

Winn, Adam. *An Introduction to Empire in the New Testament*. Atlanta: SBL Press, 2016.

New Testament Opposing Empire

Crossan, John D. *God and Empire: Jesus against Rome, Then and Now*. New York: HarperOne, 2009.

Horsley, Richard A., ed. *In the Shadow of Empire: Reclaiming the Bible as a History of Faithful Resistance*. Louisville: Westminster John Knox, 2008.

———, ed. *Paul and Empire: Religion and Power in Roman Imperial Society*. Harrisburg, PA: Trinity Press International, 1997.

———. *Paul and the Roman Imperial Order*. London: Trinity Press International, 2004.

Thatcher, Thomas. *Greater Than Caesar: Christology and Empire in the Fourth Gospel*. Minneapolis: Fortress, 2009.

Wright, N. T. *Paul: In Fresh Perspective*. Minneapolis: Fortress, 2009.

New Testament Negotiating Empire

Barclay, John M. G. "Why the Roman Empire Was Insignificant to Paul." In *Pauline Churches and Diaspora Jews*, 363–88. Grand Rapids: Eerdmans, 2016.

Kim, Seyoon. *Christ and Caesar: The Gospel and the Roman Empire in the Writings of Paul and Luke*. Grand Rapids: Eerdmans, 2008.

McKnight, Scot, and Joseph Modica, eds. *Jesus Is Lord, Caesar Is Not: Evaluating Empire in New Testament Studies*. Downers Grove, IL: InterVarsity, 2013.

Advanced

Heilig, Christoph. *Hidden Criticism? The Methodology and Plausibility of the Search for a Counter-Imperial Subtext in Paul*. WUNT 2/392. Tübingen: Mohr Siebeck, 2015.

Kahl, Brigitte. *Galatians Re-Imagined: Reading with the Eyes of the Vanquished*. Paul in Critical Contexts. Minneapolis: Fortress, 2010.

Rowe, C. Kavin. *World Upside Down: Reading Acts in the Graeco-Roman Age*. Oxford: Oxford University Press, 2009.

TEN

Women in Leadership in the New Testament

The Church of England ordained their very first female bishop, Libby Lane, in 2015. One part of the service involved the presiding bishop asking the congregation present at York Minster Cathedral, "Is it your will that she should be ordained?" While the vast majority in attendance jubilantly shouted, "It is," one outraged clergy member in attendance blurted out loudly, "No! Not in the Bible!"

Needless to say, there can be very strong views on the subject of women in authoritative church leadership. There is a spectrum of views on what roles women can and should have in church leadership, but I will address this in terms of two main views: *hierarchical male authoritative leadership* (men viewed as exclusively authorized to hold authoritative positions over a congregation that includes men) and *egalitarian authoritative leadership* (men and women viewed as equal in respect to positions of authoritative leadership in the church).

Preliminary Concerns

If you Google the subject of the Bible and women in ministry, you will see thousands of websites and blogs that share opinions on the matter, but as often happens with the internet, there is much heat with too little light. Before we address the relevant, debated biblical texts involved in the discussion, it behooves us to address some preliminary matters.

Pastors?

Sometimes writers on this subject (for or against women in ministry leadership) frame the discussion in terms of whether or not the Bible says women can be pastors. The fact of the matter is, though, that while the pastor is the dominant ministry role in many Protestant churches today in the West, it is not the dominant term for ministry leadership in the New Testament. In fact, in most English translations, the word "pastor" appears in only one biblical book, and in one single verse (Eph. 4:11) with no comment on the role! What we learn from careful study of ministry roles in the New Testament is that, in the first century, church leaders were generally recognized for their work (1 Thess. 5:12) rather than for a particular church office. Also, a group of *elders* seemed to be primarily responsible for the leadership of the church, with a variety of other gifted individuals participating in that leadership as well (see Acts 20:17; 1–2 Timothy; Titus; cf. James 5:14; 1 Pet. 5:1).

Cultural Trends and Prejudice

It is not uncommon to hear that those who advocate for women in church leadership are merely swept up in cultural trends, trading in biblical faithfulness for secular fads. Or you may hear that those who believe in male-only leadership are self-centered and infatuated with their own manliness and prejudice against women. There can obviously be extreme views that come from immature thinking, but it is best to approach this subject with the knowledge that there are intelligent and mature thinkers on both sides who have a serious interest in careful examination of and faithfulness to the biblical witness. As with any of the issues in this book, due attention should be paid to the best logical arguments from skillful study of the Bible. Very little will be accomplished by perpetuation of harsh stereotypes and flippant labeling. I propose that discussions should avoid labels like "fundamentalists," "chauvinists," "left-wing/right-wing," or "liberals."

Hierarchical Male Authoritative Leadership

Those who subscribe to a view of hierarchical (male authoritative) leadership (HL) believe that, while women should participate in the active life of the church and may be called by God to give some forms of leadership in the church (usually in service to children or other women), they are not biblically authorized to hold roles that would put them in direct authority over men. For most HL proponents, this is not meant to denigrate the dignity or intelligence of women. Rather, the most common defenses regarding the logic behind HL are that, first, women (generally speaking) are gifted in different ways than men—and it happens that men have a stronger, innate aptitude for leadership—and that, second, women are viewed as especially gifted for and called to nurture and raise children when they have a family, and the commitment to church leadership could jeopardize the care of family in the home. It bears noting that some HL proponents appeal only to the second matter and urge that the significance of prohibiting women from authoritative teaching has nothing to do with intelligence or capability but rather is about God-given gender roles and proper spheres of influence.

The following represent key biblical texts and patterns that HL proponents often turn to in support of their views. The included expositions reflect their general readings of these texts.

Adam and Eve (Gen. 1:26–28; 2:18)[1]

While it is clear men and women were both created in the image of God, Adam, the first male, was created first; thus God accorded to him a special honor. Eve was created because it was not good for Adam to be alone, and a suitable helper and companion was necessary (Gen. 2:18). Thus, the creational order identifies woman as playing a supportive function in relation to man.

Male Leaders of Israel, Male Jesus, Male Disciples

When one looks at the history of God's covenantal dealings with the patriarchs and Israel, all of the key figures are men: Abraham, Moses, Joshua, Samuel, David, Solomon, and so on. The priests of Israel were exclusively male. This is consistent with the above reading of Genesis 1–2. The same could be said for the Messiah Jesus being a male—a key indicator of the restoration of all humankind through the "last Adam," who represents the whole of humanity in redemption. Furthermore, Jesus chose only men as his cohort of disciples whom he trained and sent out as apostles.

1 Corinthians 11:2–16

All scholars recognize that Paul's discussion of head coverings, church order, and decorum is puzzling and the modern reader is not privy to much of the context and history of Paul's relationship with the Corinthians that led to this teaching. However, two elements of this passage are relevant to the discussion of gender and authority. First, Paul refers to the man as the "head"

---

1. Obviously I am noting here Old Testament texts (in a textbook about issues in the New Testament), but it is simply the case that the New Testament itself appeals to the Old Testament on this matter on occasion, and scholars (rightly) tend to look at the Bible as a whole in this discussion. Also, a text like Gen. 1:26–28 is so foundational to the whole Bible that it requires careful study no matter what side of the debate one is on.

(*kephalē*) of his wife (11:3). While it is noteworthy that Paul uses "head" (*kephalē*) here in a number of ways, especially as a play on words because the subject at hand is "head coverings," many scholars take the language of "head" in 11:3 to refer to authority.[2] The second element of significance in this passage is the argument from creation; Paul makes the case that a man should not cover his head "since he is the image and glory of God; but woman is the glory of man. For man did not come from woman, but woman from man; neither was man created for woman, but woman for man" (11:7–9 NIV). If woman was created for man, a case can be made that she cannot or should not serve in authoritative leadership over him.

1 Corinthians 14:34–36

Regarding the orderly nature of worship in Corinth, Paul urges that "women should be silent in the churches. For they are not permitted to speak, but should be subordinate" (14:34). This is not taken by any respectable scholar to mean that women ought not to open their mouths but rather is understood to mean that they ought not to be disruptive. Nevertheless, the principle of submission strongly implies that they should not have roles of authoritative leadership in the church.[3]

1 Timothy 2:11–15

Perhaps the strongest and most direct injunction against women in leadership appears to come from 1 Timothy, where Paul[4] writes, "A woman should learn in quietness and full submission. I do not permit a woman to teach or to assume authority over a man; she must be quiet. For Adam was formed first, then Eve. And Adam was not the one deceived; it was the woman who was deceived and became a sinner" (1 Tim. 2:11–14 NIV). Women, here, are

2. While it is true that *kephalē* can have various metaphorical meanings, a glance at the uses of this word in the Septuagint shows that it was employed as a term in reference to "heads" of groups; see the Septuagint of 2 Sam. 22:44; Ps. 17:44; Isa. 7:8–9.

3. There is some disagreement regarding the relevance of 1 Cor. 14:33b, where Paul writes, "as in all the churches of the saints." It is possible that this statement goes with what comes *after*—namely, Paul's teaching that women should remain silent and submissive (so the flow of the ESV). Others argue that it belongs with the statement that came *before*, "For God is not a God of disorder but of peace [as in all the churches . . .]" (see NIV).

4. Scholars debate whether Paul himself wrote this text, or if it was written years after Paul's death by someone else in his name. The jury is still out on this in scholarship, but even if Paul did not write 1 Timothy, most scholars interested in the subject of women in church leadership still consider 1 Timothy to be Scripture, and thus, it is relevant what this passage says as part of the Word of God, whether or not Paul himself authored it.

prohibited both from teaching and from having authority over men, and this is reinforced by an argument from creation.

1 Timothy 3:1–12

Paul's instructions regarding both "overseers" (*episkopoi*) and "deacons" (*diakonoi*) in the church make reference to these men being "the husband of [only] one wife" (see 1 Tim. 3:2, 12 NET), implying that these roles are for men only.

Egalitarian Authoritative Leadership

Those who advocate for egalitarian leadership in the church (EL) argue that God can give women gifting and calling to have authority in the church, even teaching and executive authority over men as well as women. This is borne out of not a liberal feministic agenda but rather a sense that churches led by both men and women are best equipped to serve a church of men and women. This perspective urges that men do not carry any inherent authority unique to their gender; rather, leadership is part of God's gifting and calling to whomever he wishes to grant it, regardless of gender.

First I will address how an EL perspective responds to the biblical texts and their interpretation as presented by the HL perspective above. Then I will note the formative arguments in favor or representative of the EL perspective.

Responses to Hierarchical Leadership Texts and Interpretations

On the matter of Genesis 1–2, EL scholars tends to argue that women were created to "help" men not in a submissive role but rather as true equals in all ways, especially in view of the fact that "helper" can be a term used of God (e.g., Exod. 18:4). When it comes to creation order (Adam first, then Eve), while there is an assumed logic of *primogeniture* (special rights to the firstborn) in the Bible, this precedent is often overturned by God himself, most notably in the case of Ishmael and Isaac, Esau and Jacob, and the fact that King David was the last born in his family.

As for the matter of male leadership throughout the Bible, those advocating *now* for EL can look at this history and argue that God was accommodating to a male-centered culture; but that accommodation does not necessarily represent his ultimate vision for leadership (this can also apply to the narrow discussion of male-only overseers and deacons in 1 Tim. 3:1–12).

Regarding 1 Corinthians 11:2–16 and "headship," those favoring EL point out that the meaning of *kephalē* ("head") is highly contested. Some argue that it is not referring to authority, but rather it means "head" as *source*, like the "head" of a river—that is, where the river comes from. Others advocate a meaning of *kephalē* as "most prominent part," understanding "head" as *representative*, not authority. Furthermore, while Paul does mention that woman came later (she came "from man"; 11:8), he concludes his discussion on the note of mutuality; man comes *through woman*; thus, they are interdependent. In the case of 1 Corinthians 14:34–36, this is viewed by some scholars not as standard teaching for all churches but, rather, as a specific issue of women being disruptive. Paul's concern is much less with gender roles than it is with harmony in the church service.[5]

What about 1 Timothy 2:11–14? It should be noted that the meaning of the verb "to have authority" (*authenteō*) is unclear—it appears only here in the whole New Testament, and the verb is extremely rare in extant Greek literature from Paul's time. While some translators urge that it means "to have authority" in a neutral or positive sense (see NIV, ESV), others argue that it means "to domineer" or "to usurp authority" in a negative sense (see KJV, CEB). If it means the latter, Paul is not making a blanket statement that denies female teaching authority, but rather he is prohibiting women from trying to domineer over men, a situation that may have been going on in Ephesus, where Timothy was residing. If Paul had simply meant "to have authority," why would he have not used the more common word *exousiazō*, as he does in 1 Corinthians (6:12; 7:4)? This should be an indicator that Paul is dealing with a highly contextualized problem, and thus, overgeneralizing his teaching here is unwise.

Formative Texts for Egalitarian Leadership

Genesis 1:26–28

The first statement that Genesis makes about humanity comes in 1:26–28, where humankind is made in God's image, male and female, and *both* are called to rule over creation. Woman was not created to serve or even "support" man, but both of them were created to serve in partnership as caretakers of Eden and representatives (image bearers) of God.

---

5. Some scholars also note that some of the Greek manuscripts we have of 1 Corinthians have this passage (1 Cor. 14:34–36) in a different part of the letter. This could be a sign that Paul did not actually write these verses, but rather that they were inserted into the text later by a scribe. In that case, they don't belong in 1 Corinthians and should not be taken as apostolic teaching.

Deborah and Huldah

In a few places in the Old Testament, we do see women playing important, even authoritative, roles in the life of Israel. In Judges 4:1–24, Deborah is noted as judging Israel for a period of time (4:4). Israelites, including men, came to her for the settling of disputes (4:5). She called upon the military leader Barak to partner with her in defeating the enemy Sisera (4:6–24). In the book of Judges, she is the only female judge, and the only judge who is portrayed at length in a fully positive light.

According to 2 Chronicles 34:22–29, a prophetess named Huldah is consulted by King Josiah's royal officials, and Josiah acts upon the prophetic word of Huldah. It is significant that many male prophets were active around Josiah, but he chose Huldah and trusted her counsel.

Women in the Gospels

While it is obvious that the twelve disciples were all men, still it is noteworthy that Jesus had a wider entourage of disciples who followed him around, including women. Luke 8:1–3 makes note of several women who not only traveled with Jesus but supported his ministry financially. Furthermore, many scholars consider it significant that Mary Magdalene was called upon by the risen Jesus to tell the other disciples about him, and she did so faithfully (John 20:16–18). Some scholars consider this entrustment of the resurrection witness an apostolic activity.

Paul and a New Age of Equality

Paul writes in Galatians 3:28 that part of what it means for a people to be united as one in Christ is that "there is neither Jew nor Greek, there is neither slave nor free, there is neither male nor female" (RSV). Before the appearance of Jesus Christ, Jews alone could serve as priests and leaders in the worship of Israel's God, but "in Christ" there is no longer a distinction between Jew and gentile in this regard. When it comes to male and female, the same could be said. This finds further support in Acts 2:17–21, where Peter gives his famous Pentecost speech, in which he proclaims the fulfillment of the prophecy from Joel 2:28–32: "I will pour out my Spirit upon all flesh, and your sons *and daughters* shall prophesy" (Acts 2:17, emphasis added). In the new age of the giving of the Holy Spirit, women are inspired with prophecy to share with God's people. Women ought not to be barred from authoritative teaching *as women* but should be considered as members of a new humanity "in Christ."

Women as Church Leaders

In Philippians 4:2, Paul names two women, Euodia and Syntyche, who ought to "be of the same mind in the Lord." That Paul would call out these women in particular might imply they were prominent, even leaders. After all, he refers to them as his fellow workers in the gospel. While this is somewhat ambiguous, more evidence for women in leadership appears in Romans 16. Phoebe is called a *diakonos* from the church of Cenchreae (16:1). It is unclear what Paul means by *diakonos* (deacon? servant?), but she is also called a "benefactor" or "patron" (*prostasis*) of Paul (16:2). The very fact of her being sent from Cenchreae to Rome seems to imply some level of prominence, and there is good reason to believe Paul entrusted Phoebe with the task of delivering the Letter to the Romans, and perhaps also reading and explaining it to the church in Rome.

Paul also mentions a woman named Junia[6] and her husband Andronicus, and he refers to both as "prominent among the apostles" (Rom. 16:7). This appears to suggest that Junia was considered a female apostle. Finally, according to Acts 18:26, the couple Priscilla and Aquila came alongside the zealous preacher Apollos and "explained the Way of God to him more accurately." Many supporters of EL identify Priscilla as someone who is presented in Scripture as competent to instruct the man Apollos in the Christian faith.

Responses to Egalitarian Leadership Texts and Interpretations, from Hierarchical Leadership Perspective

Here we will briefly consider how HL proponents respond to the EL reading of their key scriptural arguments. First, HL scholars do not accept the inference that women and men are both called by Genesis 1:26–28 to corule over all creation in the same way. They serve as partners of equal value, but not identical in roles. When it comes to figures in the Old Testament like Deborah and Huldah, they can be understood as exceptions, not the norm. Also, some

---

6. There is some debate over the gender and status of this person called "Junia" in Romans. Some translations refer here to "Junias" (the name of a man). Others, "Junia," the name of a woman. There is little reason to believe that this person was a man, because Junia was a common name at the time, and we do not have evidence for the name Junias (though some argue that "Junias" could have been a short form of the known male name Junianus). Scholars (and English translations) in the last fifteen years or so have nearly all moved to the position that Junia (female) is the right interpretation, though there is still debate about whether the phrase "prominent among the apostles" is *inclusive* (prominent *as* an apostle) or *exclusive* (prominent *in the eyes of* the apostles) with reference to Junia. For an important, though technical, study on this subject, see Eldon J. Epp, *Junia: The First Woman Apostle* (Minneapolis: Fortress, 2005).

posit that Deborah was not "raised up" to lead in the way the male judges were; furthermore, it is argued that Deborah did not have unique authority over Barak. She gave counsel, but not as Barak's authority. As for Huldah, she can clearly be praised for her wisdom in prophecy, but this does not require one to see her as an authoritative teacher. This, similarly, has implications as well for what it means that "daughters" in the New Testament will prophesy (Acts 2:17).

The women in the Gospels do not receive direct authority from Jesus to preach or teach, even if they were with him as followers. In the case of Mary Magdalene, despite her role in testifying to the resurrection of Jesus, she was not formally recognized in the first century as an apostle.

When it comes to Galatians 3:28, the statement "no longer male and female" is not a statement about church leadership, and Paul does not engage in gender issues in this letter, which detracts from its significance in the discussion. Paul has no interest in disregarding gender differences. His goal is to unify the church and avoid rivalries and any sense of superiority based on gender, class, or ethnicity.

What about women leaders in Paul's churches? The roles of Euodia and Syntyche are unclear; Paul never states what they did. Similarly, we have too little information to develop a proper understanding of what it meant to call Phoebe a *diakonos* (servant) and *prostasis* (patron) in Romans 16:1–2. As for Junia, one can take the statement "prominent among the apostles" in two ways (both in the original Greek and in English). It *could* mean that Junia and Andronicus *were apostles themselves* (noteworthy *as* apostles), or it could simply mean that the *apostles* found these nonapostles noteworthy; that is, Andronicus and Junia were found by the apostles to be important, but these two did not fall within that group. Just reading the Greek text of this phrase does not easily settle this matter, and there is much debate about how to understand the preposition *en* ("among"). On the last point, about Priscilla, some would say that she was not an independent instructor of Apollos, and that she did not teach him in any official sense.

Reflections

Clearly this is a convoluted issue with many texts and dimensions to consider. Even in this chapter I could barely scratch the surface of the topic. However, this brief introduction to the textual arguments reveals the key pressure points of the debate. It is helpful to reflect on the central hermeneutical questions involved.

Culture and Truth

Much of the debate revolves around how to understand the nature of culture and how one finds timeless truth in the midst of culture-embedded texts. Is male hierarchy central to the biblical model of human life in community, or is it a feature of one culture or set of cultures? One way that this issue is manifested relates to church and home. Advocates of HL sometimes argue that women *could* be successful teachers and executive leaders in the church, so it is not a matter of skill. But the problem is that woman was created to care for family and tend to affairs in the home. Proponents of EL often reply that nearly all women were married in the first century, and it was simply a cultural assumption that women managed the household. But in a modern world with a different education system for kids, and gadgets and appliances to simplify housework, women are freed up for ministry. Could it not be that the first-century assumptions could not imagine the modern household? So, as you can see, there is tension in relation to how the testimony of Scripture is understood as a *product* of its culture and as a testimony that can *transcend* its ancient culture.

Protology (Creation and "First Things") and Eschatology (Redemption and Final Consummation)

Both sides of the discussion, when they are at their best, try to pay careful attention to creation (protology) and new creation (eschatology): How does the way God made the world point us to how men and women should relate and live in society and church? How does Scripture's vision of new creation, a world renewed and restored from the dominion of sin, imagine men and women together?

Analyzing Narratives

Narratives and the significance of certain characters play some role on both sides of the debate (e.g., Deborah, Huldah, Mary Magdalene, Jesus, the disciples/apostles). How do we study biblical narratives in a way that we can learn about how they contribute to this discussion when explicit statements about authority are absent? How can we tell if narratives are meant to be *descriptive* or *prescriptive*?

Experience and Hermeneutics

On one side of the discussion, a woman might say, "I feel called to be a pastor." On the other side we might hear, "I have never heard a good female preacher." Both sides of the discussion can appeal to some form of personal experience. What role can and should human experience play in the study and interpretation of Scripture and ethical discernment?

What does the future of the study of women in leadership and Scripture look like? The debate in scholarship rages on, but probably the most pressing matter requiring further research is the question regarding the nature of gender itself. What is gender, and how does the Bible understand gender? What makes a man a "man"? What makes a woman a "woman"? If men are uniquely gifted to lead and teach, does that mean women are less intelligent or skilled? If men and women have equal capacity and gifting, how has God made them different as male and female? A second dimension of this issue is how gender and culture are related. Are the definitions of masculinity and femininity fixed? Can they change over time from period to period and culture to culture, or, if they don't change, can they change in their expressions? A third matter relates to exceptions: If men and women have gendered strengths and weaknesses that make men more fit for teaching and leadership, are exceptions possible for one unique woman here or there, and what can and should churches do with that option? What are the possibilities, and what are the limitations?

The reason why this has become such an important debate in the study of Scripture is that it touches on matters pertaining to real life in the church. How one interprets this issue affects ministry leadership in the church. The matter cannot be chalked up to personal preferences or even deciding which texts of the Bible are more important or authoritative on the matter (e.g., whether 1 Tim. 2:11–14 or Gal. 3:28). Alongside these problems we have questions regarding the nature of Scripture itself, how it relates to culture and experience, and what it means to be obedient to God in our time now. Charity is too often difficult to find in this debate, but we would do well to let grace flow from humility as we recognize the complexity of this discussion.

Suggested Reading

Beginner

Beck, James R., and Craig L. Blomberg, eds. *Two Views on Women in Ministry.* Grand Rapids: Zondervan, 2001.

Hierarchical Male Authoritative Leadership

Doriani, Daniel M. *Women and Ministry: What the Bible Teaches.* Wheaton: Crossway, 2003.

Piper, John, and W. Grudem, eds. *Recovering Biblical Manhood and Womanhood: A Response to Evangelical Feminism.* Wheaton: Crossway, 1991.

Egalitarian Authoritative Leadership

Belleville, Linda. *Women Leaders in the Church: Three Crucial Questions.* Grand Rapids: Baker Books, 2000.

Pierce, Ronald W., and Rebecca M. Groothuis, eds. *Discovering Biblical Equality: Complementarity without Hierarchy.* Downers Grove, IL: InterVarsity, 2005.

Advanced

House, H. Wayne. *The Role of Women in Ministry Today.* Nashville: Nelson, 1990.

Husbands, Mark, and Timothy Larsen, eds. *Women, Ministry and the Gospel: Exploring New Paradigms.* Downers Grove, IL: InterVarsity, 2007.

Johnson, Alan F., ed. *How I Changed My Mind about Women in Leadership: Compelling Stories from Prominent Evangelicals.* Grand Rapids: Zondervan, 2010.

Keener, Craig S. *Paul, Women, and Wives: Marriage and Women's Ministry in the Letters of Paul.* Peabody, MA: Hendrickson, 2004.

Kostenberger, Andreas, and Thomas R. Schreiner, eds. *Women in the Church: An Analysis and Application of 1 Timothy 2:9–15.* Grand Rapids: Baker Books, 2005.

Webb, William J. *Slaves, Women & Homosexuals: Exploring the Hermeneutics of Cultural Analysis.* Downers Grove, IL: InterVarsity, 2001.

ELEVEN

Justification by Faith and Judgment according to Works

In the 1990s DVDs were all the rage. If you wanted to rent a movie, you drove to your local Blockbuster video-rental store. It was not cheap to rent a new release; you might pay up to eight dollars. As web-based companies began to offer monthly DVD subscriptions for rentals that mail to your home (like Netflix, before they did streaming), Blockbuster struggled to compete. In 2004, they hatched a plan—*no more late fees*. You could go to your Blockbuster store, pick out a movie, and pay for the rental, but you weren't beholden to a late-return charge. Of course the idea was that it only takes an hour or two to watch a movie, so a person would pick up the movie, watch it, and return it in a few days at his or her own leisure.

Simple, right? In reality, there was no way that this could work as a business strategy, so they had to put in place limitations. For example, if you kept the movie longer than seven days, you would be charged for the full purchase price of the movie (minus the rental fee) unless you brought it back, in which case you would be refunded the purchase price minus a $1.25 "restocking fee." Confused? So was everyone else; needless to say, this plan did not work out well for Blockbuster. Ultimately, consumers were receiving mixed messages; one message told them that they could experience a unique kind of freedom and relief when they rented a movie —*no more late fees!* But eventually consumers would come to learn that penalties for keeping movies did exist. "No fees" did not mean "free."

Without trying to force this analogy too far, there is a similar paradox involved with the study of salvation in the New Testament. On the one hand, the concept of free grace is paramount in the New Testament, as evident in a text like Ephesians 2:8–9: "For by grace you have been saved through faith, and this is not your own doing; it is the gift of God—not the result of works, so that no one may boast." Similarly, when Paul explains how Abraham was justified before God, he writes, "Now to one who works, wages are not reckoned as a gift but as something due. But to one who without works trusts him who justifies the ungodly, such faith is reckoned as righteousness" (Rom. 4:4–5). And the notion of "justification by faith" is famously stated by Paul in Galatians 2:16: "We know that a person is justified not by works of the law but through faith in Jesus Christ. And we have come to believe in Christ Jesus, so that we might be justified by faith in Christ, and not by doing the works of the law, because no one will be justified by the works of the law." What these texts seem to communicate is that justification (and salvation) come to the believer not by what he or she *does* but as a free gift from God.

The challenge comes with the fact that as often as the New Testament talks about salvation and justification by *faith*, it also addresses the idea that believers will be judged according to *works*. Never do the New Testament writers say that judgment will focus on faith, nor do they say that judgment will be skipped or diverted due to initial justification. Judgment is taken as a serious matter for which believers ought to prepare, though certainly not a judgment where one expects to meet an unjust God. Paul reminds the Corinthians that "all of us must appear before the judgment seat of Christ, so that each may receive recompense for what has been done in the body, whether good or evil" (2 Cor. 5:10). This is also reinforced in Romans, where Paul teaches that God "will repay according to each one's deeds" (Rom. 2:6). God will grant eternal life "to those who by patiently doing good seek for glory and honor and immortality" (2:7). On the other hand, wrath and fury are in store "for those who are self-seeking and who obey not the truth but wickedness" (2:8). Later Paul bluntly concludes, "God does not show favoritism" (2:11 NIV).

This has created no small amount of confusion and debate among Christians over the last two thousand years. Is salvation a free gift received only by faith? Or is it partially or completely dependent on the weighing and consideration of works? How can grace and obligation coexist?

An interesting case study involves a very public (print) debate between John Piper and N. T. Wright. In 2007, Piper published a book called *The Future of Justification: A Response to N. T. Wright.*[1] One of the main concerns for Piper was how Wright conceived of the relationship between initial justification and final salvation. Piper argues that Wright has lost the essence of

---

1. John Piper, *The Future of Justification: A Response to N. T. Wright* (Wheaton: Crossway, 2007).

the gospel when Wright argues that the verdict of initial justification will be confirmed at the final judgment on the basis of an evaluation of the life lived.[2] Piper argues that for grace to be true grace it must be separate from any judgment based on works. In 2009, Wright published a book offering a study of his view called *Justification: God's Plan and Paul's Vision*.[3] In that book Wright explains that Paul's understanding of future justification is not about *earning* anything, but Paul does write about a real reckoning of what humans have done. This involves human choices, but only in tandem with the work of the Spirit.[4] Wright fears that Piper's perspective could lead to passivism, and Piper believes that Wright has tainted Paul's pure gospel with a works requirement. And so it goes!

It is difficult to navigate this discussion because, first, it touches several complicated areas of theological study including free will and predestination, the meaning of justification, the center of Paul's theology, the nature of the Judaism of Paul's time, and Paul's own relationship to that Judaism. It also requires trying to synthesize the various texts of the New Testament, something that some scholars find difficult, and some even find impossible to do! Furthermore, many scholars simply cannot choose one side and end up falling into what we will call "the messy middle." I will discuss the divergent views on this issue using the following terms: "faith-determinative judgment" and "works-oriented judgment."

Faith-Determinative Judgment

While it is true that the New Testament *does* talk about judgment in reference to *works* (Rev. 20:12: "The dead were judged according to their works"), in the end almost no Christian perspective understands this to mean that judgment is *purely* about works; otherwise Christ died for nothing (see Gal. 2:21). Wright makes a point to observe that whatever one does is by the grace of God through the Spirit. Stephen Travis represents a perspective that views works (under judgment) as *evidence* of a relationship with God. In that sense, the works are not the most important thing, but rather what matters is what these works demonstrate or show. So Travis explains, works "bear testimony to the depths of a person's character, and show whether their relation to

2. See N. T. Wright, *What Saint Paul Really Said: Was Paul of Tarsus the Real Founder of Christianity?* (Grand Rapids: Eerdmans, 1997), 129.
3. N. T. Wright, *Justification: God's Plan and Paul's Vision* (Downers Grove, IL: InterVarsity, 2009).
4. See Wright, *Justification*, 192–94.

God is fundamentally one of faith or unbelief."[5] Salvation, Travis argues, is dependent on not the Christian's works per se but whether they have put their trust in Christ. So he summarizes: "Paul therefore believes in a final judgement for every person. Its primary function will be to disclose whether each belongs to Christ or not, and to determine their destiny accordingly. For those who through faith in Christ have come into relationship with God, the verdict anticipated in justification and demonstrated in their lives will be confirmed. For those who have rejected Christ, their condemnation will be confirmed."[6] According to this perspective, justification and final judgment are not two entirely separate events. It is not that one is saved (in theory) by initial justification, but only on the proviso that enough works are done to merit salvation at final judgment. Rather, final judgment *reveals* what is hidden. Its purpose is to bring the active faith of the believer to light.[7] Works are not works alone; they are done by people. When the New Testament talks about "works," that is shorthand for talking about works that reflect in some way on *persons*. The works reveal the heart and life of the person, and judgment is designed to see the righteousness of Christ at work.[8]

Part of the reason that some come to the conclusion that *faith* is what matters at judgment and not *works* relates to holistic statements made in the New Testament to the effect that faith in Jesus settles the question of salvation. So, we might look at texts like Luke 7, where Jesus tells the penitent woman who washes Jesus's feet with her tears, "Your sins are forgiven" and "Your faith has saved you" (Luke 7:48, 50). Or consider the language of belief and eternal life in the Gospel of John. Jesus states plainly, "The one who believes in the Son has eternal life. The one who rejects the Son will not see life, but God's wrath remains on him" (3:36 NET; 5:24; 6:40, 47; cf. 1 John 5:13).[9] In Acts, Paul and Silas tell the jailer, "Believe on the Lord Jesus, and you will

5. Stephen Travis, *Christ and the Judgement of God: The Limits of Divine Retribution in New Testament Thought* (Milton Keynes, UK: Paternoster, 2009), 94.

6. Travis, *Christ and the Judgement of God*, 99.

7. See Dane C. Ortlund, "Justification by Faith, Judged according to Works: Another Look at a Pauline Paradox," *Journal of the Evangelical Theological Society* 52, no. 2 (2009): 323–39, at 337.

8. So Mark Seifrid, "Justified by Faith and Judged by Works: A Biblical Paradox and Its Significance," *Southern Baptist Journal of Theology* 5, no. 4 (2001): 84–97, at 90–91. Seifrid writes, "These works . . . are nothing more than faith at work, the apprehending of Christ's work in situation after situation of daily life. They are, as Paul says, the 'reckoning' that we have died to sin, but are alive to God in Christ Jesus" (95).

9. Note the analogy in John 3:14 between the "lifting up" of the Son of Man (i.e., crucifixion) and the "lifting up" of the bronze serpent by Moses (Num. 21:9). Those Israelites who were bitten by poisonous snakes in the wilderness were cured by God when they simply looked upon the serpent. This would serve as a testimony to ultimate divine mercy.

be saved, you and your household" (Acts 16:31). Similarly, Paul writes to the Romans, "If you confess with your lips that Jesus is Lord and believe in your heart that God raised him from the dead, you will be saved" (Rom. 10:9; cf. 1 Cor. 1:21; 15:2). In these texts and others, initial justification or salvation seems to supersede anything else, even with final judgment in view.

Works-Oriented Judgment

Despite the above considerations, some scholars insist that Paul and other New Testament writers treated final judgment as a serious matter and that human works will be assessed, which would lead to a certain salvific outcome.[10] So, for example, Paul talks to the Corinthians about his ministry and life's work and uses this as an occasion to talk about how the work of each person will be tested on the day of the Lord (1 Cor. 3:10–13): "If what has been built on the foundation survives, the builder will receive a reward. If the work is burned up, the builder will suffer loss; the builder will be saved, but only as through fire" (3:14–15). More directly Paul communicates to the Corinthians in his second letter: "For all of us must appear before the judgment seat of Christ, so that each may receive recompense for what has been done in the body, whether good or evil" (2 Cor. 5:10).[11] Judgment in these terms is viewed as a kind of final balancing of the scales or the ledger, as in Ephesians 6:8: "Whatever good we do, we will receive the same again from the Lord" (cf. 2 Thess. 1:1–6). Life choices *must* be addressed and responded to (Gal. 6:8). The book of Revelation (a text highly reverential toward the supremacy of Christ and his work) reflects the central nature of human judgment on the

10. For a clear but extreme view of this position, see Chris VanLandingham, *Judgment & Justification in Early Judaism and the Apostle Paul* (Peabody, MA: Hendrickson, 2006); for a more tempered view, see Karl P. Donfried, "Justification and Last Judgment in Paul," *Interpretation* 30, no. 2 (1976): 140–52. Donfried summarizes his view in this way:

> Paul affirms that the person who has received the gospel of God's gracious mercy by faith and who has been justified through it will receive the final gift of salvation at the last judgment. This is purely an act of God's grace which the believer will receive if he remains obedient to the gift of God and his Spirit. For the person who has been justified but who then makes a mockery of God's gift by his gross abuse and disobedience, such a one will not receive the gift of salvation at the last judgment; and he will suffer the wrath of God. Thus the final criterion at the last judgment is, for Paul, not how many good works one has performed—this is irrelevant since it is the Spirit which enables man to do those deeds of love—but whether one has held fast and remained obedient to his new life in Christ. It is the criterion of the obedience of faith (Rom. 1:5 and 16:26) which will enable us to understand many of the Pauline last-judgment texts. (145–46)

11. In reference to false apostles, Paul exclaims that "their end [i.e., fate] will match their deeds" (2 Cor. 11:15; cf. Col. 3:25).

final day: "And the dead were judged according to their works, as recorded in the books [of life]" (20:12c).

Some have tried to argue that there are two separate kinds of final judgment. Unbelievers will be subject to a judgment according to works, but believers will bypass that judgment due to Christ because their salvation is secure through faith. Believers will be called to account for their choices, but this will lead to rewards (or lack thereof) and is not determinative of salvation.[12] If this were the case, though, how would one explain John 5:29, where Jesus says that in the final hour the dead will be raised and called to account unto their final destiny, "those who have done good, to the resurrection of life, and those who have done evil, to the resurrection of condemnation"?

While this works-oriented view of judgment tends to have difficulty squaring with the notion of divine grace and justification, the reason some find this perspective compelling is simply due to the sheer number of occasions where the Bible concentrates on the reality and even the reverential fear of final judgment, not in the sense that one's fate is completely unknown, but more that it is a real test of human conviction, commitment, and choice. A number of other factors give weight to this perspective.

First, those who put weight on the biblical concern for final judgment for believers point to the foundational covenantal obligations. Especially in the Pentateuch we learn that Israel—though this people was called according to divine grace (Deut. 7:7)—was held accountable for faithfulness to the covenant. The path to life was through trust and obedience (e.g., Deut. 30:19). Again, while Israel knew the generosity, clemency, and forbearance of their God, still we see throughout the Old Testament an expectation that one's actions will reflect one's fate. Thus, in the account of Solomon's prayer of dedication of the temple, he prays that the Lord would act according to his character, "condemning the guilty by bringing their conduct on their own head, and vindicating the righteous by rewarding them according to their righteousness" (1 Kings 8:32; cf. 8:22–53).[13]

The Old Testament prophetic literature presupposes the covenant with Israel. While some texts focus on comforting a troubled people, several prophetic books call out the sins of Israel and threaten divine judgment on their disobedience, hard hearts, hypocritical behavior, or idolatry. In Jeremiah, Israel is reminded, "I the LORD test the mind and search the heart, to give

---

12. For this viewpoint, see Robert N. Wilkin, "Christians Will Be Judged according to Their Works at the Rewards Judgment, but Not at the Final Judgment," in *Four Views on the Role of Works at the Final Judgment*, ed. Alan P. Stanley (Grand Rapids: Zondervan, 2013), 25–50.

13. Many such examples are discussed in Kent L. Yinger, *Paul, Judaism, and Judgment according to Deeds* (Cambridge: Cambridge University Press, 1999), 19–63.

to all according to their ways, according to the fruit of their doings" (Jer. 17:10).

This view of the Old and/or New Testament has sometimes been called "legalistic" or "Pelagian," but those who emphasize the reality of a works-oriented judgment urge that grace and faith are not rejected or absent. Kent Yinger explains his understanding of the Old Testament in this way:

> The invitation to, and provision for, life within God's covenant favor and protection (= *salvation*) proceeds solely from God's grace. However, as would be natural in an ancient Near Eastern covenant arrangement, entry into and continuance in this gracious covenantal relationship requires walking in God's *ways*. This was seen not as *earning* a covenant status one did not yet have, but as the only proper response of love and trust in the covenant God who had already bestowed life in fullness. One's works of obedience are not viewed as *merits*, each to be recompensed in atomistic fashion, but instead as the observable manifestations of the covenant loyalty of the unseen heart.[14]

Those who adopt this sort of perspective on Scripture relate this to the teachings of Jesus, such as we find in the parables. While Jesus's parables are often meant to be surprising, they also appeal to a sense of justice and the expectation that good will overcome evil and evil will be punished. Consider the parable of the rich man and Lazarus. Poor Lazarus is mistreated in his life; the rich man, conversely, is well off but apparently not overly concerned with others. The rich man goes to Hades. Lazarus goes to a much better place (with Father Abraham). Their afterlife is seen as a reversal of the extremes of their earthly life. Abraham tells the rich man, "Remember that during your lifetime you received your good things, and Lazarus in like manner evil things; but now he is comforted here, and you are in agony" (Luke 16:25). We are not immediately told why their fates are as such, but later we come to learn that the rich man did not live a righteous life, and he was *unrepentant* (Luke 16:30). Thus, Jesus presents a picture of the afterlife whereby the scales of justice are somehow rebalanced.

Consider also Jesus's teaching on judgment in Matthew 25. Jesus portrays the final judgment like a shepherd who divides up the sheep and the goats. Those who are deemed righteous receive the kingdom, and those who are deemed unrighteous will be cast out into eternal fire. Jesus makes it clear that those who are righteous are those who fed, clothed, and cared for "the least of these" (25:40). Those who refused to tend to "the least of these" are the condemned.

14. Yinger, *Paul, Judaism, and Judgment*, 62.

On the matter of the relationship between faith and works, Protestants tend to emphasize the writings of Paul that focus on justification by faith and the ultimacy of divine grace. But those who put weight on a final judgment of deeds point to texts like James 2:14–16 as an important corrective to a "faith only" view. James makes much of the fact that some might rely on faith (in a highly cognitive sense) and end up with a religion devoid of good works, which does not glorify God. Simply affirming the right facts about God does not save; even the demons know the truth and fear God (and yet will be condemned), James argues (2:19). James gives the example of Abraham, who faithfully took his son Isaac to the altar of sacrifice (2:21). So he posits that faith and works act together, and "faith was brought to completion by the works" (2:22). Just as the human spirit is the animating power of the body (and the body is dead without spirit and breath), so works are the living activity of true faith (2:26).

It might be helpful at this point to offer the Catholic view of works, justification, and final judgment. Here we will summarize the perspective articulated by Catholic New Testament scholar Michael P. Barber.[15] Barber sets out to defend his view of Scripture that works *are* meritorious at the final judgment but that these works are able to be done only through Christ and by his grace. Barber begins by citing the *Catechism of the Catholic Church*, from which he draws significantly (though his concern for proper biblical interpretation is obviously central): "The charity of Christ is the source in us of all our merits before God. Grace, by uniting us to Christ in active love, ensures the supernatural quality of our acts and consequently their merit before God and before men. The saints have always had a lively awareness that their merits were pure grace."[16]

From the start, Barber rejects any view of Catholic theology that treats salvation as earned or the Christian life as legalistic. Catholics, Barber underscores, base their theology on "the unlimited power of God's grace."[17] Salvation is not just about rescuing humans from damnation but is also about saving them for new life in communion with God through Christ. Divine

15. Michael P. Barber, "A Catholic Perspective: Our Works Are Meritorious at the Final Judgment because of Our Union with Christ by Grace," in *Four Views on the Role of Works at the Final Judgment*, ed. Alan P. Stanley (Grand Rapids: Zondervan, 2013), 161–84; see also Joseph Fitzmyer, "Justification by Faith in Pauline Thought: A Catholic View," in *Rereading Paul Together: Protestant and Catholic Perspectives on Justification*, ed. David E. Aune (Grand Rapids: Baker Academic, 2006), 95–107.

16. *Catechism of the Catholic Church* §2011. See "III. Merit," *Catechism of the Catholic Church*, The Vatican, accessed April 25, 2019, http://www.vatican.va/archive/ENG0015/_P70.HTM.

17. Barber, "Catholic Perspective," 162.

empowerment is a gift from God, but it expects human responsibility and accountability. Barber notes how Jesus calls his disciples toward perfection (Matt. 5:48); even though it is not fully attainable in this life, being like God—holy and righteous as God is—is something that believers are told to strive for.

Barber also points out that Jesus often taught about life within the framework of works and reward or punishment. Using Matthew 6:1–6 as an example, Barber observes how Jesus calls out religious hypocrites for broadcasting their acts of piety to get noticed. He warns that this earthly fame is their only payment, and they will not receive a heavenly reward.[18] Barber concludes that Jesus portrayed final judgment as a kind of "settling of accounts" (see Matt. 16:27; cf. 18:23).[19] So what does that mean for a robust theology of grace? Barber explains that, for Catholics, when one is united with Christ, he or she can flourish in doing good by the power of God within. This is not just possible but inevitable because the Spirit of Christ within transforms the human heart and life.[20] When it comes to the final judgment, Catholics do in fact believe that the focus is on the works, and these works do determine final salvation. But as Barber has explained it, this is possible only because of the grace of God, and in fact Christ himself is the source (within the person) of the good works.

Reflections

The debate regarding the relationship between justification by faith and judgment according to works has a long and distinguished history. In some ways this can be frustrating, like a puzzle that either seems to be missing pieces or simply cannot be solved. At the same time, there is some comfort in this conundrum because it probably means both sides have something important to emphasize. Those who put the emphasis on grace and faith in justification underscore the point that Scripture makes salvation about what God has done in Jesus Christ, and this is something believers cannot do for themselves; thus, it is a gift. For those who argue that works are the focus of the final judgment, the point is that the Bible portrays this as a climactic moment in history and life where one's deeds will be carefully examined. This is not so because God counts actions and weighs the good against the bad. Nor is it because God is wrathful or vengeful. Rather, it is because humans were

18. Barber, "Catholic Perspective," 176–77.
19. Barber, "Catholic Perspective," 176.
20. Barber, "Catholic Perspective," 180.

created in God's image and were always meant to be an active blessing and source of goodness on the earth (so Eph. 2:10).[21] Judgment is meant to be an event toward which believers carry a sense of sobriety and awe, not doubt and shame.

Here, in reflection on this debate, I wish to draw attention to two matters. First, it is worthwhile to consider the binaries that we tend to use. It is not uncommon to talk about faith and works as if they were opposite, as if *works* were something active that you have done and *faith* were something passive. It is this sort of problematic polarization that fuels the debate about justification and judgment. If we view faith and works as opposites, no wonder the divine plan of salvation seems obscure. It is well noted that the Greek word for "faith," *pistis*, has a wide range of meanings and can mean "belief," "trust," and even "faithfulness." In many cases, the word "trust" comes closest to what the New Testament writers mean when they talk about *pistis* toward or in God. When we refer to justification by *faith*, that does not mean non-action or even something completely separable from works. Nor does talk of judgment according to works discount the centrality of faith. While we might not know about or agree on the precise relationship between justification and judgment, a robust biblical theology will lead one to see faith and works somehow *together* rather than separately.[22]

Second, we ought to be very careful about the language used about judgment in the New Testament. The typical way that it is discussed is judgment *according to* works, and not judgment *by* works (see Rom. 2:6; 1 Pet. 1:17; Rev. 20:13). This may seem like hairsplitting semantics, but I think it is more important than that. If judgment were *by* works, then it would imply something of a tit-for-tat, what we think of as *earning* salvation. But several "judgment" texts use the Greek preposition *kata*, which carries a sense of standard or concern. In such a case we can be sure that in the situation of judgment, God has works in view, but *kata* does not directly presume that works are the specific criterion. This seems to me to have the effect of reinforcing that

21. Martin Luther, the great champion of justification by faith alone, seemed to still have a robust understanding of the importance of Christian good works in this regard. He writes, "God is satisfied with my faith. . . . Therefore he wants me to do works to benefit my neighbor. . . . He doesn't need my works at all. . . . God is rich enough himself without me and without my works. He lets me live on earth, however, so that I may show the same kind of friendship to my neighbor that God has graciously shown to me." Luther, Weimarer Ausgabe 20:513, quoted in Paul Althaus, *The Theology of Martin Luther* (Philadelphia: Fortress, 1966), 133.

22. See Ortlund: "Our understanding of NT faith must avoid the twin pitfalls of mere mental assent, on one side, and synergism on the other"; "Justification by Faith, Judged according to Works," 336.

judgment is indeed *about* works, but in a holistic way more than in the sense of mathematical or economic accounting.

As with any of the discussions of complex subjects in the New Testament, in the case of initial justification and final judgment it is difficult to synthetically outline a single view that fits all New Testament texts. Themes of both absolute divine grace *and* human responsibility and accountability are underscored in the New Testament. What most scholars debate is how a framework can be articulated that can make sense of these in relation to one another.

Suggested Reading

Beginner

Stanley, Alan P., ed. *Four Views on the Role of Works at the Final Judgment*. Grand Rapids: Zondervan, 2013.

Faith-Determinative Judgment

Piper, John. *The Future of Justification: A Response to N. T. Wright*. Wheaton: Crossway, 2007.

Travis, Stephen. *Christ and the Judgement of God: The Limits of Divine Retribution in New Testament Thought*. Milton Keynes, UK: Paternoster, 2009.

Works-Oriented Judgment

Rainbow, Paul A. *The Way of Salvation: The Role of Christian Obedience in Justification*. Eugene, OR: Wipf & Stock, 2012.

Wright, N. T. *Justification: God's Plan and Paul's Vision*. Downers Grove, IL: InterVarsity, 2009.

Advanced

Barclay, John M. G. *Paul and the Gift*. Grand Rapids: Eerdmans, 2017.

Barclay, John M. G., and Simon J. Gathercole, eds. *Divine and Human Agency in Paul and His Cultural Environment*. London: T&T Clark, 2007.

Green, Bradley G. *Covenant and Commandment: Works, Obedience and Faithfulness in the Christian Life*. Downers Grove, IL: InterVarsity, 2014.

Westerholm, Stephen. *Justification Reconsidered: Rethinking a Pauline Theme*. Grand Rapids: Eerdmans, 2013.

Yinger, Kent L. *Paul, Judaism, and Judgment according to Deeds*. Cambridge: Cambridge University Press, 1999.

TWELVE

The Old Testament
in the New Testament

In the history of Christianity obviously the authority and interpretation of the New Testament have taken center stage, and for good reason, since it testifies concerning the life, death, and resurrection of Jesus Christ. For the vast majority of Christians over the centuries, the Old Testament has been included within the Bible, but it often plays an unclear role in the distinctively *Christian* study of Scripture.[1] Unfortunately, it is neglected and even disparaged by some traditions and communities. Old Testament scholar John Goldingay has made a strong effort to reclaim the importance of the Old Testament for Christians. He argues that because of the Old Testament's foundational significance for how God has chosen to reveal himself, the New Testament is more of a capstone to the great story-structure the Old Testament builds. Perhaps with a bit of extra provocation for effect, Goldingay writes that the New Testament's witness as fulfillment to the Old Testament makes it something like a series of footnotes to the Old Testament![2]

Whether you agree with Goldingay or not, it *is* clear when one reads the New Testament that it constantly presupposes ideas, events, and teachings of the Old Testament and often quotes or alludes to specific Old Testament texts. The actual statistics vary based on the criteria for the calculation, but

1. A 2017 study of systematic theologians has shown that their works contain very little attention to Old Testament texts; see Caleb Lindgren, "Sorry, Old Testament: Most Theologians Don't Use You," *Christianity Today*, June 13, 2017, http://www.christianitytoday.com /news/2017/june/old-testament-systematic-theology-top-100-verses-logos.html.

2. John Goldingay, *Old Testament Theology*, vol. 1, *Israel's Gospel* (Downers Grove, IL: InterVarsity, 2003), 24.

most scholars recognize that the New Testament quotes directly from the Old Testament hundreds of times; one scholar claims that the Old Testament is quoted about every twenty-two verses on average![3] When it comes to allusions, because it is clear the New Testament writers were soaked in Scripture, so to speak, reflections of Old Testament terms, ideas, and phrases appear virtually everywhere in the New Testament. (Some have put the count of Old Testament allusions at over two thousand in the New Testament.)[4] It is difficult to deny that the New Testament depends on the Old Testament.[5]

That the New Testament writers regularly quote from the Old Testament—always authoritatively and positively, it ought to be noted—is quite easy to demonstrate. The more challenging issue involves understanding *how* the New Testament writers used the Old Testament. Sometimes the use of an Old Testament text is rather straightforward, as when Jesus rebuffs Satan's invitation to worship him by quoting Deuteronomy 6:13: "Worship the Lord your God, and serve only him" (Matt. 4:10). The command from Deuteronomy prohibits the people of Israel from honoring false gods, and thus Jesus appeals to this text to rebuke Satan. There are many occasions where New Testament writers use the Old Testament in just this kind of straightforward fashion, where the application or employment of the text appears to fall in line with the meaning of the text from its original context.

However, this would be a very short discussion if that were the end of the story. There are a number of times in the New Testament where the writer brings up the Old Testament in a way that seems loose or irresponsible with respect to the Old Testament author's (original context) meaning. Consider the following example. Matthew quotes Jeremiah 31:15 in regard to Herod's slaughtering of the innocent children in his attempt to murder Jesus: "A voice was heard in Ramah, weeping and loud lamentation, Rachel weeping for her children; she refused to be consoled, because they are no more" (Matt. 2:18). Matthew is demonstrating that what happened to these helpless babies is a

3. See Roger Nicole, "New Testament Use of the Old Testament," in *Revelation and the Bible*, ed. Carl F. H. Henry (Grand Rapids: Baker, 1958), 137–51, at 137. This average statistic is helpful in terms of showing how important the Old Testament is to the New Testament, but it can also be misleading; some books directly quote the Old Testament frequently (such as Matthew), while others may allude to the Old Testament often but never quote verbatim (such as Revelation).

4. R. T. France, "Relationship between the Testaments," in *Dictionary of Theological Interpretation of the Bible*, ed. Kevin J. Vanhoozer et al. (Grand Rapids: Baker Academic, 2005), 666–72, at 667.

5. So classically argued by C. H. Dodd, *According to the Scriptures: The Substructure of New Testament Theology* (London: Nisbet, 1952).

tragedy, and only tears and wailing can follow. However, a modern reader may be left wondering why Matthew quotes the Jeremiah text in particular, as if it were a prophecy seen to be fulfilled in this act of Herod, while the context of Jeremiah 31:15 obviously relates to the Babylonian invasion of Judea that happened centuries earlier.[6] Are the New Testament writers sometimes wrenching Old Testament verses out of their original context in order to use them as proof texts? Questions like this are at the heart of a vigorous debate in New Testament scholarship.

Setting Up the Discussion

Because this is one of the most complex discussions in New Testament studies, it is necessary to set up the discussion before engaging the two major views on the subject. It is easy to assume today that first-century readers of the Old Testament thought and read just like us. Given, though, the great distance of time, space, and culture, it behooves us to try to better understand how early Jews and Christians thought about Scripture (their official Scripture in the first century being the Old Testament or Hebrew Bible). James L. Kugel did a study of how ancient Jews (around the time of the New Testament) read and interpreted the Old Testament. He was especially interested in their operating assumptions about what kind of text Scripture was, what it was for, and how it was unique and holy. For heuristic purposes, he came up with these four assumptions following his analysis:

1. The Bible is cryptic. That is, there is often, within the text, more than meets the eye. Scripture does not merely disseminate information; those with eyes to see and ears to hear will often discover hidden meaning.
2. The Bible is a book of lessons. While the Old Testament clearly refers to people and events in the distant past, it continues to have relevance and meaning for the present and the future. Jews would not have viewed the Bible as arcane or outdated.
3. The Bible contains no contradictions or errors. Jews operated with the assumption that all the pieces of the Old Testament fit together perfectly. There are no contradictions, only what may *look* like contradictions.

---

6. See Klyne Snodgrass, "The Use of the Old Testament in the New," in *Right Doctrine from the Wrong Texts? Essays on the Use of the Old Testament in the New*, ed. G. K. Beale (Grand Rapids: Baker, 1994), 29–51.

"In short, the Bible, they felt, is an utterly consistent, seamless, perfect book."[7]

4. The Bible comes from God. All parts of the Bible, whether narratives, psalms, or prophecy, come from God. This book of Scripture holds a special place among written literature because of its unique origin and inspiration from above.

Kugel's four assumptions pertain to Jewish interpreters of early Judaism generally. It is difficult to assess exactly how the New Testament writers related to this list, but there is hardly good reason to think they would have deviated from widespread Jewish assumptions such as these. How this list helps us on the subject of the New Testament writers' use of the Old Testament is clear: they filtered all of the unusual events and happenings in their life (e.g., the coming of Jesus as Messiah, his death and resurrection, the birth of the church, the welcoming of gentiles, the reality of persecution) through Jewish Scripture, knowing that the holy text would shape and guide them, perhaps clarifying uncertainties and justifying seemingly unprecedented activities. The Bible (here the Old Testament) for the New Testament writers was the living voice of God, not frozen into an ancient period merely to be dusted off for the sake of the historian. It was a vibrant, active Word of God. It is no wonder, then, that the Old Testament appears in quotations or allusions on nearly every page of the New Testament.

Having established these foundational assumptions about the text from a Jewish perspective, we will turn now to consider the nature of scriptural quotations in the New Testament. First, we must understand that the earliest autographs (the original Greek texts) of the New Testament did not contain quotation marks. So how do you know when someone was quoting? Literary context is the main indicator. We are used to using quotation marks in modern English, but most of the time we can understand texts without them. For example:

My wife reminded me as I was walking out the door don't forget to pick up Aidan from school.

Do you know what my wife reminded me of? Of course you do! Often, context aids us in figuring out when someone is quoting someone else. Now, once in a while, it is actually unclear when a quote ends, and when a writer or narra-

---

7. See James L. Kugel, *How to Read the Bible: A Guide to Scripture, Then and Now* (New York: Free Press, 2014), 14–15.

tor picks up again.[8] But this phenomenon of not using punctuation to mark quotations should remind us that there would have naturally been less of a concern to get the wording down perfectly all of the time.

Alongside that, we must remember the cultural gap between first-century Jews and twenty-first-century Westerners when it comes to formal citation.

> The ideal of "accurate" quotation is quite a modern one. It belongs to a culture in which written texts are easily accessible for reference. But in the NT world, in which literacy was perhaps no higher than 20 percent, a scroll of a single OT book, whether in Hebrew or Greek, was an expensive luxury, available to few apart from the Hebrew texts kept in the synagogues. It was also more inconvenient to consult than the compact, paged books we know, and there were no chapters and verses to guide readers through the scroll. The Scriptures were therefore known and experienced primarily through oral repetition and quoted normally from memory.[9]

Second, the main Bible of most Jews in the first century CE was the Septuagint. The Septuagint is the Greek-language version of the Old Testament that served the needs of study and worship in a time and place where Greek was used as a common language. The Septuagint, most of the time, resembles the Hebrew and Aramaic Old Testament texts that are the basis for our English translations today. However, sometimes the Septuagint has important differences. Some texts are longer in the Septuagint than the Hebrew text,[10] and some texts are shorter.[11] A certain verse may be significantly different, as it sometimes happens, in Proverbs for instance.[12] A word may be noticeably different on occasion. So, in Matthew 21:16, Jesus says, "Have you never read, 'Out of the mouth of infants and nursing babies you have prepared praise for yourself'?" Here he is quoting Psalm 8:2, but if you flip back to your text of Psalm 8 in your (Protestant or Catholic) English Bible, it reads, "Out of the mouth of babies and infants, you have established *strength* because of your

8. For example, in the well-known Gal. 2:15–16 passage, it is unclear whether what Paul says here is part of a quote directed in conversation to Peter, or whether Paul has transitioned to writing directly to the Galatians.

9. France, "Relationship between the Testaments," 667.

10. A good example is Hosea 13:4, which in Hebrew simply reads, "I am the Lord your God from the land of Egypt" (RSV). However, the Septuagint reads this way: "I am the Lord your God who makes heaven firm and creates earth, whose hands created all the host of the sky. And I did not display them for you to follow after them. And I brought you up from the land of Egypt."

11. In the Septuagint, the book of Jeremiah is about one-eighth shorter than the Hebrew.

12. The Hebrew text of Prov. 11:7 reads in English: "When the wicked die, their hope perishes, and the expectation of the godless comes to nothing" (NRSV; cf. JPS). The Septuagint text reads in English: "When a *righteous* man dies, hope does not perish, but the *boast* of the impious perishes" (NETS); cf. Prov. 10:5.

foes" (ESV). What is going on here? Did Jesus make a mistake? No, Jesus's quote seems to fall more in line with the Septuagint text of Psalm 8, where the text reads "praise," not "strength."

Third, we must be careful about how we understand New Testament language of "fulfillment." Typically we think of prophecy and fulfillment going together; the Old Testament anticipates and promises something in the future, and it happens at a later time. Sometimes the New Testament does refer to prophecy fulfilled (e.g., Luke 4:18–19; see Isa. 61:1–2), but it may come as a surprise to many readers that the New Testament writers claim fulfillment for a wide variety of texts that Jews before them did not really consider a prophecy. For example, John cites Psalm 22:18 as fulfilled at the crucifixion of Jesus when the Roman soldiers confiscate his clothing and say, "Let us not tear it, but cast lots for it to see who will get it" (John 19:24). John sees this event and conversation as a fulfillment of a Davidic psalm where the king laments as he is hounded by troublemakers. When David says, "They divide my clothes among themselves, and for my clothing they cast lots" (22:18), there is no noticeable sense in which he is looking ahead to a future suffering messiah. If it is not a (conscious) prophecy, then in what way does John conceive of it being fulfilled?

Again, we must learn to think about fulfillment in a bit of a different way. Let us begin with the fact that the Greek verb "to fulfill" (*pleroō*) simply means "to fill," like filling a cup or bucket with water. When referring to prophecies, we can call this "fulfilling" in the traditional sense. But what about other texts like Psalm 22:18? Going back to the basic sense of "filling," the New Testament writers in some way see the Old Testament texts they cite as less than full prior to the revelation of Jesus Christ. Somehow Scripture was previously *undercommunicating*, or *not yet done speaking*. Not simply the "prophecies" but apparently many more kinds of texts (narrative, speeches, psalms, etc.) were waiting to be "(ful)filled." It is almost as if the New Testament writers see the Old Testament texts as narrating their ancient stories in black and white. Their tales are told with a sense of completeness in their own time (as in Ps. 22 communicating the apparent full intent of David's lament). But the New Testament writers look back on the Old Testament, after the revelation of Jesus Christ, as a fund of divine revelation and testimony that, though complete in one way (in black and white), is still in need of bursting into full color to reach their culmination. Once a narrative, psalm, or speech plays its ultimate Technicolor role, it can finally meet its fulfilled end. In the next section, which introduces the two approaches, you will see how scholars disagree on how fulfillment operates, but it is important at this point to be disabused of the notion that the New

Testament writers were always working with technical prophecies when they talked about fulfillment.

The last thing I want to introduce is the influence of certain Jewish interpretations and methods or approaches on the New Testament authors. Matthew and Paul were not reading the Old Testament in a vacuum when they wrote their texts; rather, they (as Jews) had grown up hearing these texts and inheriting traditions and certain interpretations of them. We have a wide variety of ancient Jewish texts that help us become acquainted with some of these traditions. For example, in Galatians Paul mentions that Christ can offer redemption from the curse of the law "by becoming a curse for us—for it is written, 'Cursed is everyone who hangs on a tree'" (Gal. 3:13). In his quotation of Deuteronomy 21:23, Paul takes "hanging on a tree" as relevant to Jesus's crucifixion on a wooden cross. However, Deuteronomy is not talking about crucifixion. Rather, it refers to the shameful exposure of a dead body *after* the person has already been killed. Indeed, the "tree" would have assumed a literal tree. So what is Paul doing linking this text to crucifixion? Is he just making it up as he goes along? Not really. We learn from other Jewish texts (before his time) that Jews came to identify this text (Deut. 21:23) with crucifixion. Paul was not fabricating a sense of relevance; he was following an existing interpretation.[13]

As for methods or approaches, it is clear from extant Jewish literature from around the time of the New Testament that there were many different ways to read and interpret the Old Testament (in line with Kugel's four assumptions mentioned above). Understanding these is important, because they may not seem intuitive to modern, post-Enlightenment readers of Scripture.

Jewish Rabbi Hillel, a near contemporary of Jesus, passed down seven rules for interpretation. Three became especially prominent.

Qal wahomer: a meaning that applies in a less important case also applies in a more important case (see Heb. 1:1–4).

Gezerah shawah: when the same words appear in two different texts, those texts can be read together (see 1 Pet. 2:2–8).

Dabar halamed me'inyano: the meaning of a text is illuminated by attention to its context.

When the Dead Sea Scrolls were discovered, scholars were introduced to the Qumranists' unique approach to fulfillment; the scrolls demonstrate a type of interpretation that connects elements of the Old Testament to fulfilled elements

13. This understanding appears in one of the Dead Sea Scrolls, the *Temple Scroll* (11Q19).

in the present time that have come to eschatological completion. There are some clear comparisons between this approach—called *pesher*—and how the New Testament writers use fulfillment language, though obviously the latter emphasize the centrality of the appearance of Jesus as the Messiah.

Some Jewish interpreters appealed to allegory, where one draws out of a passage a symbolic, deeper meaning that is not apparent on the surface of the text. This approach is common in the works of the Jewish writer Philo of Alexandria.

This brief survey of some interpretive methods used in early and rabbinic Judaism does shed some light on the fact that Jews did not have one standard way of engaging with Scripture. This opens our eyes to the context in which the early Christians also were interpreting Jewish Scripture. Many scholars, though not all, believe that the New Testament writers (most of whom were Jews) employed many of the same (or similar) methods as fellow Jews of their time.[14]

Now we turn to two main views on how New Testament writers interpreted the Old Testament. The first view makes a case that when New Testament writers quoted the Old Testament, by and large they were not concerned with the original Old Testament context of the quoted author and text. The second view affirms the opposite, that the New Testament writers did indeed take care to respect the original context of the Old Testament text cited.

Out of Context: New Testament Writers Were Not Concerned with Old Testament Context

For quite a long time it was assumed among most scholars that when the New Testament writers were quoting the Old Testament, they were not actually reading the Old Testament texts in their own context but rather were plucking out verses here and there that appeared to confirm their point. This was called, in scholarship, "atomistic exegesis"—the smallest atom (a phrase or verse) was removed from its moorings in the Old Testament and placed into a New Testament text to secure a point.[15] Some scholars have argued that, very early on after Jesus's resurrection, followers of Jesus collected a running list of relevant verses from the Old Testament that could be used for spreading the good news of Jesus Christ. If this were the case, and such small portions of text

14. See especially Richard Longenecker, *Biblical Exegesis in the Apostolic Period*, 2nd ed. (Grand Rapids: Eerdmans, 1999).

15. See Henry J. Cadbury, "The Titles of Jesus in Acts," in *The Beginnings of Christianity*, ed. Kirsopp Lake and F. J. Foakes-Jackson, 5 vols. (London: Macmillan, 1933), 5:354–75, at 369–70.

were stitched together for teaching purposes, it is not too much of a stretch to think that individual verses could lose their grounding in their original context (out of sight, out of mind). There might be evidence for the use of such lists (called "*testimonia*") in a place like Romans 3:10–18.[16] However, this theory has lost much steam in recent years due to lack of more concrete evidence.[17]

A more compelling argument (that New Testament writers did not read Old Testament texts in context) involves the philosophy and mind-set behind the use of Scripture. When the New Testament writers appeal to the Old Testament, they tend to rely on its testimony to Jesus Christ or a reality that has emerged because of the Christ event. This has led some scholars to label the general approach of the New Testament writers as christological interpretation—not that every text quoted is *about* Christ per se, but rather that Christ is the key that unlocks the meaning of the Old Testament. Thus, the New Testament writers were not as concerned with reflecting the original meaning of the text as they were with reading those texts in a distinctly *retrospective* fashion in view of the revelation of Jesus Christ. All Old Testament texts, thus, become signs and pointers to the unique time of fulfillment ushered in by Jesus.

This may be a helpful place to introduce the idea or theory of *sensus plenior* ("full sense"), which refers to "that additional, deeper meaning, intended by God but not clearly intended by the human author, which is seen to exist in the words of a biblical text (or group of texts, or even a whole book) when they are studied in light of further revelation or development in the understanding of revelation."[18] An appeal to the sensus plenior imagines that there is something more, something hidden before but revealed later, that was not understood even by the original author of an Old Testament statement. This is what the New Testament writers are sometimes bringing to the surface in their use of a text. For the early Christians, this "fuller sense" is driven by the appearance of Christ, and the New Testament writers "pore[d] over their Scriptures in an effort to demonstrate that what God did in Christ is what gives Israel's entire story its coherence. It is the OT as a whole, particularly in its grand themes, that finds its *telos*, its completion, in Christ."[19]

16. See also Rom. 11:25–27; 12:19–20; 15:9–12; 2 Cor. 6:16–17.
17. This view has experienced a revival since the discovering of the Dead Sea Scrolls, since *testimonia* were apparently in use in Qumran; nevertheless, it is still unclear whether this really strengthens the possibility of their use in early Christian teaching.
18. Raymond E. Brown, *The Sensus Plenior of Sacred Scripture* (1955; repr., Eugene, OR: Wipf & Stock, 2008), 92.
19. Peter Enns, "Fuller Meaning, Single Goal," in *Three Views on the New Testament Use of the Old Testament*, ed. K. Berding and J. Lunde (Grand Rapids: Zondervan, 2008), 167–217, at 214.

For instance, Paul warns the Corinthians to learn from the mistakes of the Israelites in the desert. They disobeyed God and displeased him despite having received his divine guidance. The Israelites were all fed the same miraculous food, and they drank from "the spiritual rock that followed them, and the rock was Christ" (1 Cor. 10:1–4). If there were any Jews reading this letter written to the Corinthian church, they would recognize Paul's appeal to the wilderness wandering according to Exodus and acknowledge the scriptural testimony of divine provision of food in the desert. Perhaps there was even a Jewish tradition of a wandering rock. But they might be quite puzzled at the idea that this Jesus Christ was *there* following along with them. How was he there, *and why was he a rock?* According to the kind of christological interpretation proposed by some scholars, Christ is seen so much as the climax of Christian faith that he is "rediscovered" at such key moments in the history of the people of God.

Context Matters: New Testament Writers Were Concerned with Old Testament Context

Many modern readers of the New Testament experience confusion and frustration when it comes to understanding their interpretation of the Old Testament precisely because there are so many moments when it seems like those New Testament writers are not paying close attention to the original context of the Old Testament passage. Hence, a well-known essay collection on the topic is called *The Right Doctrine from the Wrong Texts?*[20] And, yet, we (today) experience this discomfort precisely because we naturally look to the original text's historical context to discern the meaning of the writer's words. Is it really possible that the New Testament writers felt comfortable playing fast and loose with Scripture, the Word of God? Those who advocate for the New Testament writers' respect for the original Old Testament context begin with the assumption of their best intentions and their attempt to be faithful to divine revelation as it was given in the Old Testament. It may be helpful at this point to explain that biblical scholarship suffered from anti-Semitic and anti-Judaism bias (which often included suspicion of the Old Testament) in the modern period up until about the middle of the twentieth century. Thus, at the beginning of the twentieth century, for example, it was common for scholars to assume that someone like the apostle Paul was *not* significantly influenced in his thought by the Old Testament; rather, he was *more* influenced by Greek (pagan) religious ideas. In the last half century or so, there has been a strong

20. Beale, *Right Doctrine*.

recovery of the *Jewishness* of New Testament theology, and particularly how dependent the New Testament writers were on the Old Testament to shape their own understanding of the gospel and life in God through Jesus the Messiah. It may seem like a foregone conclusion now, but it was rather controversial in the 1950s when C. H. Dodd famously argued that New Testament writers "often quoted a single phrase or sentence not merely for its own sake, but as a pointer to a whole [Old Testament] context."[21] This has been a particular emphasis of Richard Hays, who urges that most of the New Testament writers would have been so steeped in Scripture that they would have known the texts in context extremely well and may have committed them to memory. When the writers alluded to a scriptural text, it was often meant to establish a point of contact with the wider literary context of that Old Testament passage.[22]

What about christological interpretation and sensus plenior? Some scholars have expressed serious misgivings about these explanatory approaches. There is concern that they make the New Testament writers seem irresponsible and arbitrary in their appropriation of the Old Testament. Walter Kaiser, the most vigorous modern proponent of an "original meaning" view of how the New Testament writers use the Old Testament, states this concern about sensus plenior in particular: "God, who is viewed in this analysis as the principal author, is depicted as supplying to later interpreters of the text additional and subsequent meanings, thereby relegating the human authors of Scripture to, at best, a secondary level, if not a nuisance for getting at the really deep things of God."[23] Kaiser insists that, if we do not hold that the original human Old Testament author's meaning is still central, even when the text is reexpressed in the New Testament, then the authority of the Old Testament text will be undermined by Christians today and the Old Testament will not be read in its historical context in the long narrative of God's redemption; rather, various bits will be "stripped for parts," so to speak, in view of a divine meaning drawn out in the New Testament.

How might the original-context approach explain a text like Acts 15:13–18 in its use of Amos 9:9–15, where the text of the Old Testament prophet is used to validate the welcoming of gentiles into the people of God? Could Israelites in Amos's time have conceived of a time of full unity between the people of God, Israel, and the gentiles? Proponents of the original-context approach would urge that the prophets would have been far more in tune

---

21. C. H. Dodd, *The Old Testament in the New* (Philadelphia: Fortress, 1963), excerpted in "The Old Testament in the New," in Beale, *Right Doctrine*, 167–87, at 176.

22. See Richard B. Hays, *Echoes of Scripture in the Letters of Paul* (New Haven: Yale University Press, 1989).

23. Walter C. Kaiser, "Single Meaning, Unified Referents," in Berding and Lunde, *Three Views*, 45–89, at 49.

with a wider sense of the divine plan of redemption than we often give credit, though obviously they did not know all the details. If we assume the New Testament writers removed the Old Testament from its original setting in Israel's own history, in view of a new meaning in their Christian text (like Acts), this would run the risk of deconstructing the Old Testament and its very purpose as testimony to divine history that anticipates the Messiah.

A key argument made by those who believe the New Testament writers were concerned to use the Old Testament properly is that often the early Christians were interpreting the Old Testament *typologically*. "Typological interpretation" can be defined as "the study which traces parallels or correspondences between incidents recorded in the OT and their counterparts in the NT such that the latter can be seen to resemble the former in notable respects and yet go beyond them."[24] Certain figures or events from the Old Testament are established as types. In light of unfolding revelation, figures and events in the New Testament relate to and become culminating appearances of these types. An example may be helpful to illustrate typology. Going back again to Matthew 2:15, the evangelist writes about Joseph, Mary, and Jesus's departure from Egypt after the death of Herod, "This was to fulfill what had been spoken by the Lord through the prophet, 'Out of Egypt I have called my son.'" This is a direct quote from Hosea 11:1. But was Hosea prophesying Jesus's flight from Egypt commanded by God? If we read Hosea itself, it would seem not. Hosea 11:1 begins, "When Israel was a child, I loved him, and out of Egypt I called my son." Hosea 11 points back to the exodus, where God called Israel out of slavery in Egypt. In the remaining chapters of Hosea, the Lord impresses upon Israel the folly of their disobedience and calls them to repentance, so that he may not punish them but may bless them and cause them to flourish: "I will be like the dew to Israel; he shall blossom like the lily, he shall strike root like the forests of Lebanon" (14:5).

So, what is Matthew trying to communicate? Matthew portrays Jesus as reenacting Israel's exodus journey, and the exodus becomes a typological pattern that is repeated in his own experience. And the general perspective on typology is that an Old Testament type is not fulfilled in just one subsequent historical event—the potential for the text's typological meaning is inexhaustible in that respect.

When the New Testament writer reads an Old Testament text typologically, the goal is not to interpret the Old Testament text in its own context

---

24. I. Howard Marshall, "An Assessment of Recent Developments," in *It Is Written: Scripture Citing Scripture*, ed. D. A. Carson and H. G. M. Williamson (Cambridge: Cambridge University Press, 1998), 1–21, at 16.

per se but to see how a wider pattern is set in Scripture and history, freshly understood in light of Christ. There is a newness to this reading (because of the new eschatological vantage point), but the new meaning does not negate, cancel out, or diminish the original meaning of the Old Testament text.

Reflections

The debate over whether the New Testament writers' use of the Old Testament is responsible and fair is even more complex than I have represented here. Still, I will try to identify the key points of tension. Before I do so, we should remember that there is a great variety of so-called uses of the Old Testament in the New. Sometimes we see summaries of God's history with Israel (e.g., Acts 13:16–41). At other times, the New Testament writer is making a claim for explicit prophetic fulfillment. On other occasions, the Old Testament is appealed to for the sake of reinforcing a moral concern. And even still, analogies are drawn from the Old Testament. Sometimes it feels that the Old Testament text is used out of context, while on other occasions it seems less of a concern. What causes tension among some scholars is determining the overall disposition of the New Testament writers: how they tended to view and use the Old Testament, generally speaking.

Christological Interpretation

Virtually all scholars agree that the New Testament writers had a unique element in their appropriation of Scripture, and that was tied to the Christ event. As Ross Wagner aptly states (in this case with Paul's reading of Scripture in mind), "The crucifixion and resurrection of Christ are the focal point of God's plan for the ages, the single center from which all else derives its significance. Paul interprets all reality 'outward' from the cross and resurrection."[25] The question is how this christological perspective shaped and reshaped the reading of the Old Testament.

Progressive or Retrospective Reading?

Did not the New Testament writers turn to Scripture to make sense of what was going on in their own time, making meaning of the crucifixion of the

25. J. Ross Wagner, "Paul and Scripture," in *The Blackwell Companion to Paul*, ed. Stephen Westerholm (Malden, MA: Wiley-Blackwell, 2011), 154–71, at 168.

Messiah? His resurrection? The persecution of the church? The welcoming of the gentiles? For any Jew, it would have been natural to appeal to the wisdom and authority of Scripture (especially in light of Kugel's four assumptions, listed above). Echoing the provocative title of Hays's book about the Gospel writers' use of the Old Testament, it appears too that the New Testament writers had a habit of "reading backwards."[26] That is, they tended "to reinterpret Israel's Scripture in light of the story of Jesus."[27] Ultimately, Hays acknowledges that the New Testament writers did both; they read *forward* from the Old Testament to Jesus, and they read *backward* using the light of Christ to shed new light on the Old Testament. The question is, *Is there priority in one of these directions?* Which carried more authority, the ancient testimony and truth of the Old Testament, or the revelatory power of the Christ event? Or is this a false dichotomy?

Dual Authorship?

Hebrews 1:1 explains that, in previous times, God spoke *through* the prophets in many ways. This certainly gives us a sense of how Jews and Christians viewed the authorship of Scripture. Prophets (and kings and leaders) put their own minds to work in Scripture, but somehow this was divine speech as well. A key tension point for the debate about the Old Testament in the New revolves around this issue of dual authorship (divine and human). If the New Testament writers uncover "new" or "hidden" meanings in Old Testament texts, meanings that are inspired, does this bypass or supersede the original intentions of the Old Testament author? Those who think the New Testament uses the Old Testament out of context tend to argue that the original meaning of the Old Testament authors is being neglected. Some of those who argue that the New Testament writers wished to respect the Old Testament context think that, while the Old Testament authors could not have imagined Jesus Christ (or his crucifixion), or the welcoming of gentiles, perhaps they had a vague sense that something deeper was going on in a prophecy or in their words than meets the eye.

Fulfillment Language

A final area of tension takes us back to the matter of fulfillment. Is fulfillment an objective reality, a prophecy waiting for completion? Or is it more fluid, like a theme being revisited typologically? Are there a set number

26. Richard B. Hays, *Reading Backwards* (Waco: Baylor University Press, 2014).
27. Hays, *Reading Backwards*, 104.

of fulfillments of a prophecy? Can there be multiple? Are the possibilities infinite?

Conclusion

What does the future look like for the study of this subject? While I don't expect there to be a consensus anytime soon, a few notes can still be made here. First, as mentioned earlier, scholars do tend to allow for a combination of options for how the New Testament writers approach and use Scripture. It would seem that the apostles were not necessarily tied to a one-size-fits-all method of interpreting the Old Testament.[28]

Perhaps a key insight that has emerged in recent years is the recognition that the New Testament writers were not simply using the Old Testament but rather *interpreting* it. There was energy put into *finding meaning* in Scripture. They believed that the Bible did not simply dispense wisdom—it must be sought out and found. Jews spent much time discussing and debating torah precisely because this was a process of discovery and part of what it meant to walk with God.

With this in mind, perhaps one way forward in this discussion is to glean insight from studies in translation theory—after all, good translators know precisely what it means not just to transfer words from one language to another but to carry over the appropriate meaning that both respects the original and also makes sense to the new recipient. A few years back I was watching a foreign film (*Crouching Tiger, Hidden Dragon*), and the subtitles were automatically included to serve English speakers. For a bit of fun, I also turned on the English audio dubbing. To my surprise, the subtitles text and the audio dubbing, though sometimes similar, were often quite different. When one looks at what translators do and how and why they do it, one learns that it is not a cookie-cutter exercise. Translation is an art that requires understanding both the text or information you want to convey *and* the audience that will receive the translation. Again, the translator has a duty simultaneously to be faithful to the original information and also to make the translation relevant and intelligible to the receivers. By analogy, if Paul, like a translator, cared about fidelity to the Old Testament text *as well as* impacting his particular readers with the right meaning, his "quotations" would not necessarily look

28. See Craig Blomberg, review of *Three Views on the New Testament Use of the Old Testament*, ed. Kenneth Berding and Jonathan Lunde, *Denver Journal*, March 3, 2009, https://denverseminary.edu/resources/news-and-articles/three-views-on-the-new-testament-use-of-the-old-testament/.

like how we quote texts in a formal manner. As Roy Ciampa puts it, "Paul's goal, aim, or end was not so much to show them how to carry out exegesis of the type that people today might recognize and endorse but to help them understand Scripture as a book which has them and their needs in mind and which addresses their particular challenges."[29]

This perspective hardly resolves neatly all the questions we have been looking at in this chapter, but it does remind us that the New Testament writers were not handling texts in a style directly analogous to our understandings of citation and historical interpretation in academia. It also reminds us of the apostolic dual convictions of looking back with faithfulness to the past, as well as recognizing the larger impact of the revelation of Jesus Christ.

Suggested Reading

Beginner

Hagner, Donald A. "The Old Testament in the New." In *Interpreting the Word of God*, edited by Samuel Schultz and Morris Inch, 78–104. Chicago: Moody, 1976.

Hays, Richard B., and Joel B. Green. "The Use of the Old Testament by New Testament Writers." In *Hearing the New Testament*, edited by Joel B. Green, 122–39. 2nd ed. Grand Rapids: Eerdmans, 2010.

Moyise, Steve. *The Old Testament in the New*. London: T&T Clark, 2001.

Advanced

Beale, G. K. *Handbook on the New Testament Use of the Old Testament*. Grand Rapids: Baker Academic, 2012.

———, ed. *The Right Doctrine from the Wrong Texts? Essays on the Use of the Old Testament in the New*. Grand Rapids: Baker, 1994.

Berding, Kenneth, and Jonathan Lunde, eds. *Three Views on the New Testament Use of the Old Testament*. Grand Rapids: Zondervan, 2008.

Carson, D. A., and G. K. Beale, eds. *Commentary on the New Testament Use of the Old Testament*. Grand Rapids: Baker Academic, 2007.

Docherty, Susan E. *The Use of the Old Testament in Hebrews: A Case Study in Early Jewish Bible Interpretation*. WUNT 2/260. Tübingen: Mohr Siebeck, 2009.

Hays, Richard B. *The Conversion of the Imagination: Paul as Interpreter of Israel's Scripture*. Grand Rapids: Eerdmans, 2005.

29. Roy Ciampa, "Approaching Paul's Use of Scripture in Light of Translation Studies," in *Paul and Scripture: Extending the Conversation*, ed. Christopher D. Stanley (Atlanta: SBL Press, 2012), 293–318, at 308.

————. *Echoes of Scripture in the Letters of Paul*. New Haven: Yale University Press, 1989.

Kaiser, Walter C. *The Uses of the Old Testament in the New*. Chicago: Moody, 1985. Reprint, Eugene, OR: Wipf & Stock, 2001.

Porter, Stanley E., ed. *Hearing the Old Testament in the New Testament*. Grand Rapids: Eerdmans, 2006.

THIRTEEN

The Application and Use of Scripture

Sometimes on Facebook and other social media I see Christians post a meme or poster to this effect: "God said it. I believe it. That settles it." The idea is that—on whatever issue—the Bible is right and everyone else is wrong. Sometimes, though, I want to respond with another short meme: "It's complicated." Now, once in a while it is *not* complicated to interpret the Bible. When the Bible says, "Do not commit adultery," that's pretty straightforward. I agree with the famous quote (supposedly from Mark Twain), "It ain't those parts of the Bible that I can't understand that bother me, it is the parts that I do understand." Nevertheless, often enough it doesn't "settle it" merely to claim a command or prohibition written in the Bible.

Sometimes biblical readers lean toward interpretive errors on opposite ends of the spectrum. The first common error is what I call the "direct-universal approach" to applying Scripture. This approach presumes that whatever commands or prohibitions are written in the Bible are *always* applicable and are so *directly*. The attractiveness of this approach is that it *seems* natural and sensible—you see a command, and you feel it is the Word of God written for you: "Do not worry." "Do not judge." "Love your neighbor." But what happens when we carry out this mentality for *every* biblical command or prohibition? What if we try to make every single command in Scripture direct and universal? A journalist named A. J. Jacobs did an experiment a while back where he spent a year trying to follow all of the prescriptions in the Bible *literally*, and he proved that (a) it is impossible and (b) it is foolish.[1] It

1. See A. J. Jacobs, *The Year of Living Biblically: One Man's Humble Quest to Follow the Bible as Literally as Possible* (New York: Simon & Schuster, 2008).

is foolish because the Bible is not a law book composed of rules for Christians (e.g., like a book of driving laws). The Bible contains narratives, letters, poems, parables, prophecies, and prayers. When we decontextualize the Bible, ignore literary techniques and genres, and flatten it out into a running list of commands, we are bound to get some of it—perhaps much of it—wrong.

For example, Proverbs 26:4 says, "Do not answer fools according to their folly, or you will be a fool yourself." *OK, don't get into arguments with fools. Got it.* The next verse says, "Answer fools according to their folly, or they will be wise in their own eyes." *Wait, what? Do I answer fools or not?* What we learn in Scripture is that not all commands have the same objectives, expect the same responses, or have the same contexts. Those folks who claim, "God said it, I believe it"—do they think that women shouldn't braid their hair (1 Tim. 2:9)? Do they always greet one another with a kiss in church, as mentioned regularly by Paul (Rom. 16:16; 1 Cor. 16:20; 2 Cor. 13:12; 1 Thess. 5:26)? I recently read about a young Christian intent upon obeying "the literal truth of Scripture"—having read Matthew 5:29, where Jesus tells his listeners to remove their eye if it sins, he gouged his eye with a screwdriver! Ouch![2]

Speaking of dangerous misinterpretations of the Bible, let us consider the phenomenon of snake handling in some churches. The practice of snake handling began in the early twentieth century when a Tennessee preacher tried to interpret Mark 16:18 literally: "They will pick up snakes in their hands, and if they drink any deadly thing, it will not hurt them; they will lay their hands on the sick, and they will recover." In the last century, a variety of churches have held up snake handling as a practice that demonstrates faith in a powerful God. Today some churches continue the practice of snake handling, believing that this act of faith is a testimony to the literal interpretation of Scripture.[3] Sadly dozens of unfortunate deaths have occurred.[4]

If some people default to the direct-universal application approach, others gravitate toward the opposite, what I call the "à la carte method." This approach is usually taken unwittingly where one simply picks and chooses what one prefers to apply from the Bible. In reality, it is hard to find a church or denomination where there isn't *some* selective application. Too often Christians slip into an à la carte approach to applying Scripture due to cultural

2. See Daniel Wallace, *Greek Grammar beyond the Basics* (Grand Rapids: Zondervan, 1996), 681.
3. Ted Olsen, "They Shall Take Up Serpents," *Christian History* 58 (1998), http://www.christianitytoday.com/ch/1998/issue58/58h025.html.
4. Nicola Menzie, "Snake-Handling Christians: Faith, Prophecy and Obedience," *Christian Post*, June 5, 2012, http://www.christianpost.com/news/snake-handling-christians-faith-prophecy-and-obedience-75985/.

blinders. For example, a Christian community may go to great lengths to obey all commands related to praying, evangelism, and fellowship, but that same community may underplay or ignore those texts expecting care for the poor (Mark 10:21; James 1:27). Sometimes it is pointed out that Christian tradition has placed strong emphasis on Christians sharing the bread and the cup because Jesus said, "Do this in remembrance of me" (Luke 22:19), but very few churches do footwashing even though Jesus plainly says, "So if I, your Lord and Teacher, have washed your feet, you also ought to wash one another's feet. For I have set you an example, that you also should do as I have done to you" (John 13:14–15).

Neither the direct-universal method nor the à la carte approach is ultimately a satisfactory approach to applying Scripture. So what else is there? Biblical scholars have put quite a lot of thought into this question, especially as it is so crucial to the life of Christians, but despite some agreement there is ongoing debate. The two main perspectives differ on the nature of the biblical canon and whether or not Christian life today should be guided *by Scripture alone* (from-the-Bible application) or *from and beyond Scripture* (beyond-the-Bible application). This debate in some ways revolves around the perceived *limits* of the Bible—what it can and cannot do, what it is for and what it is not for—and what is needed for Christian life and ethics beyond the Bible.

From-the-Bible Application

The first perspective in biblical use and application could be called "from-the-Bible application," because this view holds that what is written in Scripture is wholly sufficient for guiding Christian life and ethics. What separates this from-the-Bible (FTB) approach from the direct-universal method mentioned above is that the FTB proponents recognize that the biblical books were written in a different time and culture and, to quote L. P. Hartley, "the past is a foreign country: they do things differently there."[5] Typically, those who take the FTB approach interpret and apply Scripture based on two guiding assumptions: (a) the text carries universal meaning in terms of its guiding *principles*, not the specific in-culture commands; and (b) there is an unfolding of God's will throughout the biblical story, such that Jesus is the ultimate consummation of the wisdom and righteousness of God. We will treat each of these elements in turn.

5. L. P. Hartley, *The Go-Between* (London: Penguin, 1958), 7.

Focusing on Principles

As hopefully demonstrated above, it is unwise to apply the biblical text to our own time and place without accounting for the clear cultural differences between here and now, and there and then. For example, when the apostle Paul learns that his coworker Timothy has an upset stomach, he advises him: "No longer drink only water, but take a little wine for the sake of your stomach and your frequent ailments" (1 Tim. 5:23). If we took the direct-universal approach, we might think that God intends for us to partake of wine any time we have an acid reflux episode! On a more serious note, we could appeal to the famous Proverb: "Those who spare the rod hate their children, but those who love them are diligent to discipline them" (Prov. 13:24). While Christian groups disagree on whether spanking is appropriate, very few today emphasize it is only biblical spanking if it includes a literal "rod." Also, when the "rod" was used in ancient Israel, it was used on the *back*, not the bottom—most Christians today who support spanking would not smack the back. There are, though, a large number of Christians who believe that spanking is not a biblical command for us today *at all*, but rather what the text of Proverbs 13:24 (and other texts about discipline, e.g., Prov. 12:1; 13:1) teaches us today is the *principle* of taking discipline seriously. When Paul instructs parents in Ephesians, he warns them, "Do not provoke your children to anger, but bring them up in the discipline and instruction of the Lord" (Eph. 6:4).

Let's go back to the issue of women braiding their hair. Now, I have two young daughters who look quite lovely with braids. However, more than once in the New Testament women are told not to braid their hair (1 Tim. 2:9; 1 Pet. 3:3). Should my daughters avoid braids? What about ponytails or pigtails? We should be reminded that when biblical commands or prohibitions are given, we ought to know or determine the *rationales* for them. It is clear enough from the context of 1 Timothy 2 that Paul was calling women *not* to focus on their outward appearance to attract attention but to focus on "good works" (1 Tim. 2:10). In 1 Peter, outward adornment is contrasted with "the inner self with the lasting beauty of a gentle and quiet spirit, which is very precious in God's sight" (1 Pet. 3:4). What seems most important in applying this text is not the letter of the law (do not braid your hair!) but the wider principle—let others be attracted to your virtue, not your outward appearance.

We instinctually know how to extract principles from biblical texts. For instance, when Jesus says to turn the other cheek (Matt. 5:39), we know that there is a lesson here about nonretaliation that applies far beyond the sides of the face. When we pray, "Give us this day our daily bread" (Matt. 6:11), we know this applies too for the gluten intolerant. Taking a principles approach seriously means that the "usefulness" (2 Tim. 3:16) of the Bible relates to how it shapes us to do what is right before God.

Progressive Revelation

The FTB approach I have been discussing here tends to focus on principles within the text but also takes seriously that the Bible is not simply a series of principles linked together as if pearls on a string. Rather, the whole is put together in the canon as a kind of story that begins with creation, recounts the story of Israel, introduces the Messiah Jesus, and ends with the letters of the apostles and the visions of John with a view toward a future consummation of redemption. From a Christian standpoint, the life, death, resurrection, and reign of Jesus are the climax of the Bible's story of redemption. When Jesus was with the disciples on the road to Emmaus, he explained to them the fulfillment of everything written about him in the law of Moses, the prophets, and the psalms (Luke 24:27; cf. 24:44). Paul explains to the Corinthians that all God's promises find their "yes" in Jesus (2 Cor. 1:20)—he is the summation of divine wisdom, righteousness, sanctification, and redemption (1 Cor. 1:30).

The concept of progressive revelation means that God chose to reveal himself, his will, and his plan for redemption over time (hence "progressive"), such that earlier stages show a less-complete picture of this than later stages. And this can be applied to biblical commands and behavioral expectations as well—the biblical commands *later* in the story tend to be closest to the ideal that God desired his people to attain. For example, in the Old Testament, Israel was called to adhere to very specific regulations regarding clean and unclean food. In the New Testament, though, Jesus emphasizes what comes *out* of the body in relation to purity (e.g., lies, slander, adultery), rather than what goes *into* the body; hence, all foods are "clean" (Mark 7:19).

To illustrate further the concept of progressive revelation, we might take the ethical example of polygamy versus monogamy. In the Old Testament, the law gives allowance for multiple wives (Exod. 21:10a) but places expectations on how the wives are treated for their protection (Exod. 21:10b–11; cf. Deut. 21:15–16). Still, many of Israel's leaders had multiple wives, sometimes hundreds, and neither God nor the prophets formally punished Israelites for this in Scripture. However, in the New Testament it is explicitly stated that a Christian leader must have only one wife (see 1 Tim. 3:2). The final ideal for exclusive marriage is only *explicitly* commanded in the New

Testament, though it is presupposed in Genesis 2:24 ("and they become one flesh").

Now, why would God reveal his ethical will *progressively* instead of all at once? Why not tell Israel from the start what is ultimately right and good? Walter Kaiser offers a classic answer to this question: "The process of revelation was pedagogically graded for our learning as the race grew, studied, and profited from the former revelations. Hence the law prepared the way for the prophets, and the earlier prophets prepared the way for the later prophets. Finally, it was necessary for the demands of obedience to be proportioned to the development of the person or of the age."[6]

When studying ethics and the application of biblical texts, then, the assumptions of progressive revelation dictate that, as Dennis Hollinger states, "the safest principle is to interpret the Old Testament in light of the fuller New Testament." Hollinger goes on,

> When the Old Testament directives are clearly affirmed in the New Testament, we must affirm them as normative for our moral actions and character. When practices and directives go contrary to the New Testament, the latter clearly take precedence. When practices in the Old Testament are not explicitly contrary [to] or affirmed in the New Testament, we must weigh the moral teaching or example in light of the larger contours of biblical teaching. This should in no way imply an inferiority of the Old Testament or an evolutionary stance on moral development. Rather, the notion of progressive revelation is tied only to the process of God's self-disclosure.[7]

To sum up, the FTB approach recognizes that it is nonsense to simply try to apply every command in Scripture willy-nilly without any understanding of the ancient context or the literary genres. First, there is an appreciation for the theological values and *principles* that support the life of God's people. Behind every text there is a principle that can guide human life for the better. Second, many who take this FTB approach read the Bible as a grand story of a God who reveals his person, his plan, and his will over time, not all at once. What this means is that *later* parts of Scripture give us a greater sense of the most complete will of God. What is earlier is not necessarily wrong, but rather it was right for its own time, place, and context. What would be wrong is to copy *now* the expectations of that former era.

---

6. Walter C. Kaiser Jr., *Toward Old Testament Ethics* (Grand Rapids: Zondervan, 1983), 63.
7. Dennis P. Hollinger, *Choosing the Good: Christian Ethics in a Complex World* (Grand Rapids: Baker Academic, 2002), 159; see also the popular work by G. D. Fee and D. Stuart, *How to Read the Bible for All Its Worth* (Grand Rapids: Zondervan, 2002), especially 165–80.

Beyond-the-Bible Application

What was described above regarding the from-the-Bible approach to the use and application of Scripture may sound familiar because it has a long heritage of explication in academic and church contexts—in fact, much of it seems like common sense. When we hear stories (whether in the Bible, or even in movies and novels), we often click with some value or principle in the story, whether it be individuality, charity and selflessness, unconditional love, or desire for justice. Also, we instinctively know that the *ending* of the story is where we will finally see the point of the tale most clearly or poignantly articulated.

Nevertheless, there are some scholars who, while neither denying that we can study principles in Scripture nor forsaking the idea of progressive revelation, believe that the Bible does not always give us the final or complete picture of how to live rightly in the world. These scholars believe we must interpret it in a way that may go *beyond the Bible*. I will present two key views within this category of "beyond the Bible" (BTB).

Redemptive-Movement Hermeneutics

The first theory we are going to describe comes from the influential work of William J. Webb and is explained and defended at length in his book *Slaves, Women & Homosexuals: Exploring the Hermeneutics of Cultural Analysis*.[8] Webb's hermeneutical approach actually begins with foundations already laid out in the explanation of progressive revelation above—God has a perfect will and desire for his people and his world, but he did not choose to reveal it all at once; instead, he moved them bit by bit over time toward his final standard for holiness and obedience. What we see in any particular case in the Bible is that the people of God are given divine instruction and revelation to move *toward* the final vision of the good and holy, but they are not given the most ideal standard. Where God desires for humans to change their behavior toward an ideal, we can see what Webb calls a "redemptive spirit"—that impulse that drives the people of God forward and contrasts their behavior with that of the surrounding culture. This sounds a lot like the application of the mindset focused on progressive revelation above; but here is a key difference: one can sometimes trace a redemptive spirit moving along a trajectory through Scripture toward an "ultimate ethic" (as Webb calls it), and that ultimate ethic may not be realized until long after the biblical period.

8. William J. Webb, *Slaves, Women & Homosexuals: Exploring the Hermeneutics of Cultural Analysis* (Downers Grove, IL: InterVarsity, 2001).

Webb engages with the topic of abolition of slavery as a case study. In the Old Testament, slavery as practiced by Israel under torah was more humane than in the surrounding cultures, but clearly abolition was not called for in the Old Testament itself, and slaves had lesser status and privileges than nonslaves in Israel. In the New Testament, we see more divine light shed on the matter; for example, Paul says that in Christ "there is neither slave nor free" because all are one in Christ (Gal. 3:28 RSV). Paul was *not* saying that all slaves should go free—he never made such a statement explicitly in his letters. He wanted slaves to be treated on equal footing with the nonslaves in the church, but Paul did not directly advocate publicly for abolition as far as we know. (Neither did Jesus for that matter.) But Webb would argue that divine revelation and guidance in Scripture demonstrates a redemptive movement in the canon toward abolition, though the trajectory does not reach the ultimate ethic in the biblical period. Put another way, just because the New Testament does not call for abolition of slaves doesn't mean that God did not expect the church *after* the New Testament period to aspire to a final goal of abolition. Undoubtedly those of us who believe in the importance of no slavery think that God would ultimately want it this way.

Now, some have criticized Webb's hermeneutical proposal, arguing that Webb's trajectory approach devalues the sufficiency of Scripture, as it continues beyond the biblical period in search of an ultimate ethic. To be fair, though, Webb believes that his ethical hermeneutic is an *evangelical* hermeneutic that takes Scripture with defining seriousness and commitment. He clarifies his use and view of Scripture in this way: "Understanding the NT as final and definitive *revelation* does not automatically mean that the NT contains the final *realization* of social ethics in all of its concrete particulars."[9]

An important element of Webb's redemptive-movement hermeneutic has yet to be mentioned and is significant for his proposal. Scripture does not always use a *trajectory* to reveal the divine will. There are some areas where the ethic is static insofar as there is no movement. For example, the Ten Commandments state, "You shall not murder" (Exod. 20:13). It is not as if the Old Testament says, "Limit murder," and the New Testament goes further toward prohibiting murder. Rather, murder (as premeditated killing of another) is forbidden from beginning to end (already foreshadowed in the early chapters of Genesis with the curses on Cain for killing his brother in cold blood; see Gen. 4:1–16). Sometimes, again, there is no *movement*, no waypoints along a trajectory toward an ultimate ethic.

9. See William J. Webb, "A Redemptive-Movement Model," in *Four Views on Moving beyond the Bible to Theology*, ed. Gary T. Meadors (Grand Rapids: Zondervan, 2009), 215–48, at 246.

How do you know, then, when you are dealing with a situation where there is *no* movement, and where there *is* movement? In Webb's book, he offers eighteen criteria for analysis. We will not review all of these, but suffice it to say that where there is a redemptive-meaning movement toward an ultimate ethic, Webb would expect to see in Scripture a clear sense of some movement in the canon toward that final vision, key statements that give the principle that drives that vision (which he calls "seed ideas"), and ideally "breakout" moments where one catches glimpses of the ideal. On the subject of women in Scripture, Webb urges that we have a key seed idea articulated by the apostle Paul in Galatians 3:28: "There is no longer male and female" for those who have been baptized into Christ. The seed statement sows the seed of the concept that eventually leads to an ultimate ethic. As far as breakouts of women in leadership in Scripture, Webb points to people like Deborah (Judg. 4–5) who, contrary to the norm in culture, show strong and independent authoritative leadership over the people of Israel. Webb identifies such breakouts as pointers toward an ultimate ethic and evidence that a trajectory is indeed in motion.

Drama Improvisation

The second perspective on a BTB approach I refer to as "drama improvisation." This view is relatively new in the history of biblical hermeneutics but has caught the interest of many biblical scholars for its dynamic nature. The drama-improvisation approach begins, much the same as Webb's hermeneutic, with the notion that it is problematic simply to mimic today the culture of ancient Israel or the early church. Twenty-first-century Christians are not meant to glean from the Bible that we should wear head coverings (or veils), avoid muzzling our oxen, or wear tunics. That is far too static of an approach to the Bible, one that presumes that Scripture is little more than a big rule book. Rather, this approach begins with the notion that the Bible tells a story, a story that begins with God's creation of the world, narrates the chaos that results from sin, the new hope of God making a covenant with Israel, the redemptive work of the Messiah Jesus, and the activity of the church in serving as agents of redemption in the Great Commission and the greatest commandments (love of God, love of neighbor). But the story does not conclude with the era of the apostles. The story continues in the life (or lives) of the church all across the world and throughout the centuries until now and even beyond.

From that perspective, the Bible's authority must somehow speak and reach beyond its own era (hence "beyond the Bible"). N. T. Wright is one of the proponents of this approach (though he himself does not use the language of "beyond the Bible"), and he explains his viewpoint in his book *Scripture and the Authority of God*.[10] Scripture has no independent authority, Wright argues; rather, it is attached to the authority of God himself (Father, Son, and Spirit). When we talk about Scripture having "authority," it is not meant to be directives for the legalist. Rather, God invests his authority in people: prophets, priests, kings, apostles, and so on. They are taught and sent to be delegates of God's redemptive power and work. So, Wright urges, "it is through the spoken and written authority of anointed human beings God brings his authority to bear on his people and his world."[11] And the teachings of many of these leaders are recorded not in dictums and laws per se but particularly in narratives. And it is in the great story that the Bible tells where we see the authority of God. The story itself, the meaning of the story and its worldview, points to a particular truth about the way things are and the way they ought to be. Indeed, "a story can be told with a view to creating a generalized ethos which may then be perpetuated this way or that."[12]

Wright prefers not to speak of "application" of the Bible but rather draws from the world of theater and drama and talks about Christian obedience to scriptural revelation as a kind of "improvisation."[13] Wright offers a poignant illustration. Imagine that a previously unknown play from Shakespeare has recently been discovered. We know the play has five acts, but the last act is missing. How can the play be performed? Wright conceives of the possibility that the play is put into the hands of expert Shakespearean actors who study those first four acts carefully. In their effort to produce that fifth act, it would make no sense merely to repeat what came in the earlier acts—the story must continue. That last act must be consistent and resonant with the first four acts while not parroting it. What is required, then, is a faithful *improvisation*, an act that requires creativity and development, but within the boundaries of the nature of the whole play itself.

Analogously, Wright believes that the Bible flows like a series of four acts (creation, fall, Israel, Jesus) and anticipates a fifth act of the church's ongoing mission. That last act happens mostly *after* what is recorded in Scripture. The church's challenge involves how to be *faithful* to the story and how to

---

10. N. T. Wright, *Scripture and the Authority of God: How to Read the Bible Today* (New York: HarperOne, 2011).

11. This quote comes from an essay by Wright called "How Can the Bible Be Authoritative?," *Vox Evangelica* 21 (1991): 7–32, http://ntwrightpage.com/2016/07/12/how-can-the-bible-be-authoritative/.

12. Wright, "How Can the Bible Be Authoritative?"

13. See too Kevin J. Vanhoozer, *Faith Speaking Understanding: Performing the Drama of Doctrine* (Louisville: Westminster John Knox, 2014).

be *influenced* by the biblical story without making the mistake of simply repeating what is there.[14]

To summarize briefly, a BTB approach treats the Bible as authoritative but does not believe that the Bible reflects the final revelation of how Christians should live. While the Bible is the foundation, and it sets the trajectory and direction of Christian discipleship and ethics, there is a critical role for the church to discern how to carry *forward* the moral vision contained within Scripture.

Reflections

We can affirm again as we did in the introduction: it's complicated. We have introduced four different approaches to the use and application of Scripture (direct-universal, à la carte, from the Bible, and beyond the Bible). The first two of these are clearly loose and irresponsible approaches. But when it comes to the latter two, there are very intelligent, mature articulations and defenses of their positions. I will discuss the tension points between these two views in what follows.

The Unique Inspiration and Authority of Scripture

One dimension of the discussion pertains to the uniqueness of Scripture. Christians in some way adhere to the belief that the Bible reveals God's work, will, and ways better than any other form of knowledge. Both the FTB and the BTB views take this with the utmost seriousness. The more challenging matter relates to how one circumscribes and interprets the authority of Scripture. Is it an authority that is complete in and of itself? Is the canon a closed interpretive system, offering the fullness of divine revelation, or does it function as a foundation and arrow pointing toward commitments, convictions, and behaviors that may go beyond the biblical period? This is not a direct criticism of the Bible; after all, the Bible does not directly address many pressing issues of our time such as climate change and ethical use of technology.

Spiritual Discernment

Intricately related to these questions is the matter of spiritual discernment. One of the reasons why the direct-universal approach is so weak is that it

14. That does not mean that Wright does not believe some commands should be obeyed directly and universally; his comments are of a more sweeping nature about how to relate biblical authority to Christian responsibility.

requires little thought or discernment from the Christian—it is a matter of just doing what is written. Now, there is nothing wrong with simple obedience per se, but Scripture quite comprehensively promotes patient wisdom in the area of discerning God's will, in tune with the Spirit of God and in conversation with the people of God. Again, the Bible is not a rule book, and although it includes some guiding principles and rules, it is obviously not comprehensive; it does not comment on every possible life scenario. The FTB and BTB approaches both require a measure of spiritual discernment in using and applying the Bible, but one of the key differences is that the BTB approach (e.g., with its "improvisation") expects a lot from the modern person and community in terms of sensing how to live in tune with Scripture, but not necessarily repeating what happened in Scripture. Some are uncomfortable with and troubled by this openness and personal application due to its inherent ambiguity, and others find it freeing and conducive to contextualization.

Universality and Cultural Contextualization

On the subject of contextualization, another point of disagreement on this subject pertains to how one thinks the Bible relates to what is universal and what is cultural. On the one extreme, the direct-universal approach treats Scripture as applicable in a literal fashion to all people in all cultures at all times. On the other hand, the à la carte approach lends itself to a maximum sense of personal and cultural preference or applicability. One might say that the former puts a premium on comprehensive authority of Scripture to guide all Christians, while the latter emphasizes how the Bible comes from a singular or limited cultural perspective and it is unwise to force that upon everyone in every situation. While we are dealing with several hermeneutical factors and questions, at the very least these competing views remind us of the complexity of the affirmation that Scripture is inspired by God but written by mortals.

Conclusion

At the end of the day, questions come easily on this topic of the use of application of Scripture, but answers are harder to find. At the very least, it is important to start with "it's complicated," so that we may recognize the many factors and considerations in this discussion pertaining to the nature of Scripture, the divine-human dimensions of its authorship and its purposes, and the ways that God's people ought to be seen as a unified people of consonant behavior and yet also a discerning people who read and assimilate Scripture as guided by the Spirit and in community.

Suggested Reading

Beginner

Duvall, J. Scott, and J. Daniel Hays. *Grasping God's Word: A Hands-On Approach to Reading, Interpreting, and Applying the Bible.* Grand Rapids: Zondervan, 2012.

Fee, Gordon D., and Douglas K. Stuart. *How to Read the Bible for All Its Worth.* 4th ed. Grand Rapids: Zondervan, 2014.

Good, Meghan Larissa. *The Bible Unwrapped: Making Sense of Scripture Today.* Harrisonburg, VA: Herald, 2018.

From-the-Bible Application

Doriani, Daniel. *Putting the Truth to Work: The Theory and Practice of Biblical Application.* Phillipsburg, NJ: P&R Publishing, 2001.

Kaiser, Walter C. *Toward Old Testament Ethics.* Grand Rapids: Zondervan, 1983.

Beyond-the-Bible Application

Webb, William J. *Slaves, Women & Homosexuals: Exploring the Hermeneutics of Cultural Analysis.* Downers Grove, IL: InterVarsity, 2001.

Wright, N. T. *Scripture and the Authority of God: How to Read the Bible Today.* New York: HarperOne, 2011.

Advanced

Meadors, Gary T., ed. *Four Views on Moving beyond the Bible to Theology.* Grand Rapids: Zondervan, 2009.

Schneiders, Sandra M. *The Revelatory Text: Interpreting the New Testament as Sacred Scripture.* 2nd ed. Collegeville, MN: Liturgical Press, 1999.

Smith, Christian. *The Bible Made Impossible.* Grand Rapids: Brazos, 2011.

Author Index

Scripture Index

Old Testament

Genesis

1–2 137
1:1 31
1:26–28 135, 138, 140
2:18 135
2:24 179
4:1–16 182

Exodus

18:4 137
20:13 182
21:10 179
21:11 179

Leviticus

19:18 51

Numbers

21:9 148

Deuteronomy

6:4–5 51
6:13 158
7:7 150
21:15–16 179
21:23 163
27:26 78
30:19 150

Judges

4–5 183
4:1–24 139
4:4 139
4:5 139
4:6–24 139

2 Samuel

22:44 136

1 Kings

8:22–53 150
8:32 150
19:18 61

2 Chronicles

34:22–29 139

Psalms

8:2 161–162
17:44 136
19:7 72
19:8 72
19:10 72
19:11 72
22:18 162

Proverbs

10:5 161n12
11:7 161n12

12:1 178
13:1 178
13:24 176
26:4 176

Isaiah

7:8–9 136
34:4 62–63
40:9 61
52:7–10 61
61:1–2 162
64:1 62

Jeremiah

17:10 150–151
31:15 158, 159

Ezekiel

1:10 33

Hosea

11:1 168
13:4 161n10
14:5 168

Joel

2:28–32 139

Amos

9:9–15 167